SONS OF ABRAHAM

SONS OF ABRAHAM

*A Candid Conversation about the Issues
That Divide and Unite Jews and Muslims*

Rabbi Marc Schneier
and Imam Shamsi Ali

Foreword by President Bill Clinton
Introduction by Samuel G. Freedman

BEACON PRESS

BOSTON

Beacon Press
Boston, Massachusetts
www.beacon.org

Beacon Press books
are published under the auspices of
the Unitarian Universalist Association of Congregations.

18   17   16   15   8   7   6   5   4   3   2   1

This book is printed on acid-free paper that meets the uncoated paper
ANSI/NISO specifications for permanence as revised in 1992.

Text design and composition by Wilsted & Taylor Publishing Services

Library of Congress Cataloging-in-Publication Data
Schneier, Marc, author.
Sons of Abraham : a candid conversation about the issues that divide
and unite Jews and Muslims / Rabbi Marc Schneier, Imam Shamsi Ali ;
[foreword by] President Bill Clinton ; [introduction by] Samuel G. Freedman.
pages cm
Includes bibliographical references and index.
ISBN 978-0-8070-6119-0 (paperback) — ISBN 978-0-8070-3308-1 (ebook)
1. Islam—Relations—Judaism. 2. Judaism—Relations—Islam. 3. Islam—United States.
4. Judaism—United States. I. Ali, Shamsi, author. II. Title.
BP173.J8S344 2013
296.3'97—dc23   2013023021

To my beloved son, Brendan.
I pray that the sentiments reflected herein
will inspire his generation to fashion a world
of greater understanding, cooperation, and peace.
Rabbi Marc Schneier

To my parents,
who have been a source of strength, courage,
and inspiration to me my whole life.
Imam Shamsi Ali

CONTENTS

FOREWORD

The end of the Cold War laid bare, and in some cases rekindled, long-existing conflicts rooted in racial, ethnic, and religious differences. At the heart of many of these conflicts, from the Balkans to Russia to China to Indonesia to Africa and most recently in Myanmar, is religious identity. Sometimes they involve persecuted minorities. Sometimes the involve fighting within a religion, as when Sunni fight Shia. Sometimes they involve terrorism and false claims that the killing of innocent civilians, even others of the same religion, is sanctioned by God or a prophet.

Of course, the conflict with the most profound consequences beyond its borders is the long dispute between Jewish Israelis and Muslim Palestinians and their Arab supporters. It echoes across the world. It is at the root of how Jews and Muslims understand and misunderstand each other in the United States.

As president, I worked for a just and lasting peace in the Middle East to create a Palestinian state in the West Bank and Gaza, used the power of the United States to stop the oppression and slaughter of Muslims in Bosnia and Kosovo, and engaged in regular consultations with Muslim Americans on a wide range of issues. I also worked hard to prevent terrorist attacks on the United States and other nations. Many attacks were thwarted, both before and after I left office, but not at our embassies in Kenya and Tanzania in 1998, or the USS *Cole* in Yemen in 2000.

After 9/11, the wars in Iraq and Afghanistan, and dozens of terrorist acts across the world—most recently the Boston Marathon bombings—it is tempting to say this is an unsolvable conflict, a clash of civilizations that cannot be defused. Of course, this overlooks the fact that the vast majority of Muslims in the United States and elsewhere are law-abiding, peace-loving, hard-working people who want to live in harmony with both their neighbors and their faith. The situation is not hopeless.

For the last several years, my daughter, Chelsea, has served as cochair of the advisory board for the Of Many Institute, the largest interfaith student group in the United States, at New York University. Led by Rabbi Yehuda Sarna and Imam Khalid Latif, these students live, talk, and do service projects together. NYU also offers a minor in interfaith leadership.

Still, there are too few people committed to reconciliation through honest dialogue. That's why the efforts of Rabbi Marc Schneier and Imam Shamsi Ali to bring Jews and Muslims together, not only in the United States but also in Europe and the Middle East, are so important. Like true friends, they honestly face issues that divide Jews and Muslims, as well as what unites them as "sons of Abraham." They not only talk the talk, they walk the walk. And their personal friendship is a poignant example of what is possible among people of deep faith and goodwill.

I have been inspired by their example, and I hope you will be, too, as you read this important book.

PRESIDENT BILL CLINTON

INTRODUCTION

On the weekend before Thanksgiving 2012, in principle a time to celebrate fellowship, the news of Muslim and Jewish interaction was a depressingly familiar tale of bloodshed and wrath. Israel and Hamas were in the midst of an eight-day confrontation that would ultimately claim nearly one hundred sixty lives. Israel had assassinated a terrorist leader in Gaza several days earlier, Hamas had responded by launching lethal rockets into the civilian areas of Israeli cities, and Israel's retaliatory bombing had killed innocent Palestinians as well as armed militants. In their intractable enmity, the two sides not only seemed bound to endlessly make war on one another but also to irreparably poison relations between Muslims and Jews throughout the world.

Certainly, the toxin was already loose in the United States. The nation had just concluded a presidential campaign in which Jewish voters were implored to choose the Republican, Mitt Romney, who accused Barack Obama of having "thrown Israel under the bus." While this strategy did not work, or at least not well enough for Romney to win, it compounded the divisive mood in the country. During Romney's drive toward the GOP nomination, several of his challengers for the nomination outdid themselves trying to be the most anti-Muslim—one promising never to have a Muslim in his Cabinet, another flourishing the canard that Muslims want to install Shari'a religious law, a third claiming that the Muslim Brotherhood had insinuated itself into the State Department. Well before the 2012 election had even begun in earnest, a congressional committee had conducted hearings on supposed Muslim subversion. In all of these demagogic episodes, American Jews were being asked implicitly or explicitly to take sides against American Muslims.

Yet on that same weekend before Thanksgiving, the members of a Jewish temple and Muslim mosque on Long Island came together to donate blankets, clothing, and food to the thousands of people uprooted by Hurricane Sandy. In Denver, Jewish and Muslim volunteers made a thousand peanut butter sandwiches to feed homeless and hungry people on the street. In suburban Detroit, young men, both Muslim and Jewish, played pickup basketball and then talked together about ways to improve the city. Just outside Washington, DC, Muslim and Jewish teenagers cleared debris and put down mulch in a park, then socialized over pizza. In the Bay Area of northern California, young professionals from Jewish and Muslim communities jointly discussed each religion's teachings on business ethics.

These collaborations, set vividly against the backdrop of the Middle East missiles and the rancorous presidential campaign, were part of a larger program of "twinning" that matched up Jewish and Muslim congregations—primarily within the United States but also from as far afield as Baku in Azerbaijan. And that congregational program arose from and attested to the extraordinary collaboration of two brave and bold men, Rabbi Marc Schneier and Imam Shamsi Ali. This book is the story of these men: their lives, their friendship, their commitment to coexistence work, and their vision of the future for Muslims and Jews in America and beyond.

Sons of Abraham is a book of optimism, but not of naivete. Rabbi Schneier and Imam Ali are not what one might call the "usual suspects" of ecumenical efforts—clergy who are reliably liberal, if not congenitally touchy-feely, on all theological and political matters. Rabbi Schneier is entirely a product of Orthodox Jewry. Imam Ali studied Islam in a madrassa and university that largely followed the stringent Saudi Arabian model. Both men, for a period of their adult lives, uncritically accepted the biased view of Jews and Muslims as being innately, inherently enemies.

Over time and with study and experience, however, both of these men grew, and eventually dared to challenge the conventional wisdom within their own religious communities. Against no small amount of criticism from their own coreligionists, they forged their alliance. And Rabbi Schneier and Imam Ali did so in the bitter, frightened, polarized years after the September 11 attacks. Their credibility is built on what might be called, to borrow a term from sports such as diving and gymnastics, the degree of difficulty.

The strength of their partnership also lies in their ability to disagree. Too often, interfaith dialogue operates under a well-intentioned kind of self-censorship in which controversial topics are avoided rather than engaged. No wonder so many otherwise laudable efforts can be so easily ridiculed as if they were folk songs being sung around the campfire. As this book demonstrates, Rabbi Schneier and Imam Ali trust their friendship and their common cause deeply enough to address any issue. They take on anti-Semitism in the Muslim world and bigotry against Muslims among Jews. They delve into sticky theological issues, like the idea of chosenness in Judaism and the concept of *Kheir Ummah*, or *best nation*, in Islam. They even address the third rail of Israel and Palestine, and find a respectful, civil rhetoric with which to contend and dispute.

No one who knows of their work, and no one who learns of it from this book, can fail to be heartened. These are men of substance doing work of substance, taking significant risks against significant odds. I recall seeing them on the afternoon of September 9, 2011, two days before the tenth anniversary of the Al Qaeda terrorist attack on America. Hundreds of congregants were entering the Islamic Cultural Center, the largest mosque in Manhattan, for the Friday *jummah* service, the Muslim equivalent of Sabbath morning worship in a synagogue or Sunday Mass in a Catholic church. Beneath the center's soaring dome, the congregants gathered, wearing Brett Favre jerseys or business suits or salwar kameez and covering their heads with crocheted skullcaps or Yankee caps turned backwards in hip-hop fashion. They had come to hear the weekly homily from their spiritual leader, Imam Ali. And they had come, too, to hear from the imam's special guest, Rabbi Schneier.

The tenth anniversary of 9/11 offered an especially vivid test of their alliance, and that was why they made a point of appearing together at the Islamic Cultural Center. There was no way to mark this day without squarely facing the damage it had done—not only the three thousand deaths, not only the destruction of iconic buildings, but the way it had desecrated the image of Islam and damaged relations between Muslims and non-Muslims in America. Uttering mere niceties, the bromides of brotherhood, would not suffice at this *jummah* service. Neither would the lamentations of victimhood.

"My brothers and sisters," Imam Ali said at one point, "the best way to meet the challenge in the days ahead is to engage minds, to change others' perceptions, to talk to them, to make friends of them. We must be just to everyone, because justice is written in the Holy Qur'an. We must change our perception of others, and change their perception of us, to one of mutual respect. We have the responsibility to make it better. We are here as Muslims participating in all aspects of American life. Each one of you, without exception, must be an ambassador of Islam."

Then, after welcoming several visiting ministers, Imam Ali introduced "one of my best friends," Rabbi Schneier. He called him "my brother." "This guy," Imam Ali said, "is there every time we have a challenge in front of us." Members of the congregation lifted up their smartphones and digital cameras to take photographs of the rabbi.

"We should not underestimate the importance of remembering," Rabbi Schneier said. "The question is what to remember, how to remember, who to remember. Three thousand people were killed in the World Trade Center and the other tragedies—three thousand Christians, Jews, Muslims, Sikhs. Let us remember that every life is sacred, that every life counts. And how do we remember that? By keeping the light of understanding. We share a common faith, and we share a common fate. And we, as Muslims and Jews, stand shoulder to shoulder."

The book that Rabbi Schneier and Imam Ali have written offers eloquent evidence of that light. It tells us that human beings can grow beyond their prejudices. It tells us friendship and collaboration can survive civil disagreement. It tells us what has been done, and it tells us, most importantly, what those of us who care about the inevitably, inextricably shared future of American Muslims and American Jews still must do.

SAMUEL G. FREEDMAN

PART ONE

Who We Are

CHAPTER ONE

Child of the Soil

IMAM SHAMSI ALI

I came from a humble family in a village called Tana Toa on the island of Sulawesi in Indonesia. It was a very small place, very traditional. The nearest city was five hours away by car, and we had very little contact with the outside world—no cars, no TVs, no phones. People just followed the local customs. Most people in my village would call themselves Muslims, but they never studied Islam, they did not learn the Qur'an, and they held on to a lot of superstition. Some people even claimed that the Prophet Muhammad was born there in the village. And that is the reason why it's called Tana Toa—the name means "the old land."

My dad was a farmer and my mom was a housewife. I have four brothers and a sister; I was number three out of the surviving five. As a child, I did farmer things, playing with horses, with cows. I was barefoot almost all the time. We used to walk seven miles every day to school. I didn't pay much attention to school as a child. When I felt lazy, I would just go do something else, and then tell my parents that I'd been to school. Some of the people in the area had graduated school and yet they just went back to work on the farm, so sometimes I'd ask myself, What is the reason to study?

I grew up rebellious, and I think it is my basic nature. I led the village kids in what some would call gangs, fighting with kids from other villages. If any kids came over and they had cows or horses, we would fight them. That is just what we did. I also think I rebelled because I wanted the village to be developed and I saw every day that nothing developed and nothing ever changed. In the city, I knew, people had electricity, cars, and phones. We had nothing. I remember there was only one truck in the whole village, and it belonged to someone who lived in the city. Some of the people in the village went to the city to work, and when they came back, they were able to purchase things that we could not, whether a house or a bicycle. They would tell us about the marvels of the city.

My father basically didn't know anything about religion at the time. Prayer was only once a week, on Friday, but my father did not pray. He fasted during Ramadan because it was something that all people observed. The only good Islamic practice I can pinpoint with my parents was that they wanted me to learn to read the Holy Qur'an in Arabic, and so they sent me to a special teacher. They used to say, "You have to learn because this is our Muslim holy book." I think I was six or seven when I started learning to read the Qur'an in Arabic. My teacher's name was Puang Tambang. I was very close to him and still consider him a second father.

Around that village, some teachers were harsh—they might beat you or yell. But Puang Tambang was a very kind person. He was wise and gentle and easily got along with students. I still remember his voice was very soft. His wife was very motherly. Sometimes, if I didn't wash my feet properly, she would take me back to her house to do it the right way. We didn't pay the teacher anything really, but in our village it was difficult to get water from a well, so every time we went to class, we would bring water for the teacher as a charity. Puang Tambang's house was a normal village house, very simple, made of wood. All the students would gather in one room, having the Qur'an in front of them and reading it one by one.

Why I fell in love with learning the Holy Qur'an is still a mystery to me. I didn't like school at all—especially math! But if you gave me something easy to memorize, I would fall in love with it, and perhaps that was the key for me. Before I even started identifying the alphabet in order to read the passages, I had already memorized some short *suras* (chapters) from the Holy Qur'an. My teacher always praised me in front of the other students, and that pushed me to go further; I wanted to be the best. Normally the teacher would teach half a page at a time and call on the students to recite the day's lesson. When the teacher came to me, he would realize that I knew the whole page. He would quiz me on the half page we studied, but I already knew the next lesson. So I finished learning the Holy Qur'an in a very short time. Usually, it takes two years or more, and if I'm not mistaken, I did it in about seven or eight months. When I finished, the teacher appointed me as an informal assistant and that pushed me too. I was about seven or eight years old, and he would take me to any celebration that he attended. For example, when someone died, for forty days people would gather to read the Qur'an for the deceased. My teacher used to take me to those gatherings and ask me to lead the people reading the Qur'an. I felt important, which in turn increased my love for study and my feelings of responsibility for getting it right.

But outside of madrassa, my tendency was still to be rebellious. Out of the five boys in our family, I was considered the laziest. My father would ask me to bring grass for the horses, but I would instead go out and play with the other kids. I didn't like to work on the farm; it was hot and humid, and it was not my nature to work there. After I finished my primary school, my father was very confused about what to do with me since I was not interested in school and I was not interested in the farm.

Luckily, at that time (I was about twelve) my oldest brother, Bato, already lived and studied in the city, in Makassar. He was studying at a vocational high school. When Bato saw that my father was confused about what to do with me after my graduation, he spoke to the landlord of the house where he lived in the city. The landlord told my brother that there was a school called a *pesantren* that would be good for me. A pesantren is a school that is highly disciplined. My dad then asked my brother to talk to his host about enrolling me. They brought me to the city and to the home where my brother lived, and the following day we went to the pesantren.

It was a privilege to be a village boy going to the city for the first time. You knew it was something special, something greatly different. In the city you saw cars, you saw electricity all around you; it was all very impressive. The person who owned the house where my brother lived happened to be someone who also came from my village. He was working as a nurse, and in my village that job was considered very prestigious. The school was in a remote area outside of Ujung Pandang, the capital of south Sulawesi, housed in a very simple building. When I went there for the first time, we met with the founder and the leader of the pesantren, whose name was Kyai Haji Abdul Djabbar. (*Kyai* means "religious and spiritual leader," the same as *maulana*, for example, in South Asian countries.) He was a very humble, simple man. Everything about the place and the people was humble but exotic at the same time. I recall seeing a bicycle for the first time and longing to learn to ride—at the time, even a bicycle was exotic to me.

My name was originally Utteng, not Shamsi. When the Kyai saw my primary school certificate, he asked me what Utteng meant, but none of us knew. He was a very religious person and didn't feel I should have a name with no Islamic meaning, and it was then that he asked my family to change my name. The pesantren leader wanted me to be called Shamsi because it means "sun" in Arabic, and Ali, which means "high." Basically, he said, I was to give light and sun to others. I respected and accepted that he changed my name, and after that people in the school called me Shamsi. And gradually I began to think there was wisdom behind it.

In the beginning it was very tough for me to move away from home. The pesantren was a boarding school, and it was my first time living away from my parents. I was very homesick. We had to take care of ourselves fully, except for cooking. We washed our own clothes, we cleaned our own rooms. It was a tough life for us at twelve, thirteen years old. We were only allowed to go back to the village twice a year. Despite the overwhelming homesickness, I think the most difficult part for me was the fact that I had to be disciplined and was expected to follow all their rules very strictly. My rebellious nature resisted this and often during those early days I called the pesantren a "holy jail."

Luckily, three months after I started, it was Ramadan and we were given permission to go home. I went back and celebrated Eid al Fitr—the end of Ramadan—in the village. I also began to notice things I'd not noticed before.

The village people back home claimed to be Muslim but still clung to pagan practices. Outside my village, in the middle of the jungle, there is a huge rock, and people used to visit it for ritual services, for cures and such. I still remember that my mother and father used to do that—if any of us were sick, they would go there and pray and say that if we were cured, they would slaughter a chicken in front of the rock. In my house, there was a stone that was believed to be inherited from our communal grandparents, and it was considered sacred. My mother used to make special food and present the food to that stone.

After my three months in the pesantren, I had certainly learned something about Islam, the Prophet, and the oneness of God. When I had come home, out of her joy and happiness, my mother had prepared special food for me. But before giving it to me, she presented it to the rock, to bless it. And I understood at that time that this was wrong. Secretly, I threw that food in the garbage. When my mother knew what I had done, she was so scared that she got sick for three days. She was scared that this sacred rock would curse us.

I tried to explain that the rock had no power, but she didn't understand. She had a very strong belief in that practice and she had no knowledge about the truth of God. People in the village grew up traditionally and had no knowledge about the real religion of Islam. But in the pesantren, I realized, I was learning many things my people back home did not know.

At the school, daily and early, we would pray *Fajr*, the prayer before sunrise, and often the teacher would come to us and see who wanted to pray even earlier—4:00 or 5:00 a.m. Then we would listen to the Kyai's speech until sunrise, then we would shower, have breakfast, and go to class. The actual classes would start at 7:30 a.m. We studied math, science, and the secular subjects until noon, when we would have prayer and lunch. Then we would delve into Islamic studies—Arabic language, Islamic law, Islamic history, and so on—until around 5:00 p.m., when we prayed *Asr*, the late-afternoon prayer. Then you could choose an exercise to practice, such as soccer, badminton, or *silat*, a martial art that is like Indonesian kung fu. Almost every day we trained, and silat was wonderful because I found I could express my rebellious nature in a constructive way.

In the pesantren, we were only allowed to speak Indonesian for the first three months after arriving. My native tongue was a dialect, so this took some effort. We also began learning English the first year there. Once we started learning, we were strictly held to practicing Arabic four days a week and English three days a week. Although we were learning English, I found myself looking forward to Arabic lessons more. Every afternoon, teachers would teach us some Arabic vocabulary, perhaps ten words or so. After we learned a word in Arabic, we were allowed to use that word only in Arabic. So, for example, if we had been taught the Arabic word for "door" but used the Indonesian word for it, and someone around heard us, we would get into trouble; we would get punished. The punishment was usually cleaning the bathroom or the mosque. I was thus encouraged to speak Arabic very quickly. And I fell in love with the language.

The beginning of faith came to me through the Kyai. He would come to our rooms late at night and in his very gentle voice would wake up the students and ask them to pray the night prayers, known as *Tahajjud* or *quyamul lail*. Sometimes these nighttime prayer sessions were so peaceful because the pesantren was outside the city and very quiet. I was influenced not so much by the Kyai's speeches as by his actions, and it was these that later made me realize what it meant to believe in God. His patience when he dealt with us—some of the students were in the pesantren because they were rebellious and their parents could not handle them—was quite extraordinary. But the Kyai was very wise and very serene. I never saw him outwardly angry; he would only smile, and that became to me the reflection of what religiosity was. It touched me spiritually and psychologically. His humbleness and humility and perseverance motivated me to follow his way of being and act as he did. My rebellious nature was still there, but I slowly learned to deal with it in a better way. The Kyai influenced me to control myself, to resist my ego sometimes.

Also, God blessed me with what I was told was a beautiful voice, and when I was in school I used to compete with friends to do the call to prayer, the *azzan*. I enjoyed going to the mosque earlier than the others in order to do the call, and I enjoyed sitting in the front row, behind the teacher. I tried to make my voice as beautiful as I could. I still remember the sound system: it was so huge. There were two campuses, one for boys and the other for girls, and the voice carried on that sound system could go all the way to the other side, from our campus to the girls' campus. It was a source of a pride for me that the girls could hear me all the way on their campus. We competed among ourselves: who was chosen to do the call, who was studying well, who was on time, who behaved the best. It was a type of training and discipline that was completely the opposite of how I had lived in the village.

I came back to the village for a second time after almost one year away. In the pesantren we had informal classes in addition to formal ones, one of which was public speech. Every night we had two or three students practicing how to speak in public, and I practiced too. Back in the village, I had an opportunity to deliver a sermon on Islam. I still had a defiant nature, and I gave a speech that was highly critical, disdaining the rituals I felt were pagan, like the sacredness of the rock. People were very surprised by my attitude, but they were not angry with me. I was only about thirteen, but they saw me as someone studying in the city, so they considered me a source of pride for the village. In addition, because I was studying in a pesantren and learning about Islam, they gave my words a certain respect, thinking that I should know better than they did. I called them on their *shirk*, which means taking partners beside God or objects other than God in worship, such as the practice of worshipping stones. And they listened, even if they didn't change their ways.

In the pesantren, we didn't have television; we didn't have radio or newspapers. In fact, we were not allowed to have those because they were considered distractions. We were only there to study and to concentrate on studying. We were preparing there for the future, whether it was further education or integrating into society. We even had a small farm there where we learned to grow rice. These things were all in preparation for when we left, so that we could be productive and would have some skills and something to do. There was training in construction, for example—how to build buildings. The Kyai used to say: "You are studying here not just to nourish your minds, but to know how to live your lives." Later in my life, I came to know that this is a part of Islam, but I didn't think of it that way at the time.

To be honest, I didn't have much information about the outside world until the second year of senior high school. A teacher from Al-Azhar, the famous Islamic university in Cairo, was appointed to teach Arabic in Jakarta and came to visit our school. He was the first foreign person I ever saw. I felt proud that we could speak to him in Arabic. Later on, a group of Pakistanis who were part of the Tabligi Jamaat (TJ)—a group of Muslims who normally invite other Muslims to come to the mosques and remind them to practice their religion—visited our school and stayed several days. They were wearing turbans and *shalwar kameez* and long beards, and spoke to us in English, and again we felt a source of pride that we could communicate with outsiders in another tongue.

As far as learning about the city, while most of the Islamic studies and Arabic teachers were residents of the pesantren, most of the teachers of our secular subjects lived outside the campus and came from the city. Sometimes they would talk about life in the city, about movies and contemporary goings-on. Indonesians are very influenced by Bollywood movies, and we would hear about those. Some students would sneak out and have adventures—smoking and seeing movies mainly.

One adventure I had took place in my junior year. There was a student named Mustafa, who was physically bigger and taller than me. We had to take our bowls and such back into the kitchen in lines, and one day he cut the line and I became angry about it and told him so. He gave me a "So what?" kind of response, and we got into an argument, whereupon he challenged me to fight. I was very well trained in self-defense from silat at the time, and so we went behind the school and I beat him very badly. I was about seventeen at the time and was not very worried about getting kicked out of school. But Mustafa's uncle was in the police, and the following day I was arrested and put into jail. I stayed there for two weeks. My Kyai, who was very well known and respected in the city, intervened, and that is why my stay was only two weeks. If he hadn't intervened, I might have stayed in jail longer and have had to go to court.

When I got out of jail and Mustafa got out of the hospital, the Kyai influenced us very strongly to make peace. We actually did become friends, and our families reconciled. The Kyai talked about how God was forgiving and loving and overlooked his servants' mistakes and sins. He asked us to consider this: if God was willing to forgive his servants who committed every type of sin, why would we not be willing to forgive? I still remember those words. This became a big life lesson for me. People can make mistakes, and sometimes they are huge mistakes—but then everything can be healed, and that is what reconciliation is about.

After graduating from the pesantren, I really had no plan about what I would do next. I ranked second in the graduating class, but I didn't want to go to university; I wanted to stay where I was. I had really fallen in love with living in the pesantren, and I had already become a trainer in silat, and I liked that very much too. So my teacher agreed to let me stay, and I became a teacher there.

After some months, a scholar came from the International Islamic University in Islamabad, Pakistan. He'd been invited by the Indonesian minister of religious affairs to visit different religious schools. He spoke to my teacher—I didn't know this at the time—and said that he wanted two students from the pesantren to study at his university. He also said there was a scholarship from the Muslim World League, an international Muslim organization based in Mecca, Saudi Arabia, to cover the costs. So my teacher said he would offer his best students and later came to me and another student to ask us if we'd be interested. This was about seven or eight months after I had graduated.

Of course we were interested and wanted to go. We were happy that we had an opportunity to study abroad, mainly because we saw it as a prestigious step to take. The problem was that we had to buy our own tickets to Pakistan, and this was very expensive—about eight hundred US dollars, which was a lot at the time. My father was even willing to sell some of his farmland to help me, but he could not find a buyer. Finally, the day before we were to travel, the teacher said, "Prepare." But we still didn't have tickets. I think he wanted to test our seriousness. My dad spoke to the teacher and told him that we didn't have the money, so we thought it would all be canceled. But the teacher said, "OK, we will use the pesantren's money, but we will need something as a guarantee," and my father gave the certificate to our family lands as the guarantee.

The next morning, I had a lot of friends come to the airport to see me off. This was the second high privilege I had in life—the first was going to the city to study at the pesantren, and the second was going abroad to study. It was June 1988, and I was twenty years old and had never left Indonesia. I still remember entering the security check and walking toward the airplane. It was the first time I had seen a plane, and I marveled at the whole flight experience: how the plane looked inside, how people were served food on it, takeoff and landing. At the time we planned to leave Jakarta, the capital of Indonesia, I did not have the visa for Pakistan yet. And so we stayed several days in Jakarta to obtain both the Indian and Pakistani visas.

There is a special and beautiful place in Jakarta called Ancol and a famous doctor called Dr. Noor, who helped us there. We stayed in a mosque, and people brought us food and other people arranged visas for us to visit India and Pakistan. After a week, once we obtained the visas, I boarded the KLM flight to India. This was the first time I had seen foreign ladies in my life—European and Indian stewardesses.

We arrived in India and took a very old taxi to a Tabligi Jamaat building in New Delhi called Nizaamudeen. We arrived at night and were assigned to open rooms, where many people slept on simple beds. In the morning when we woke, I was surprised to find thousands of people—some Arab, some European, some Indian, some African—mostly dressed in white garments. I was moved by the breadth of the *ummah*, the Muslim community, which I now saw. We prayed our morning prayer in congregation, but there was no microphone used. I chose to sit all the way in the back in order to observe those crowds, so I could not hear the imam's voice clearly.

After the prayer we listened to a long speech, which I think was in Urdu but which was also translated into Arabic and English. Then we ate our breakfast with all these people, eating quite fancy food—meat, roti, yogurt, and certainly *chai*. Looking at the food and the number of people made me wonder where the Tabligi people got the money to prepare such food for thousands of people three times every day. I was very impressed by the community there, by the generosity we saw and received, and I tried to absorb it all. They assigned us to a region called Khanpur, an area with a large Muslim population, to preach. We stayed there for three days, listening to lectures, praying, eating, and preaching. It was a whole new world for us.

All these years later, I can still remember what my Kyai told me before we left Indonesia. He said he could not guarantee me an easy journey or an easy life, but he had done all he could to prepare me. He reminded me about our life in the pesantren and how going abroad, being able to study in Pakistan, my ability to speak two important foreign languages, both Arabic and English, just having our education was a privilege. He said, "You have every tool possible that I could arm you with: patience, wisdom, exercise. You know how to use your heart when you judge something, not just your intellect." And he said—and this I remember so clearly—"You have learned not only knowledge, but you have learned life."

CHAPTER TWO

Child of a Dynasty

RABBI MARC SCHNEIER

My mother claims that when I was two I had the habit of standing on a table and pretending to be speaking, or preaching, like my father, Rabbi Arthur Schneier. I just had a great affinity for the synagogue and for the Jewish people. I would spend more time at the synagogue than at home. On my father's side, I was a descendant of seventeen generations of rabbis, so it was something very natural. Even as a child, I believed that you need an opportunity to contribute to something that is eternal, such as the Jewish people.

There were no children in my synagogue, Park East Synagogue in New York City. When my father came there in 1962, it was practically an old-folks' home. The president was ninety-two years old. The token children were my sister and me. I was three years old. Perhaps what I felt was more an affinity for my father than the synagogue. For example, if I had the opportunity to go to an unveiling with my father, I didn't have the patience for that.[1] He would go off and do the unveiling, and I would have a tuna-fish sandwich and sit in the car. I didn't understand what he was doing; I would be playing with a football or baseball among the cemetery monuments. But it was Sunday with my father.

---

1. The unveiling ceremony takes place at the grave after the traditional period of mourning.

There was a Jewish aristocracy on the Upper East Side. The synagogues were cathedral-like, and our homes and etiquette were refined. Jewish observance had to be done to a maximal standard of quality.

Our home was unique because of the guests I was exposed to through my father's work: many chief rabbis, visiting dignitaries. It became an international hub. I was exposed to leaders from all walks of life. I was always encouraged to participate, sometimes to the extent that I felt like I was performing. I was made to present a *d'var Torah* or discuss the weekly portion. It wasn't directed to people "in the know," who were knowledgeable about Jewish texts and traditions, but to many who were secular or non-Jewish. I think that enabled me to develop the skill to disseminate a message of Torah scholarship to people who lack the background.

Music always had a very powerful meaning for me, a very spiritual meaning, and I discovered that through my best friend growing up, David Merkin. The Merkins and the Schneiers were two of the few Orthodox Jewish families on the Upper East Side with children. Most of the Orthodox population was older. The number of Orthodox Jewish children in the neighborhood could be counted on one hand. So we were like the young princes, David and I. We were inseparable.

The Merkins had a beautiful weekend home in Atlantic Beach. The summer I was nine years old, I attended the local synagogue, and I heard this magnificent, glorious voice. I had an epiphany. I didn't know what it was, but I had never heard anything like it. It was Cantor Louis Danto. I remember asking my father, "Why don't you have a cantor of that stature?" For years I kept saying, "You have to get a great cantor!" Eventually he brought in a great cantor for his synagogue.

My mom's side of the family was from Miami, so I used to spend much time there with my grandparents. My grandfather was the first Jewish Sabbath-observant physician in South Florida, and he also founded and was a generous supporter of the Hebrew Academy of Miami Beach. I used to go down on January holiday, over the Christmas and New Year's school recess. When everyone would run and get changed—my grandparents had a beautiful pool—I would look at family pictures and listen to cantorial music in the living room. I would just sit there. Something in that music spoke to me.

From watching my father, I became fascinated with the idea of becoming a rabbi. My father broke the mold. He was enormously creative in how he grew the synagogue, built a platform, and became an international religious leader. One day I came home from school and saw someone sitting in my father's chair. I walked over and I said, "Can you please get up? That is my father's seat." I wasn't trying to be disrespectful, but I didn't know who it was. And it was Rabbi Levin, the chief rabbi of Moscow.

Then there was Rabbi Rosen, the chief rabbi of Romania, who to this day I see as one of the greatest rabbinic figures of the twentieth century. Rabbi Rosen was a surrogate grandfather. He hoped that I would succeed him one day in Bucharest. Rabbi Rosen, under Ceausescu, transferred 400,000 members of his community to Israel. Brilliant man. I remember the July when I was sixteen, I was with my father in Bucharest at a celebration of Rabbi Rosen's anniversary, I think his thirtieth as chief rabbi. The president of the Orthodox Union was at the podium, saying he was speaking on behalf of one million Jews. I was sitting next to a member of the Romanian Parliament, and very innocently he said to me, "Marc, I didn't realize there were thirty or forty million Jews in the United States. Because every American Jewish leader speaking says he is representing millions of Jews."

Until eighth grade, I went to Ramaz, a Modern Orthodox day school in my neighborhood on the Upper East Side. I graduated at the top of my class in sixth grade, and I was greatly influenced by my sixth-grade teacher, Rabbi Ephraim Buchwald. I was a student council leader in junior high school. I was very popular, but I knew I wanted to be a rabbi. In 1972, at Ramaz, Talmud study was more of a token class than the core subject it is today. So I left Ramaz to go to high school at Manhattan Talmudical Academy (MTA), which is the high school for Yeshiva University. As I explained to Ramaz principal Rabbi Haskel Lookstein, no one forced me. I wanted to do it.

My high school experience reinforced the idea that Judaism was Orthodoxy and everything else was compromise. As I think back now, I was a robot. A robot. I was programmed: this is how we daven, this is where we daven, this is how we learn and what we learn, this is how we prepare and what we don't prepare. I even thought my father was perhaps too flexible in terms of his dealings with other religious leaders, as in, "Why are you wasting your time?" "Why aren't you doing more for the Jewish people?"—that sort of insular thinking.

The irony is that that I had such a miserable experience at MTA that

I almost ended up not going to YU and not becoming a rabbi. I found MTA very limited—the administration, the teachers, the students. They could not see beyond their small community, their little Torah corner of the world. They lacked sophistication. I had very much enjoyed my time at Ramaz, but I wanted to be a rabbi and I knew I had to make certain sacrifices. I came to MTA with a certain ambivalence. I remember I started getting involved in student activities toward my junior year and I volunteered to chair the high school's Yom Hashoah (Holocaust Memorial Day) commemoration. I told the assistant principal, Rabbi George Finkelstein, I wanted to invite a family friend, Elie Wiesel, to speak. And he said, "He's not *shomer Shabbos* [orthodox]; we wouldn't be comfortable." I was appalled. Not only were his facts incorrect, but I found his comment both offensive and provincial. And that's when I washed my hands of the place. It left me with such a bad taste. I was just going to grin and bear it, and that's a pretty horrible feeling entering college. I had just sacrificed four years of high school and now I was going to going to sacrifice four years of college, all in order to become a rabbi. I felt like I was being martyred just to fulfill my dream. I was in a pretty despondent place.

When I entered YU in 1976, after my traumatic experience at MTA, I said to myself, "If I want to become a rabbi, I have to get through these four years." I was going to live at home and commute, but then I decided, "OK, let's try the dorm." And my first day in the dormitory, I saw on the walls an announcement of elections for freshman class president. I thought to myself, "You know . . ."

To make a long story short, I was the only student in the school's history who's ever gone from freshman class president to sophomore class president to school secretary-treasurer my junior year and to student body president my senior year. The school paper, the *Commentator*, would frequently comment on my leadership style. One of the headlines that year was "YU Student Government: Marxcism with a C." I ran the student government with an iron hand. And YU student government was a wonderful source of fulfillment. I had a good balance in my life at that point. Yeshiva University allowed me to go back to my roots, in terms of looking outside my little comfort zone, being concerned with others, with greater issues.

The late Ed Koch was a member of Park East, my father's synagogue, and I worked in his office on Capitol Hill in Washington as an intern in the summer of 1975, before my senior year in high school. I was a great tennis player—I taught tennis in camp, I watched tennis; really, I was obsessed with tennis. That summer, the men's finals of the US Open, I discovered, were on Rosh Hashanah. I thought this was extremely insensitive, especially as the tournament was in New York, my hometown.

So there I was, in a congressman's office, during the summer doldrums. I was responsible for responding to Ed Koch's foreign affairs correspondence—his position on Turkey, on Israel, whatever. I said to Koch, "Would you mind if I wrote a letter in your name to Bill Talbert, complaining that the Open finals are being held on Rosh Hashanah, a sacred Jewish holiday?" Talbert was the president of the US Open. Koch was thrilled I'd taken the initiative.

I sent Talbert the letter, and he wrote back something to the effect that he has to worry about blacks, about Puerto Ricans, and now about Jews. I showed it to Ed Koch, suggesting that we do something about this, and in his indomitable manner, he replied, "Go for it." We knew we couldn't change the date of the Open for that year, but Koch demanded an apology for Talbert's letter and a promise that scheduling the finals on Rosh Hashanah would never happen again. I presented Talbert with a hundred-year Jewish calendar. My passion for Judaism and sports came to the fore almost twenty-five years later when, serving as president of the New York Board of Rabbis and working with New York City public advocate Mark Green, I was instrumental in introducing kosher food concessions to both Yankee and Shea stadiums.

But until that summer of 1975, I had never been on my own. No one warned me about the fact that in Washington—this is before it had a Metro—the Jewish community wasn't geographically close. I lived at Georgetown University because it provided a student shuttle to the Capitol and because there was a Modern Orthodox synagogue, Kesher, in the neighborhood. It became famous later, when Joe Lieberman was running for vice president, because it was his synagogue. But at this time, it was much smaller. Its claim to fame was that the author Herman Wouk was a member. He always brought his German shepherd to daily services, and because Herman Wouk was Herman Wouk, no one said anything about it.

But I was rooming on the Georgetown University campus, and Georgetown is a Jesuit school. I was not told about the Washington summers, and when I got there I had to choose between sharing a room with air conditioning and having a single room without it. I was already feeling so out of place on a Jesuit campus that I took the single. When the Washington summer hit, I became the suffering servant.

And then I had to find kosher food. I remember telling my parents, "Unless you resolve this, I'm returning to New York to work in Koch's district office." So they had Lou G. Segal—the famous kosher restaurant in the Garment District, which also did kosher catering for airlines—send me about forty frozen kosher TV dinners. Then I had to figure out where to store them. We used Ed Koch's freezer, Congressman Claude Pepper's freezer, Congresswoman Bella Abzug's freezer. I became known as the "kosher intern." People were fascinated—the idea of an Orthodox Jewish intern was novel. Just seeing a young man walking around the halls of Congress with a *kippa* was novel. I showed that you could be an observant Jew and work on Capitol Hill at a time when this was unknown.

But I also remember that friends of mine couldn't understand why I couldn't go out Friday night, why I couldn't play softball on Saturday, which were big social times for congressional interns. And this was my first encounter as a high school student with young men and women my age who weren't Orthodox—who weren't even Jewish. My circle had been more provincial than theirs.

The late 1970s, when I was in college, was also a time when the issue of Soviet Jewry was at its pinnacle. My father was known for his work with Soviet Jews and Eastern European Jews, but in his own way. When most people were protesting to "let my people go," he led the movement to "let my people *grow.*" Through interfaith coalitions, he was trying to get rabbinic seminaries established; he was trying to get rabbis and other religious functionaries trained. He understood in his wisdom that even if the doors of the Soviet Union were to be opened, most of the Jews would remain. So he was trying to build as much of a Jewish life there as could be built under the Communist regime—in terms of the baking of *matzot*, in terms of bringing prayer books and *chumashim* (printed Torah) and Bibles. He was never progressive in his politics, but he was pragmatic.

I accompanied him on a number of his trips—to Romania, Hungary, Moscow, Leningrad. In July 1972, I was the first American to celebrate his bar mitzvah in the Soviet Union at the Moscow Choral Synagogue. So I was directly exposed to my father's work, to his negotiations. And I was very deeply influenced by his example. Through him I saw the importance of humanism, of cross-cultural preservation. I learned how powerful it is and productive it is to have other faith leaders fight the Jewish battles and have the Jewish community fight the battles for other faith communities. It's far more potent. If you're sitting with a government official and you have a prominent priest from the United States speaking for Jewish rights, it resonates more than hearing from a rabbi alone.

On the one hand, then, my world was expanding. But the rabbinical school at YU, where I found myself next, was more confined, more parochial, than the college itself. The students at the rabbinical school had not been my circle as an undergrad. My circle was pre-law, pre-med. I found a lot of *smicha* (rabbinical) students went in because they were unclear about their career path. I felt torn between my world outside Yeshiva and my world inside Yeshiva. The teaching rabbis I was being exposed to in the practical rabbinic program were far more conventional than the rabbis I'd seen in my own home growing up.

I remember that during my third year in the seminary at YU, just before getting *smicha*—in those years it was a three-year program, not four, as it is now—I suddenly questioned myself, "Why this religion?" I used to go to the library after my class with Rabbi Soloveitchik and study comparative religion on my own. It was like I was trying to find the absolute answer, absolute truth, which I later discovered doesn't exist. I was reading, reading whatever I could find that seemingly would prove the difference between us and other religions, that would explain why God revealed himself in front of three million people at Sinai, whereas Jesus had just been in front of a few people. I was searching for that absolute guarantee that Judaism was the one true faith. It was like I was thinking, "I'm going to commit my life to the rabbinate and I want to know unequivocally that this is a superior religion, the guaranteed way of life." There was a terrible need for that kind of security.

For me, Yeshiva was more of a process, a means to an end. For me, the end was very, very clear. I knew I was going to become the associate rabbi of Park East Synagogue. I got *smicha* in 1983. I felt nothing. It was the same way I felt when I first entered YU. It was all about getting to the end, and that was joining my father at Park East. Nothing else mattered.

CHAPTER THREE

The Struggle Within

IMAM SHAMSI ALI

In August of 1988, several weeks after I entered Pakistan to attend the International Islamic University (IIU), I was traveling with a group of students, visiting mosques for perhaps three days at a time. One of the members told us that Muhammad Zia-ul-Haq, the leader of Pakistan, had just been killed in an airplane crash.

We viewed Zia as a hero who would bring back the Golden Era of Islam. He was very committed to establishing Islamic law in Pakistan, and he was viewed by some Muslims as someone who could balance the power of the West. I still remember Zia was buried next to the Grand Mosque in Islamabad just as I was coming back from my trip. In his honor, almost all leaders of the Muslim world came to participate in his burial service. That moment opened my eyes to the international world.

What also sticks in my mind are the discussions in our student circles that the United States had designed this crash to kill Zia-ul-Haq. Even though the US ambassador also died in the crash, the students said, "See how America sacrifices its own people for its own purpose." And with the Soviet Union in Afghanistan, the sense of conspiracy strengthened: first the Soviet Union invades Afghanistan and now Zia is killed in a crash. Feelings of suspicion quickly reinforced those of conspiracy—and vice versa.

Certainly, I was an innocent young guy. I was influenced by what I heard. I can still hear the people speaking loudly about it—in the cafeterias, public squares—anywhere people got together. I was annoyed by all the talk, and I thought maybe there was a certain truth to it. But I restrained myself from becoming more involved. I kept telling myself, "I am here to study," and reminding myself of that sole purpose.

In reality, there was a very strong struggle within me regarding the Islamic issue at that time. The environment in Pakistan really pushed our views toward political Islam: *Islam should dominate the world. Islam should rule.* But at the same time, I had learned in the pesantren that Islam is about how to be a better person, spiritually and socially. So I was wrestling with these competing ideas. It took all my years in Pakistan, and perhaps more years than that, to resolve that struggle for myself.

Before I had gotten my visa to Pakistan, I travelled around India with the Tabligi Jamaat for almost three weeks, visiting different cities and villages. We went to an area called Lucknow, very well known to us because of a famous scholar there named Ali Al-Nedwy. Even in Indonesia, we had heard his name. He was a Hindi-Arabic translator for the TJ; he had his own university; and he had written a book called *What the World Is Suffering*, addressing the problems Muslims were having economically, socially, and so forth, and what the consequences of that suffering were. That book was and still is a milestone for many, many Muslims. Al-Nedwy wrote about Islam's historical and contemporary roles in civilization and posited that because of the volume and depth of the Muslim world and its resources, when Muslims are suffering, and when they are underdeveloped, the impact on the rest of the world is both tangible and affecting.

Reading this book showed me that Islam should contribute to and play an important role in all human civilization. When we met with Ali Al-Nedwy, it had a big impact on me. Meeting and listening to this great Muslim scholar made me optimistic that, despite the decline in the state of the Muslim ummah, there was hope. And I felt that as a young person it was my duty to contribute to that process. I disagreed with certain things Al-Nedwy said at that meeting, but he was so charismatic and I was so young that I did not want to debate with him; it might have been considered disrespectful. I knew even then that what he was saying was not sufficient for me, but it was an important step in my realization that Islam had a larger place in the world than what I had seen.

The TJ was always very emphatic that we should avoid discussing politics: "Don't talk about the invasion of Afghanistan or Zia-ul-Haq or the Indian government…" Back in the pesantren in Indonesia, I had learned that the prophets had come to bring change, to defend those who were oppressed by political structures. So I felt that avoiding that in our discourse was limiting, and my natural inclinations were to question this.

The subject of politics was pervasive in Pakistan. Conspiracy theories were very, very common. At the time, Muslims thought that although the Soviet Union had invaded Afghanistan, the ultimate goal was really to weaken the entire Muslim world—by going into Afghanistan, then into Iran, then into Syria—any and all places that might endanger Israel. We thought that even though America was helping the mujahideen, its intention was also to ultimately have power over Muslim countries.

The idea of "America" to many was a country held by Jews, one where, again, everything came down to the Jewish world view, with the ultimate purpose of "helping the mujahideen" really being to help Israel. This was the time of the Intifada, and we knew that Jews were killing Palestinians. So my view of Jews at the time was typical of that of many Muslims: Jews are Israel, and Israel is a repressive regime; the Jewish people hate us; Jewish people are planning to dominate the world; Jewish people are behind every bad thing that happens in the world; and Israel is the actualization of it all.

At the same time, I have to mention that the Palestinian students living in Pakistan were in some ways privileged. They received a lot of aid both from common people and from governments around the world. Some of them owned motorcycles, while we struggled to pay for our food. The Saudi Arabian government gave them more, and their scholarships were higher than our scholarships. We knew the Palestinians didn't have a state, but they seemed to be enjoying life more than we were, and to be honest, some international students like me were a bit jealous of the Palestinian students. Sometimes the non-Palestinian students would even say, "There is no difference between Palestinians and Israelis," because of the uneasiness we felt seeing Palestinian students benefiting from more than we had at the time.

Despite the ambivalence we may have felt toward our Palestinian co-students, we still felt a strong allegiance to our Muslim brethren as a community. One of my professors at the IIU happened to be Pakistani and was influenced by the jihad in Afghanistan. We got to a point where we were discussing the obligation of all Muslims to defend our rights and our dignity and our honor, and he said, "Each one of you must go out and defend our country." And he meant Afghanistan. Some people would say, "You are not brave," to those who didn't feel inclined to go and fight. They felt we didn't have the same spirit as those who wanted to fight. I disagreed with that because it also says in the Qur'an that even in times of war, not all people are obligated to go out and fight, that some must stay and learn the religion. This created some tension. But it also gave me a real understanding that Islam is not a monolith: there is no *one* way of seeing it. As I often said then and still say: "If you see three Muslims, you will probably find nine opinions, on all issues, all the time."

And so I came to the conclusion that this is the way we see our religion. Things are influenced by our cultural, social, and even political affiliations, and people will always see things differently. For example, even when we deal with purely religious issues, such as the different date projections for the beginning and the end of the holy month of Ramadan, we realize there are wide avenues for the many opinions possible for real Muslims living *their* Islam. This topic of diversity within Islam met with varying levels of resistance from my teachers. I had an Egyptian professor who had graduated from the Sorbonne. He was open minded and encouraged us to debate and push back on issues. The professor explained that we could ask any question about anything that we didn't understand. I still remember one Afghani who became very angry and upset because the professor said one could even question some verses of the Holy Qur'an. But it gratified me to see Islam understood more contextually rather than just literally from some of the professors who had graduated from Western universities and who were more open to questioning. I want to preserve the balance in the way I see teaching and learning. I am orthodox but open to new interpretations of the Qur'an.

Our university was prestigious in terms of both Eastern and Western methodologies of learning. It combined the Eastern way of learning—memorization—with the Western methods of comprehension and rationalization. The professors were Egyptian, Middle Eastern, and European. Courses were taught in Arabic and in English. I took Islamic studies, which was 50 percent in Arabic, 50 percent in English. The Shari'a faculty, whose specialty was Islamic law, was 70 percent Arabic and 30 percent English, and we also studied international law, especially British law, which Pakistan used. There was an Arabic faculty, which was about 80 percent Arabic alongside English speakers. This university was intentionally international and wanted to arm the students with an international sensibility.

The summer of 1989, I went on the hajj (the pilgrimage to Mecca) for the first time. Because it is not easy for hajjis who don't speak the language, the government of Indonesia had hired some students who could speak Arabic to be guides for the Indonesian pilgrims.[1] They hired and paid us—a major boon since our scholarships were so low and we were always in need of funding.

As I've noted, I am naturally rebellious, a little bit tough, and until then I had never cried in my life, even when I left Indonesia and my family behind. Though others cried because they didn't have any money to go back to their countries or because the uncertainty of leaving everything behind could be overwhelming, when I left Indonesia, I really gave my life over to God and felt no sadness. I cannot overemphasize the importance of going to Mecca and to hajj for me, and what an emotional experience it truly was. We landed in Jeddah, which at night seems very shiny because there is a lot of conspicuous electricity. We went to Mecca directly and entered into the Grand Mosque. It was huge. And you can imagine, as a Muslim, five times a day you pray in the direction of Mecca, so the day you find yourself there, facing that place you prayed toward, with the Ka'bah in front of you . . . For others, it is just an object, but for Muslims, there is a spiritual connection.

I was tearing up for the first time, and I just felt so humble. I thought, "I am sitting here and so young and in front of the Ka'bah and praying to God Almighty . . ." It was an absolutely overwhelmingly huge thing for me. I was only twenty years old, worshipping Almighty God in the very place that was the center of my spiritual direction. None of the people in my village—not in the entire municipality, as far as I knew—had ever been to hajj. For Indonesians, when you even mention the word "hajj,"

1. *Hajji* are people who perform hajj, or the pilgrimage to Mecca. It is interchangeable with the word "pilgrim."

it is enormous. When people in my village knew that I was in Mecca doing hajj, for them it was incomparable to anything else. Being a materially successful person would not matter too much to them, but when you say someone from this village has gone to hajj—this is an immeasurable thing. For Indonesians, the completion of hajj itself becomes part of your name, an honorary and honorific title. I had thus become "Hajji Shamsi Ali." And each hajj I've undertaken has been remarkable for me for many reasons, both spiritually and temporally.

When undertaking the hajj one performs certain rituals, like circumambulating the Ka'bah, running between the two mountains of Safa and Marwa seven times (the symbol of Haggar looking for water for Ishmael when they were alone in the desert), and going out to Arafat, a mountainous area, and standing there for almost an entire day, praying to God, performing rituals of introspection. Then you travel to a place called Muzdalifah and stay there overnight, remembering God and preparing yourself for the next day's fight against the devil, for which you collect small pebbles. The following day you go to Mina, the devil's place, to throw these stones against three pillars.[2] The biggest devil is called Jamrat-ul-Aqaba. In Mina, we proclaim the greatness of God and ask His protection from evil, while throwing the seven stones to symbolically chip away at the devil as we do so. As Prophet Muhammad said, the biggest jihad is the one waged against one's own self, and this is symbolic of that jihad—the fight against our own evils. The most difficult war is always that against the negative things in our own nature.

After the first stoning, we go to a middle mound and then to a smaller one. Once the rituals are carried out, we conclude by shaving our heads or cutting our hair. This symbolizes cleansing, that we ourselves are now clean, that we are coming into a new chapter, that we are newly born.

The most interesting discussion I had on the hajj was when we came back from the place for shaving our heads. There was a Saudi man who asked us how many times we had come to hajj. We told him it was our first time, and then we asked the same of him. He said, "Never." And he looked to be above sixty. He was a Meccan, and he had never performed

---

2. Due to the high volume of worshippers throwing stones 360 degrees around the pillars, in 2004, the Saudis erected walls to replace the pillars for pilgrims' safety.

hajj. We wondered why not. And he said, "I will do it later on, because I am here." We were surprised by that statement even as he went on to tell us he had been to New York and France and various other places. More surprising still was that he said he always prayed *outside* of the mosque. When I asked him why that was, he said that he had a gold store that he had to take care of. When the *azzan* was called, he just stood up and prayed where he was, so he didn't have to leave his shop. He had never even been inside the Great Mosque. I was quite stunned. For me, as a student, to see and feel the hajj was such an important event in life, and it was a surprise to meet people—including many Saudis—who didn't really practice their religion. Prior to that, I'd felt that "Saudi" was synonymous with "religious people." I came to the realization there and then that just because someone was Saudi, it did not mean he or she was religious. This discussion remained in my memory. It was one of the temporal aspects of the hajj that affected me greatly.

Another temporal result of (a later) hajj was finding my wife. It was my third year in the university, I was twenty-two, and I felt it was time for me to marry; twenty-two is not an early age for Indonesians. In the university, we didn't have any contact with women. It was not allowed. I didn't know any women my age, and I had no idea how to go about the proposal business. I went to work again that summer for the Indonesian government as a hajj guide. It happened that my future father- and mother-in-law were going to Mecca that year as well. Normally when people go to Mecca, they inform their relatives and friends because it is a great privilege, and I had mentioned this to my family and friends back home. My pesantren teacher and father-in-law are brothers, so I knew they were going, and in Mecca we met each other.

I mentioned to them that I wanted to go back to Indonesia to find a suitable wife, and they asked if I had anyone in mind, to which I replied no. I asked them how to prepare for a proposal, and my mother-in-law-to-be actually took me to some stores to buy gifts for my future wife. She asked me to buy a ring and some Muslim clothing from Mecca and an antique platter, the kind you can put on a table. Just simple Meccan things, but for an Indonesian, things from Mecca are a big deal. These are the things that we bought for the *mahr*, the dowry that I intended for my future bride. I had no idea I would eventually be marrying their daughter!

After hajj, I went back to Indonesia and to the pesantren to see my teacher. He took me to meet different candidates for marriage, but there were no positive results. After days enquiring with some former students of the pesantren and some family members about a possible match, nothing had materialized. Finally my teacher suggested his niece to me, one of the daughters of his brother. His brother actually had three daughters, of which my wife is the oldest. My teacher said, "You can choose one of those girls." I was surprised and shocked he said that to me, because I did not expect at all to marry from my teacher's family. We considered that family so honorable that it would be beyond my expectation to marry a girl from his circle. But my teacher assured me it was indeed suitable, and so we went to see his brother, my father-in-law-to-be, and met with him at his house.

In the beginning I was extremely shy about this meeting and asked my teacher to represent me with his brother and sister-in-law. But he insisted that I must be present to propose to one of his brother's daughters. My soon-to-be father-in-law and I both felt a slight embarrassment at realizing we had met already on hajj, but my teacher happened to be his older brother and well respected in the family, so no one said anything. Finally, the man who was to become my father-in-law said, "I have three daughters. You can meet them and talk to them." In my mind it was not traditional to talk to a girl still in the pesantren, so I said, "I don't have to talk to them," but after a short talk between my father-in-law, his brother, and his wife, I decided to choose the oldest daughter, who was seventeen. I thought choosing the oldest was appropriate because I wanted someone who could accompany me to Pakistan, someone who was relatively mature. So we all agreed, and it was decided we would marry.

When I told my family the news, my father had no objection, but my older brother, whom I considered the second father in the family, completely rejected the idea. I don't know why, but he said to me, "You are studying abroad. Why don't you marry from outside, a foreigner?" I declined that idea. I wanted someone to understand me, who came from my culture, who would travel with me to Pakistan. He did not accept it and did not agree to the marriage. Finally we arranged the marriage without his consent. When we married (in the pesantren itself), I was quite alone; my father didn't come because of his advanced age, and my brother didn't come because he objected to it. The only person who came to my marriage was the person who hosted my brother in his home during his schooling.

I had intended to go to the Middle East to continue my studies, to get a master's degree in a university in Saudi Arabia or Egypt. But now that I was married, I needed a better job. The International Islamic University hosted the largest mosque in Pakistan, the King Faisal Mosque. It is a very beautiful mosque in a mountainous area, and there was to be a selection of a *muezzin* (the mosque designate who performs the call to prayer) from among the university students. The first challenger for the muezzin position was my colleague from Indonesia, the one who had gotten to IIU on scholarship with me. He had beautiful recitation also, but I defeated him for the position and was selected. I was also selected to be the assistant imam. The imam there (Professor Mahmood Ghazi) used to be the religious minister under the Musharraf government. (He has since passed away.) He could only go to noon prayers, late afternoon, and sunset, which left the evening (*Isha*) and morning (*Fajr*) prayers for me. This position was a big privilege because, especially on Friday, thousands of people—maybe five, seven, even ten thousand—prayed there. It was a huge mosque, and I was the one who recited the Qur'an before the Friday service and the one who called them to prayer. Normally, in Pakistani culture, the imam is someone with a long beard—which was something I certainly did not have. Sometimes when I led the prayer, people didn't object until I turned my face to them, then one by one they'd come up to me and ask me, "Why'd you shave your beard? You are an imam; you are supposed to grow your beard." And I would just laugh and sometimes say, "You know, I have my beard inside," because I knew what they meant, what a beard represented. I held that position for about two years and enjoyed it very much.

When I finished my bachelor's degree, I didn't know what to do next. I thought about going back to Indonesia to my old pesantren to teach, but ultimately decided not to because I knew the salary there would make it very hard for me to support my family. God the Almighty had already blessed me with my first daughter, and because we already had a child and I needed more money to support my family, I was looking for new opportunities. At the time, the Saudi government was organizing schools for Afghani refugees around the capital, Islamabad. The salary was quite high—around five hundred US dollars monthly. In Pakistan in 1992 that was good money, and I applied to teach there. I was accepted, and I decided to continue with my graduate degree at the IIU, besides continuing to be a muezzin and working for the new Saudi school.

I finished my master's degree in comparative studies of religion in 1994. Toward the end of my teaching period in the Saudi school, a Saudi man who happened to be the director of the Islamic Education Foundation in Jeddah arrived there to observe and to recruit teachers to work for him. He was looking for teachers who could speak English and Arabic, and so the school principal came to me and said, "I have a guest. His name is Hamood Ashmimry, and he is looking for a teacher to teach back at his academy in Jeddah." I had just finished my master's degree and hadn't a clue what to do next, so I accepted the job offer. I went back to Indonesia for a few days, taking my family back home until I could set up a house for us, and at the end of 1994, I went to Saudi Arabia to work.

I saw being allowed to live and teach in Saudi Arabia as a great privilege for any Muslim, but especially one like myself who came from a faraway and remote area in Indonesia. The Islamic Education Foundation was an institute for non-Arab professionals to learn Arabic and Islamic culture. It was a great job, and in the beginning I liked it very much. The problem was that the teaching method in Saudi Arabia was very inflexible; you had to follow the method they already had established, with the books they prescribed. It was difficult for me personally, especially with my rebellious nature, to feel I had no freedom of thought. We were teaching non-Muslims mostly—Australians, British, and Americans. But the directors wanted us to talk about Islam only in the way the Saudis understand it. I do really feel I'm a committed Muslim. But I thought the Saudi people were much too strict and literalist, though I did not use the term "radical." The Wahhabi interpretation of Islam, which is the norm in Saudi Arabia, is literal and divisive in its nature, and its followers are very aggressive. To avoid tension, I normally chose to persuade them rather than to debate with them. But the prevailing attitudes created tensions between members of the community in a way that damaged the true teaching of Islam.

The inflexibility I faced there crept up in many guises. One day I was asked whether it would be correct for a woman to visit a graveyard. I said there was no prohibition, though some say that if men and women are there together, the women will get too emotional. My opinion was not consistent with the Sunnah, the Prophet's understanding of Islam in the Salafi interpretation, which was their way.[3] The next day I was called in by the director and told that what I'd said was anti-Islamic. Another example occurred within our school: the Saudis wanted to have the women students completely separated—to listen to us by voice from the next room. I said, "That is not effective teaching." There is no direct encounter with the teacher; while the male students can interrupt or ask questions, the women cannot. So I said, "Maybe the women can be in the same room, but in the back rows." To this too, the director said, "This is un-Islamic."

I wore my own clothing, such as Indonesian shirts or normal pants and *batik* (Indonesian traditional cloth), which also was not looked upon kindly. And as an Indonesian, I wasn't able to grow a long beard. I received criticism for this on a daily basis. I debated this with my professors and colleagues; I did not and do not want to be dictated to. Once I said to one of the scholars, "If long Arabic clothes are Islamic, then why did the opponents of the Prophet have them, too?" I sensed a kind of inclination from the scholar to agree with me, but he would not and did not express it. I don't know why I didn't feel the threat of excommunication, but I refused to back down.

There is an unspoken notion that non-Saudis and non-Arabs are not considered knowledgeable in Islam. That general attitude is openly stated on a daily basis as well. When I gave a public lecture, the Saudis in the audience would not pay attention because they assumed they were more knowledgeable than me. A friend of mine used to say jokingly about this: "The Prophet was sent to the Arab people—to correct attitude!"

The experience was not just a personal disappointment for me. In many ways, the larger community of Muslims is disappointed with the lives of Muslims in the Arab countries. We know Islam is open and inclusive, and suddenly we found this society that is exclusive in the very name of religion. From that time on, I felt the contradiction. We want to see the glory and beauty of Islam in the lives of people, which means re-

---

3. *Sunnah* means "traditions." Prophet Muhammad's Sunnah are his examples and his observed and noted traditions, words, and deeds.

specting their freedom and promoting social justice. Yet I found in Saudi Arabia that even Muslims could not organize religious services in their own homes without special government permits. I, for example, wanted to have lectures in my home for Indonesian expatriates, and I was not allowed to do so.

After nine months in Jeddah, although I knew it would be an adjustment for them, I finally invited my wife and daughter to join me, simply because I felt lonely and the society was very exclusive. It was really difficult for my wife. She had to cover her face—something she'd never done before. She could not go anywhere without me. And I was very disturbed by the mistreatment of Indonesian workers there. The Indonesian consulate in Jeddah organized Friday services, and I gave the sermons. After it was over, the men came to me and told me stories of what happened to female workers. We did some research about the mistreatment of Indonesian workers in Saudi Arabia. We found physical abuse, such as beating of workers, sexual abuse, and psychological abuse. There were women who ran away from their employers but could not get out of the country because the employers had taken their passports.

One of the stories that really stayed in my memory was about a woman in her twenties who jumped out of the window of her employer's house. According to her, from the very beginning of her arrival she had been abused by her employer's wife physically and by the husband sexually. One day the employer's family went away, and she was left imprisoned in the house (the house was locked from outside) for days until she ran out of food. She decided to jump from the window. I questioned myself at the time: Are these people really following Islam or what? I found Western people were treated better than Muslim people. It sadly reinforced the feeling I'd had years before on my first hajj: being an Arab or a Saudi was not a guarantee of being a better Muslim.

After my two-year contract in Jeddah was up, the institute wanted me to stay. I decided not to and left for Indonesia. In 1996, I received an offer from the Indonesian ambassador to the United Nations, Nugroho Wisnumurti, to come to New York to lead the Indonesian Muslim Community Center, later known as Masjid Al-Hikmah, in the Astoria neighborhood of Queens. And that is how my family and I came to New York.

CHAPTER FOUR

The Empathetic Imagination

RABBI MARC SCHNEIER

One day in 1968, when I was eight years old, my father showed up at the Ramaz School to take me home. I asked him why he was there, and he said, "Dr. Martin Luther King was assassinated." And I said, "Who is Dr. King?" That was my first question. I didn't even know. I remember that same year in school, I was doing a report about African Americans in the South and I used the word "Negro." And the teacher crossed it out and said, "Now we refer to them as 'black.'" I was so oblivious.

Or maybe it was worse than oblivious. I was afraid. I was afraid especially as a young man walking the streets of New York. Growing up on the Upper East Side in the 1960s, you had certain biases. I remember when I went to day camp, a lot of the kids who came from Manhattan came from the Upper West Side. I had to wait for the camp bus there. And I remember being very uneasy about *that*. So let's not even discuss Harlem or Washington Heights. Whether kids were black or Hispanic, it was all the same thing to me. I was mugged three times walking from the A Train up to Yeshiva. So that was my knowledge of the black community.

As the years passed, it got worse. Out of my ignorance, I saw blacks as the enemy, the enemy of the Jews: Andrew Young meeting with the PLO when he was UN ambassador; Jesse Jackson saying New York was "Hymietown"; Farrakhan. "They're like Arabs, they're like Palestinians," I thought. I even remember in my early days of venturing into interracial work attending a dinner where the honoree, who was African American, spoke about his visit to Israel, and he kept referring to the Palestinians as "the PLO—the People Left Out." Like blacks are left out. That was his point. I wouldn't say I had an active bias, but I had my view. Like most Jews or, rather, like most Orthodox Jews, I felt that the black community was no longer our friend and had sided with the Palestinians.

I had an epiphany in 1988. Ed Koch, who was in his third term as mayor then, held a Martin Luther King Jr. commemoration at City Hall on the federal holiday, and he asked me to deliver the invocation. It was an incredibly tense time for race relations in New York, not long after the Tawana Brawley hoax and the Howard Beach killings.[1] But Koch reached out to me, since I had worked for him in Congress and was now a rabbi at Park East. So maybe it was providential that Koch invited me, one of those forces of the universe setting me on the course to my destiny.

All I know is that when I heard the Boys Choir of Harlem singing "Lift Every Voice and Sing," that's when I had my revelation. I felt a spiritual connection. I felt the pain and the suffering of the African American community. There was something soulful about the song, the performance. Something that made me feel so connected. The feeling of wanting to help those who are struggling is very much part and parcel of who I am. I can't quite describe it. I've just always felt like a very sensitive person, an old soul. I like to use the term *empathetic imagination*. But I also recognized the fact that in the beginning, wanting to work with the black community, I had to walk on eggshells.

———

So my objective became to meet as many African American leaders as possible to understand the community and size up the playing field: to figure out who was influential, who were the movers and shakers.

In 1989, following Ed Koch's defeat to David Dinkins, I supported Dinkins heavily in his mayoral campaign. To the chagrin of many in the

---

1. Brawley, an African American teenager, claimed that a "white cop" had smeared her with feces and stuffed her into a garbage bag. Her claims, trumpeted by the Reverend Al Sharpton and accepted as true by many blacks, were later exposed as fabrications. In the Howard Beach incident, a gang of whites in that Queens neighborhood set upon several black men whose car had broken down and were looking for help. The mob chased one of the blacks, Michael Griffith, onto the Belt Parkway and into the path of a car that struck and killed him.

Orthodox community, I was known as David Dinkins's rabbi. Dinkins introduced me to his closest friends and supporters, among them the most influential members of New York's African American community. Darwin Davis was one of Dinkins's best friends. I was—what, twenty-eight, thirty? Darwin was going on sixty, and he was the executive vice president of the Equitable Life Insurance Company, clearly one of the highest-ranking African Americans in the corporate world. Darwin was part of an illustrious club, along with Ed Lewis, Earl Graves. They were the black corporate gang. And they were connected to Basil Paterson, Percy Sutton, Charles Rangel—the political pack. In their community, I felt like the minority. I was the outsider. They had their own culture and their own language. And I found it very intriguing. They were as corporate as white America and often they even had greater influence among other business leaders as the only African American leaders in their industries.

Darwin kind of adopted me. We'd have lunch together; we'd have dinner together. Sometimes I'd take him to a kosher restaurant, or he'd have me to his office. He was a wise, erudite man, a man of great wisdom. I learned a lot about family and values, and I was very inspired by his struggle. You can only imagine what a Darwin Davis went through to reach the top of the corporate ladder.

It's one thing to see the finished product—there's Darwin Davis sitting in this glamorous, opulent office, overlooking the Hudson River. But he could remember stories his parents and grandparents told him—he's two generations away from slavery. He told me of his experiences, growing up in Michigan, being in the South, being in the Army. When he got out of college with a business degree, General Motors wouldn't even hire him. He got a master's degree, but he had to be a teacher because the other doors were closed. The only reason Equitable hired him was pressure after the race riot in Detroit in 1954. I could only imagine his struggles and challenges to get to the top. I asked myself, "Do we really not have the time to step back and appreciate the struggles the black community went through?"

The most important thing I learned from my friendship with Darwin was the need for true equality. You can't come from a place of arrogance, of assumed superiority. Very often in the Jewish community, we think we can choose black leaders; we think we know what's best. *We don't.* You have to take a step back and try to understand other people's beliefs or culture and respect what *they* believe. I'm an Orthodox rabbi who believes that my orientation, my belief, my point of view is what works best for me. But there is not only one path—not in religion and not in the rest of life.

A lot of people don't know that I founded the Foundation for Ethnic Understanding (FFEU) with Joseph Papp. People remember Papp as a great producer and director—the Public Theater, the New York Shakespeare Festival, *Hair*, *A Chorus Line*. They remember the impresario of Broadway. What they don't recall is that Joe Papp was the pioneer of color-blind casting. To this day, when you speak to James Earl Jones, Morgan Freeman—they haven't forgotten that they wouldn't have had the opportunity to play Shakespeare without Joe Papp. I remember sitting in Joe's office. He disliked *The Cosby Show* just as he disliked *All in the Family*. He would say, "Why must it always be all white and all black?"

Papp taught me that if you are going to make a difference in the world, you have to work with people who are in a position to achieve that difference. I had known Joe growing up. He was conflicted about his Jewish identity for a very long time. His real name was Joseph Papirofsky. From "Papp" and the way it sounded, many people thought he was Greek. Yet he always fasted on Tisha b'Av. He'd ask me about things in the Talmud, and he was always using Yiddish. I had a larger vision, of using Jewish values and principles to impact the greater world. To get this foundation going, I needed a Joe Papp—his gravitas, his larger-than-life personality, his imprimatur.

When Joe and I were trying to come up with the name, we were toying with the Foundation for Ethnic . . . what? Ethnic Harmony? Ethnic Understanding? We realized we are not really looking for harmony. We just wanted to understand each other. And we found out that in the city of New York, there are more than two hundred ethnic communities. So you can try to do everything and accomplish nothing. In the 1980s, after Howard Beach and Bensonhurst, with race relations at an all-time low in New York, Joe and I realized we had to become specialists. I once said to Abe Foxman of the Anti-Defamation League, "Abe, you are a department store: anti-Semitism, interfaith relations, civil rights, combatting bigotry. I'm a boutique operation." That's what Joe and I set up with the foundation: a black-Jewish boutique.

Darwin Davis was introducing me to all the major African American executives he knew, and some of them were our earliest funders. We had a hard time getting traction, though, for a variety of reasons. First was the New York mayoral election in 1989. As I've noted, after Koch lost to Dinkins in the Democratic primary, I got involved hook, line, and sinker in David's campaign. I caught a lot of heat from the Orthodox community for my support of Dinkins. People were angry: *How dare you support a black candidate? Blacks are going to take over the city.* All the usual racism. The Orthodox community—and a lot of other Jews, a lot of other whites—were going to cross party lines to vote for Rudy Giuliani. And he was a much more polarizing figure than Koch had ever been: never a liberal; never a civil rights volunteer. The election went down to the wire. Dinkins narrowly won, and that was a kind of mixed blessing for me.

It was a very tenuous situation. People were sympathetic to improving black-Jewish relations. They wanted to work with me in restoring the black-Jewish alliance. But how far would they go? What would they do for the Other?

And then came the Crown Heights riots in 1991, which put black-Jewish relations probably at their lowest point in American history.[2] What I recall vividly from the riots was the lack of communication between the two communities, not only in Crown Heights itself but in general. In a tragic way, it underscored why we needed the foundation: so there'd be lines of communication, relationships, in place to defuse violence.

The Crown Heights riot was personally hard for me because of my close friendship with David Dinkins. I was very disappointed in how he responded—holding back the police from fully intervening, letting the violence go on for days. I was also disappointed in hearing in the Jewish community pillory Dinkins. *He's an anti-Semite; he's a racist.* I tried to step out of the firing line. Dinkins's personality was to avoid conflict, and in dealing with the Crown Heights riot, it did not serve him well.

In the midst of the riot, I got a call from Howard Rubenstein, the

2. Racial violence erupted in the Brooklyn neighborhood after a car driven by a Hasidic man, who was part of a motorcade accompanying the Lubavitcher rebbe, lost control and struck and killed a black child, Gavin Cato. In the ensuing turmoil, a black man stabbed to death a visiting Hasidic scholar, Yankel Rosenbaum. The riot went on for three days, with Jewish people and property under attack.

famous publicist. He asked me what seemed like the most absurd question: if I had a relationship with Michael Jordan. Now, I was probably number forty-three on the list of people Howard was asking. I said, "No, I don't. And besides, why are you asking?" And he said, "Because if Michael Jordan would get onto the streets right now, the whole thing would be over."

I never forgot that point. It was a valuable lesson. Ninety-nine percent of people are followers, and a very few are in the position to make a difference. It wasn't the David Dinkinses or the Charles Rangels or the John Lewises who would solve the problems; it was the personalities—Michael Jordan, Magic Johnson. They have celebrity power that resonates in all communities. And that's why I have always tried to bring celebrities into my work. There's strength in boldface names.

Our goal was to build a national movement with African American moderate and centrist leaders, and our breakthrough was bringing in Russell Simmons. This was in the mid-1990s. I met him, strange to say, thanks to Louis Farrakhan. Russell was very supportive of the Million Man March, of what Farrakhan represented in terms of black empowerment, pride, self-worth. But at the same time, he had thirteen Jewish partners in Def-Jam and his other businesses. One of his partners said to him, "You need to sit down with the president of the New York Board of Rabbis," which I was serving as at the time. As for me, I did know Russell Simmons was a superstar. But I knew very little about hip-hop. And I was somewhat intimidated because he was a hip-hop mogul. Could he be trusted? I wondered. Would he speak out of both sides of his mouth? I harbored a lot of stereotypes about the rap community.

As I started to get to know Russell, I sensed he was good, kind, and sincere. I think he did not understand why Louis Farrakhan evoked such negativity among Jews. And meanwhile I saw where he was coming from. No one can deny that Farrakhan, for many African Americans, was a source of empowerment. But I still didn't know exactly how we could bridge the gap between us on Farrakhan.

In 1995, I hosted Coretta Scott King for Martin Luther King Jr. Day at the World Jewish Congress, and I asked her in a private moment about Farrakhan. And she said, "You have to remember Martin's philosophy—

that you can disagree with the message, but not the messenger." And that's what Jesus also said. It's not our belief in Judaism. We will attack the messenger. So we had two belief systems in conflict. On Farrakhan, Russell and I agreed to disagree without being disagreeable.

My friendship with the King family grew even closer when, in 2000, I published *Shared Dreams: Martin Luther King, Jr. & the Jewish Community*, with a foreword by Martin Luther King III. Subsequently, Martin and I toured the country together speaking on the book and on the subject of black-Jewish relations.

The more I was involved in black-Jewish relations, the more I expanded my horizons and understanding. At Passover, Jews always talk about the parallels between blacks and Jews, and our shared experiences. We were both slaves. But I learned that we have to also appreciate what was so different post-slavery. After forty years, we entered into the Promised Land. Blacks were set free in the very land that enslaved them. Imagine if Moses had said, "Go rebuild your lives among the very people who oppressed you."

Russell Simmons came in as the secretary of the board of the Foundation for Ethnic Understanding. He was active, and together we hosted different fund-raising benefits and did some commercials. I remember in 2000, he and I filmed a commercial with Stevie Wonder with a group of black and Jewish kids. During MLK Day and Black History Month, it was shown three times a week on *Nightline*. For months, it was shown. People would call me and say, "What kind of budget do you have?" They didn't realize it was a public service announcement that *Nightline* just happened to embrace.

We also held conferences at Yeshiva University. The first conference featured Kweisi Mfume and Hugh Price, heads of the NAACP and National Urban League, respectively. We brought Jesse Jackson to YU, and the YU president, Dr. Norman Lamm, introduced the reverend as his favorite preacher. This was 1997, and Jackson was no longer a lightning rod in the Jewish community. He'd redeemed himself; he'd come a long way. He had worked with the World Jewish Congress. He'd spoken on behalf of Soviet Jewry. People could not believe that Jesse Jackson was coming to YU. But, you see, with Russell Simmons, Hugh Price, Kweisi

Mfume, Coretta Scott King, and the Congressional Black Caucus emerging as the voices of moderation, some started to realize that the train of black-Jewish reconciliation had arrived.

During the summer of 2011, the twentieth anniversary of the Crown Heights riots, I invited the Reverend Al Sharpton to speak at my synagogue in the Hamptons.[3] People couldn't believe it. They did not appreciate that people evolve, people grow. And as a result of that invitation, Sharpton wrote an open letter of apology to the Jewish community, addressed to me, that ran in the *New York Daily News*, acknowledging that the language he had used during the Crown Heights riot was inappropriate. Over the years, I have worked closely with Sharpton and have seen his commitment to the Jewish people and Israel develop and grow. I have annually spoken at his MLK Day commemoration in Harlem and have joined many government officials to speak at the Reverend Jackson's annual Rainbow PUSH Wall Street Project Economic Summit in New York City.

I have one admission to make, though. To this day, I know virtually nothing about hip-hop. Recently, Russell and I were discussing our trip to Israel, and I heard the word "ludicrous." I said, "What's so ludicrous about going to Israel?" Russell said, "Are you serious? You never heard of Ludacris?" Or the time I completely humiliated him in California at a benefit: I called Kanye West, Kanye *East*. So, for me, it has been an education.

Hip-hop has become the establishment. That is, the black establishment. To the younger members of the Hampton Synagogue, I am the coolest rabbi because I hang out with Russell, Jay-Z, Beyonce, LL Cool J, and the like. Russell probably has *the* summer party in the Hamptons to benefit his foundation for the arts. It's always on the third Saturday in July, six till eleven. And with the long summer days, I can't get there till ten-thirty because of the Sabbath. One year, I arrived while Russell was presenting an award to Susan Sarandon. He saw me walking in, and he went over to the microphone and said to eight hundred guests, "Ladies and gentlemen, Shabbos is now over!" That's our very special relationship.

---

3. The event was ultimately canceled at the request of Yankel Rosenbaum's family.

CHAPTER FIVE

From Suspicion to Trust

IMAM SHAMSI ALI

My exposure to life outside my norm was limited before coming to the United States. During my time in Indonesia and Pakistan, I did not meet any Westerners, and while I was in Saudi Arabia, most of the movies were Egyptian, Lebanese, or Syrian. In every place I had lived before coming to the United States, it was rare for me to see "the Western world," except for on television news, where one could see stories of the United States supporting Israel over the Palestinians. The notion that I had before coming here was that people in the United States wouldn't accept a Muslim—that we would not have freedom to practice our religion, that we would have to practice it secretly.

When I landed at JFK Airport in New York on a very cold day at the end of 1996, I imagined I would be received into a sea of white people, unwelcoming to a Muslim newcomer. Instead, at the airport, I saw many shades of non-white: Asians, Latins, African Americans, and even South Asians such as myself. That was the first surprise. I quickly received my second. From the airport I took a taxi to the Indonesian Mission near the United Nations in midtown Manhattan and saw my driver's name was Mohammed Reza. I thought he might be Pakistani, so I tried talking to him in Urdu. I asked, "You are Muslim?" When he replied, "Yes, I am Muslim," I quickly realized that, despite my fears prior to arriving here, the first person I had an interaction with in this country was a fellow Muslim, and that he and I were not alone in an angry sea of white Christian evangelicals.

When I started taking the subways, it was difficult for me to get used to it. I remember once buying a token, taking the R train to Forest Hills to a friend's home, and getting so lost that I walked around over an hour before finally calling from a public phone to get directions. I had no cell phone, of course, and I didn't know how to get in touch with most people, so the operator that day was my lifeline. When I got my bank account, I received an ATM card, but I didn't know how to use it. I was too shy to ask for help, but when a Chinese woman saw me looking puzzled, she taught me how to use it. Incidents like this changed the way I saw America. I came to understand that it's not just the white people's country, that we could pursue our dreams here. Another thing that really surprised me was the openness. In Saudi Arabia, women are covered from head to toe. Here, everything is in front of your eyes. It required some adjustment.

I came here to lead a small Indonesian Muslim community in Astoria, Queens. They couldn't afford to pay me, so the Indonesian ambassador gave me money for living expenses, and I worked as a public relations officer at the mission for my livelihood. I stayed with a friend from Indonesia for several days, then moved into a room in the Astoria community's mosque. The mosque, Masjid al-Hikmah, was just a year and a half old when I arrived and was a very simple structure, a former storage building. We had all kinds of people attending service: people working in restaurants, cab drivers, babysitters, people from the consulate, the UN, our mission, banks. Our biggest gathering was around two hundred people, though at the time, the five daily prayer sessions had not been established there yet. We started with the noon and sunset prayers, and I began to give lectures to the larger community and to teach in the weekend school.

Part of the adjustment I mentioned earlier was not just with the "traditional Americans" but with my congregation. I could see clearly the differences in goals between the Indonesians and the other communities I met with. Indonesians seemed to have come mainly for the economic opportunities, while Indians and Pakistanis seemed more keen on education. Most of the Indonesians I met would tell me that they intended to make money here and return to Indonesia (although I have yet to see that happen). What troubled me most upon my initial interactions was that I could sense the non-serious attitude toward religion in the community I'd been sent to lead. Indonesians coming to mosque were coming mostly for social purposes—to eat and chat—not to study and pray. I was challenged to manage myself and how I reacted to this. I was leading a community that seemed very lax about restrictions. A woman could come to mosque without her head covered, though she would cover to pray. Men would talk about mundane affairs more than spiritual ones inside the mosque. This was a marked adjustment for me to make, coming from Saudi Arabia.

The first year I was in New York I was alone, and I began to feel concerned about how my family would adapt. Every religious person has some worries about raising children with their values intact in a foreign land. After a year here, I brought my family. When my daughter was four, she went to pre-kindergarten, and we found the concern for education high but felt that the school paid more attention to what my daughter wanted than to what the parents wanted. My wife is more traditional than I am and became worried that our daughter wouldn't listen to us anymore as Muslim parents, that she would become disrespectful. And how would she dress herself in the future? So we decided to turn our home into a second school for her, so she would absorb our religious and cultural values as well as her new American ones.

At first, I was mostly interacting with the Indonesian community. But in 1997, a group of South Asian Muslims came to the mosque to tell us that they were preparing for the Muslim Day Parade, and I got involved in the planning. At first, I didn't have a clue what it meant to have a "parade." I thought it was a protest or a demonstration.

The parade was in September, ten months after I had arrived in the United States, and I felt very honored to be joining the leadership line as it was the first time that I was leading an international group of Muslims from such varied backgrounds. The gentleman behind the parade, a Pakistani Muslim, asked me to lead the noon prayer on the street, to recite the Holy Qur'an. When I did, I could sense the surprise (or disappointment) of many there, because I had no beard. Being Indonesian, I was outside the stereotype of a "proper" Muslim leader, and not having a beard and being new to the New York scene made some in the parade wary of me.

But thanks to God's grace, by the end of the day they had accepted me, and I felt even more a part of the US Muslim community.

After our first few years in Queens, we moved to a house closer to the mosque in Astoria, where we met a wonderful Irish Catholic couple in their late seventies. They lived on one floor of the house and we lived on another. They were incredibly nice people. Every morning, the man came to clean the hallway in front of our house, and we got to know each other. He might not have known that we were Muslims at first, but he did when he saw that my wife wore the hijab. But that didn't affect his or his wife's attitude at all. Every morning when I left the house to take my four-year-old daughter to pre-school, he would come out of the house to give her a hug. She used to call him "Granddad." We became very close to that couple. I began to feel like a real New Yorker.

Five years after I had arrived in New York came the cataclysmic events of Tuesday, September 11, 2001. That morning, I was on the number 7 train headed to work at the Indonesian Mission to the United Nations, and someone on the train looked out the window and noticed that there was a fire at the World Trade Center. When we arrived at Grand Central Station, I went outside to the street and watched on a television screen inside a bank building as a plane hit the second tower. At that instant, I and everyone else understood that this was not an accident but an attack. I was at the mission watching the news on television when we got word from the UN that it was necessary to evacuate all diplomatic buildings.

I left the mission and went out to the street only to find that there were no longer any subways or buses running. I walked uptown twenty blocks to the Queensboro Bridge at Fifty-ninth Street, where I was able to hail a livery car to take me back to Astoria. During the whole ride, the driver, who was Latin American, continually cursed Muslims for what had happened. He didn't know I was Muslim as I was wearing a suit and tie, and he probably just thought I was Korean or Chinese. I listened to him, very sadly, the whole time. How many people at that time hated Muslims because of what was happening? Too, too many. I couldn't respond to anything he was saying because at that moment my mind was overwhelmed by the enormous tragedy that had engulfed New York.

When I arrived home, my Irish Catholic neighbor came up to me and hugged me. He told me he couldn't really believe Muslims were responsible for the attack, because he had learned from me that Islam was a religion of peace and brotherhood. Two days later, he came to us and brought flowers and told me he understood how terrible and frightening it must be for us, especially since my wife wore a hijab and there had been plenty of attacks on women in hijabs by hoodlums in the aftermath of the tragedy. That wonderful man, more than anyone else, completely changed the way I viewed non-Muslims.

For the first days after September 11, my family stayed inside, watching the news reports on TV. A lot of people in our community called me to say they had been attacked. We decided to close the mosque for three days, to try to wait out the storm and to avoid more attacks. After several days passed, we decided to live our lives normally because we wanted to show we weren't supporting the attack. We advised women wearing hijabs to be cautious and alert.

The second day after the tragedy, the Interfaith Center of New York organized an event called Religious Leaders Respond. One of the persons who worked for the Interfaith Center was a Russian Muslim named Yuskayev Timur. He knew me and called to ask if I could come to represent the Muslim community at the event. That came to be seen as the first Muslim response to the tragedy and was widely covered by the media.

It was very difficult for me to decide how to respond. I had a mix of feelings—overwhelming sadness, confusion, and a sense of embarrassment as I struggled to adequately represent Islam at such a terrible moment, after so-called Muslims had brutally attacked the city in which I was living, killing so many innocent people of all backgrounds. Yet I knew that I had a responsibility to represent my faith in a dignified manner, because I was clear in my mind that the attack had nothing to do with my faith; it was a perversion of everything Islam stood for.

When it was my time to speak, I spoke directly from the heart, condemning the attack with every fiber of my being. I made it clear that our faith doesn't condone or justify such an act for *any* reason. I said that I was an Indonesian and a Muslim, and most strongly condemned the acts and wanted to ensure they never happened again.

Later that night, I got a call from the Commissioner's Office of the New York Police Department. They wanted me to come to a meeting at St. Patrick's Cathedral in the morning. I thought it was for an interfaith event, but it turned out to be a group meeting with President George W. Bush. We were to meet him around 11:00 a.m. to talk and then to go down to Ground Zero together for a memorial service with several pastors, Catholics, Hindus, Sikhs, and rabbis. Imam Izak-el Pasha of the Malcolm Shabazz Mosque in Harlem and I represented the Muslim community. It was so difficult shaking President Bush's hand. I felt so conflicted and so sad.

When we left St. Patrick's, we went down to Ground Zero in a motorcade. Going to that memorial service a few blocks from Ground Zero was very trying for me as I knew everyone had such ill will toward me as a Muslim. A lot of people were crying, many members of the victims' families were there crying, receiving the president. I was so saddened and touched by the situation and the pain I saw that my fears were temporarily forgotten.

Earlier on that day at the cathedral, when I spoke to President Bush, I took the opportunity to ask him personally if he could come out and state clearly that these inhuman and heinous crimes, though being committed by people with Muslim names, were in reality completely unrepresentative of Islam and Muslims. I asked him to please acknowledge that these acts were not the acts of Muslim people or of all Muslims. He didn't say yes or no, just nodded his head. The following day, however, he went to the Islamic Center in Washington and said to the media that the 9/11 attacks had nothing to do with Islam or Muslims. I felt very grateful for that statement and his goodwill in making it.

About two weeks after 9/11 there was a memorial event called the Prayer for America, held in Yankee Stadium. There were seventy thousand people there, and it was televised nationally and internationally. When I went in and walked onto the stage, I saw the emcee was Oprah Winfrey. I went to sit down and behind me were Bill and Hillary Clinton. Cardinal Egan, archbishop of New York, was there. They played the National Anthem, everyone had flags, many people were crying, there were New York Fire Department and NYPD members. Marc Anthony sang "America, the Beautiful." Mayor Rudolph Giuliani was the first speaker, and Governor George Pataki spoke as well. It was a very emotional experience.

I was honored to represent the Muslim community along with Imam Pasha. I decided to recite three verses from the Holy Qur'an. The first verse I chose is one that talks about universal human brotherhood and says that we all come from the same father and mother (49:13). The second talks about the need for peace and justice in the world (5:8). The third is about the importance of perseverance and patience in facing challenges (110:1–3). I asked a Muslim woman whom I knew to translate the Qur'an with me, and she agreed. My intention was to give exposure to women as well as to the literal words of the Qur'an in the hopes that misrepresentation of both in Islam would be somewhat rectified. When I read the Qur'an, the stadium felt very quiet.

So many people's views of Islam and of Muslims were changed by that fateful day in September, and so were mine: I came to understand the importance of dialogue. Along with meeting President Bush, this prayer service was the turning point in my engagement in interfaith work. I had done interfaith work before September 11, but it was limited. Being involved in these two events really opened the doors for me to get much more involved. Before September 11, 2001, I had never met a Jewish person, let alone a rabbi. At the prayer service in Yankee Stadium, I met several rabbis, including Joe Potasnik and Arthur Schneier, the father of Marc Schneier. And I was seated next to a female rabbi. I have to admit I was more interested in observing them than in talking with them; I was still hesitant about their motives and intentions. From my time in Pakistan and Saudi Arabia, I had this belief that Jews controlled America and that all Jews were against all Muslims.

But the female rabbi to my side was very friendly, and she smiled at me, shook my hand, and gave me her card. To my surprise, I saw her name and noted that it was Soetaro—an Indonesian name, from Java. She explained that her great-grandfather came from Indonesia, but she was Dutch. The Indonesian name was the legacy of her ancestor. This was the first rabbi I had ever met in person, and the first that I ever had a conversation with. I still remember her warmly.

Rabbi Arthur Schneier came to me and asked me if I was Indonesian. We shook hands, and I affirmed that I was. He told me he had a very close friend in Indonesia whom he really wanted to visit—it turned out to be President Abdulrahman, known also as Gus Dur. He praised President Gus Dur very highly as he invited me to his own synagogue for another memorial service and was very warm toward me. After I met Rabbi

Potasnik, I felt a pull toward friendship with him too. I began to see these rabbis as good people and as individuals I wanted to know more about. But even after meeting Rabbi Soetaro, Rabbi Potasnik, Rabbi Schneier, and many more Jewish religious leaders, I still had very limited communication with the larger Jewish population.

Around December 2001, the ambassador of Indonesia called me to say he'd gotten a call from the ambassador of Kuwait, who was then chairman of the Islamic Cultural Center of New York, which has a large mosque on 96th Street in Manhattan. The Kuwaiti ambassador wanted me to work there. Since the Indonesian ambassador was my nominal boss, I said if he wanted me to be involved, I would be. He agreed to my joining the ICC-NY, and I went to meet the Kuwaiti ambassador, who interviewed me and decided to post me at the ICC as the assistant imam on a part-time basis. He wanted me to deliver Friday sermons at least twice a month.

My job there was leading prayers and giving sermons, but I think the most important function I had was outreach. I started classes for non-Muslims to increase understanding and clarify misconceptions about Islam. We had announced this in the local newspaper, and in the beginning we had up to thirty people coming to join the class. Some came to express their anger, some came to learn, some came to ask a question and leave. But in the end, this class has been a good forum and a great teaching tool.

The first real interfaith interaction I had with a rabbi was with Peter Rubinstein of Central Synagogue, a very large Reform congregation in Manhattan. I have to give credit for this to the late Reverend Dr. Arthur Caliandro of Marble Collegiate Church, who was a great friend of mine. He called the ICC-NY in 2003 and offered to set up an interfaith gathering with Rabbi Rubinstein to be held at Marble Collegiate.

From the beginning, Rabbi Rubinstein, Dr. Caliandro, and I just clicked, and I felt that I had known them for a very long time. Rabbi Rubinstein is humble and friendly, Dr. Caliandro was kind and wise, and we called each other brothers. We frequently called each other to discuss the topics for the Thanksgiving ceremony we were preparing and engaged in discussions, and from there we followed up with many other engagements, including exchange visits among our congregations.

In 2004, on Prophet Muhammad's birth date, we invited Christians and Jews to come to the mosque and we held interfaith talks. The experience was great, and we felt the walls between us were crumbling down. We started to see the reality of the people—that they were good and kind people, and that we were all truly the same. The idea that Jewish people thought they were superior, that they wanted to destroy us, was quickly fading away.

Before I met Marc Schneier, I had the general impression that Orthodox rabbis were very exclusive and that it would be impossible to communicate with any of them. Maybe it is something like the perception people have of the Muslim community—that it is possible to talk only to the "more liberal" Sufis, not to orthodox Muslims. So when I met Rabbi Schneier, an Orthodox rabbi, I was a bit wary.

It was in the spring of 2005, when Pope John Paul II had just died. CBS wanted to interview non-Christians about their points of view about the pope. It was an early morning interview, and while I sat there in the studio, another person came in whom I immediately recognized as a Jew because of his yarmulke. He was introduced to me, and he hesitantly extended his hand to me to shake. He did not smile at me and barely looked at me. We exchanged cards; at the time, I was assistant imam at ICC-NY, and he was the president of the Foundation for Ethnic Understanding. We were interviewed together, and we both talked about being enthusiastic about furthering the cause of interfaith cooperation that Pope John Paul II had started. At the end of the interview, we said our good-byes and went our separate ways.

Rabbi Schneier and I did not meet again until almost two years later, and this meeting was far more significant. Toward the end of 2006, Marc Schneier came to the ICC-NY to meet with Imam Omar Abu Namous, then the head imam. He didn't pay me any mind, and I only knew that he was at the center because I could hear his voice. I don't know if he knew I was there, and I didn't even know that he was the son of Rabbi Arthur Schneier, whom I had met years before at the September 11 event. We did not talk during his visit to the ICC. Even though we had exchanged cards years ago, Rabbi Schneier and I were still very wary of each other. I felt that I already had a good rabbi friend, Rabbi Rubenstein, whom I was working with and who was as wonderful a human being as I knew. I thought that was enough for me.

A few months later, Marc Schneier sent his assistant to meet with me, and he invited me to be on a panel at New York University regarding Muslim-Jewish relations. It was the beginning of our communications. There were four panelists—Schneier; myself; Imam Khalid Latif, the Muslim chaplain of NYU; and Rabbi Yehuda Sarna of the Bronfman Center for Jewish Life at NYU—and the event was cosponsored by FFEU. Russell Simmons, now the foundation's chairman, opened the talk, and Joel Cohen, a well-known attorney and author, was the moderator. The discussion was lively, and I think students reacted well to my straightforward responses. We talked about Islam and Judaism and how to build bridges between Muslims and Jews. We talked about historical things, about *tawhid*, the "straight path," and other fundamentals. We came to the conclusion that of the monotheistic religions, Islam and Judaism were the most closely related.

I was listening to Marc very attentively and remember thinking, "This Rabbi is very inclusive, very sincere." He was open and genuine in the way he presented his ideas, which very much provoked my interest in him. It was another turning point for me. Marc acknowledged his past prejudices toward Muslims and that, through the process of learning about Muslims and Islam, his prejudices were changing. I was beginning to feel the same thing in my attitudes toward Jews and Judaism.

When the panel was over, I asked Marc why he had invited me instead of Abu Namous to speak. He told me Abu Namous had alienated the Jewish population at his synagogue while talking about Israel and Palestine. He had said there should be a Muslim Palestinian state where Jews *could also* live—an alarming idea for many Jews who felt his discourse was tending toward an atavistic *dhimmi* model of coexistence.[1] Rabbi Schneier did not feel that furthering the conversation with Abu Namous was perhaps the best way to invite dialogue; thus, my invitation to join that panel.

The FFEU and ICC-NY had already agreed to cohost the Imams and Rabbis Summit. Marc told me that Abu Namous had to be the figurehead as he was the principal imam in New York, but he needed me to be there and be the real force behind it. I worked very hard on the summit,

---

1. *Dhimmi* status was one granted to non-Muslim citizens living in Muslim-governed lands during the period of the Islamic empires.

and I think it went well. Some rabbis were bombastic, some imams were emotional, and some harsh words were said. But the meeting ended with some points of agreement; among those, that Muslims and Jews in North America would organize once a year for a Weekend of Twinnings, where each faith group's congregation would exchange visits with other congregational groups.

By 2008, I was the principal imam at the Ninety-sixth Street mosque (the ICC-NY), as well as at the Jamaica Muslim Center in Jamaica, Queens, and the Masjid Al-Hikmah in Astoria. Marc asked me to bring all those congregations to the New York Synagogue for the twinning. We knew that the New York Synagogue was an Orthodox synagogue, and I was very impressed that they were participating in the twinning when I came to know later that many members of the congregation were senators or congressmen and their relatives. The first time I went to the New York Synagogue, though, the people's reactions to us were not very welcoming, and we did not feel a very friendly vibe. Marc and I held a discussion, and many questions came at us both. One of the questions asked of me was about how I perceived the Jewish people. At that time, I still did have some remaining negative ideas about them, ideas I had brought from Pakistan and Saudi Arabia. But Rabbi Rubinstein had changed many of those ideas for me in a very marked way. Also, the friendship that I had begun with Marc had affected me. I spoke to them about how sometimes we have pre-assigned ideas of people that are wrong. I spoke about how going to a synagogue and trying to build friendship with Jewish people was an important step for me. Many people asked me about Israel, and my stand was the same then as it is now—since Israel was recognized by the UN, it is a valid country and it must be accepted and respected as such. Apart from this, there must be a two-party state, where Israel is left to its sovereignty, as the Palestinians should also be.

One very difficult comment came from a Jewish lady, who said it was impossible for Jews and Muslims to be peaceful because Muslims have madrassas where they are trained to kill Jews. I tried to smile and maintain an outwardly peaceful demeanor, though the accusation hurt. I told her that I was a madrassa graduate, and if I'd been trained to kill Jews, I wouldn't be there to talk with them but rather to harm them. I asked her where that conclusion came from, and she told me it was from a documentary film about the madrassas in Pakistan and other Middle Eastern countries where kids were taught to be radicals, to have animosity and hatred toward the Jewish people. I told her jokingly that I had seen many movies about this country and especially New York City as well, and what I saw in the movies about New York City were shootings all around. If I had taken my conclusion from those movies, I would never have come here at all. I challenged her to open her mind, to visit Muslim schools, to talk with Muslim people and see what they were really taught.

Later that day, someone came to me and said he knew my name was really "Muhammad Ali." I was surprised, as my full name actually is Muhammad Shamsi Ali, but he did not know me. He told me that he thought I was Muhammad Ali because I was a champion for answering that lady as I did. That really made me smile. Little comments like that one always gave me incentive to continue in the path of dialogue.

I met with Marc after this on several occasions, and we traveled together to many places—Chicago, New Orleans, California—talking about the importance of Muslim-Jewish cooperation. During those trips, oftentimes both Muslims and Jews asked the same question: How do you respond to those verses in the Qur'an and the Tanakh that are very critical about each other's faith traditions?[2] We tried to respond in as friendly and broad-minded a manner as possible, but we came to the conclusion that we needed to tackle these "difficult passages" much more intensely.

All of these experiences got me even more deeply involved in interfaith work. I was recruited by the Tanenbaum Center.[3] There I met with the president of the Jewish Theological Seminary (JTS), who is also an advisory member of the Tanenbaum Center. He was very interested in doing something with the Jewish and Muslim communities but didn't know how. He sent Rabbi Burt Visotzky to me at the ICC-NY. Rabbi Visotzky invited me to speak at the JTS synagogue in 2008, and I felt honored, as I was to be only the second non-Jew to speak there. (Desmond Tutu was the first.) It was around this time that I received some

---

2. The Tanakh is the holy scripture of the Jewish people. The first five books are the Torah, believed to have been given to Moses by God.

3. Named for the late Rabbi Marc H. Tanenbaum and founded by his widow, the Tanenbaum Center continues his life's work for interreligious relations and human rights.

additional exposure in the Jewish community with Walter Ruby's article in the *New York Jewish Week*, so I truly felt the dialogue lifting.

The ICC-NY, the Jewish Theological Center, and the Presbyterian Church on 120th Street and Broadway had agreed that we would do some social work together and collaborate on Abrahamic faith education and programs. We agreed that every three months, Jews, Christians, and Muslims would take part in organizing a soup kitchen at the Presbyterian church. The original program was sponsored by the Jewish Theological Center and the ICC, with the Presbyterian church providing the facilities and hosting events. We organized a three-day conference on life-cycle events—birth, marriage, death—with each day happening at a different place of worship. We also agreed to do the Midnight Run, a program in which volunteers go out together after midnight to distribute food and clothes to homeless people.

When I started my interfaith efforts at the Jamaica Muslim Center, I got a lot of resistance. The first thing I did when I became principal imam was to institute tripartite dialogue between Muslims, Christians, and Jews together. I pressed the congregation to become involved in hands-on efforts to build ties with other faiths. There was no tradition of that among South Asian Muslims like those found at the JMC, and many of them saw it as a betrayal of "true" faith. But I pushed ahead, and by the third year our interfaith program was fully accepted by the congregation. People went from resisting to asking me, "When are we going to do it again?"

No matter who else I worked with from the Jewish and Christian communities, though, my relationship with Marc Schneier was unique. My respect for him kept growing when I visited his congregation and realized that he says the same things to them publicly in his sermon and comments that he says to me in private. When I go back to my congregation after meeting with leaders of other faiths, my people always ask me, "Can you trust these people?" In the case of Marc, I have come to believe that yes, I truly can.

CHAPTER SIX

Growth and Evolution

RABBI MARC SCHNEIER

For many years, even after I had changed my attitude about African Americans, even after I'd begun working closely on black-Jewish relations, I still had a deep, serious bias against Muslims. Muslims, to me, were demons, the evil empire, the second class, anti-Semitic, anti-Israel. Those attitudes came from the conversations I had, and they came from the company I was keeping. They came from a place of intense Jewish pride at the expense of others, which led to the need to elevate one kind of people at the expense of putting others down.

Keep in mind that I had never actually met a Muslim. The only ones I had ever encountered were the ones at the *shuk* in the Old City in Israel. When I heard disparaging comments about Arabs, it seemed to me that Arabs and Muslims were interchangeable. They were evil in terms of what I considered their obvious object of destroying the Jewish people. They were primitive, backward people. It was a very racist, degrading way of looking at others.

Those attitudes fit completely with what were then my political views. I was a Likudnik, supporting Menachem Begin and Yitzhak Shamir, who were the prime ministers behind the Israeli settlement movement. I saw Yitzhak Rabin as a traitor for making the Oslo agreements. I considered the territories on the West Bank as being ours by right, given to us by God, ignoring the fact that there are probably ten thousand different interpretations of what constitutes the Land of Israel. Let's just say I followed the party line.

During the Persian Gulf War, in 1991, I was with the Israeli consul general, Uri Savir, doing a program for Martin Luther King Jr.'s birthday, awarding a King medal on behalf of the State of Israel to two African American leaders. This was in Uri's residence. We found out that scud missiles were falling on Tel Aviv when Uri's wife, Aliza, burst into the room and told us. We assumed then that it was chemical warfare. Instantly, the blacks and American Jews and Israelis clasped hands and in a circle sang "We Shall Overcome."

Maybe two days later, I was on the *Today* show debating whether the war was morally justifiable or not. The other panelists were an imam and Joan Campbell of the National Council of Churches. To Campbell, President George H. W. Bush was a greater demon than Saddam Hussein. I said that this war *is* morally justifiable, and I cited a number of biblical and Talmudic statements about eradicating evil. One Talmudic passage says, "Before someone rises to kill you, you should rise to kill them." So there's a basis in Jewish texts for preemptive war. And at the end of the segment, Bryant Gumbel turned to me and said, "Should I call you Rabbi Schneier or Rambo Schneier?" In one sentence, that defined who I was in 1991—*Rambo Schneier*!

If there was a tragedy, a terrorist attack against Jews in Israel, people would stand up in synagogue and say, "Every Arab should be shot." That's what they wanted to hear, and I didn't object to it. But even as I talked in very absolute, black-and-white terms, something didn't sit right with me. I looked at the people involved in these causes' institutions—the settlement movement, Gush Emunim,[1] their American supporters—and deep down I felt this just wasn't me. And that was a real conflict in me.

I was beginning to develop an empathetic imagination, which I think is one of the crucial qualities for humane and compassionate living. And probably I needed to go through the process I did with the African American community to arrive at my place now with the Muslim community. One of my greatest supporters and role models is Danny

---

1. Literally, "Bloc of the Faithful," it was one of the first and most important groups pushing settlement in the occupied territories.

Abraham, a philanthropist who's been a huge figure in trying to make peace between Israel and the Palestinians. We are extremely close. Politically, religiously, we are soul mates. And Danny would offer me his opinion both from an Arab and a Jewish perspective. And it occurred to me that this man, who is now Mr. Peace, was one of the original funders of the JDL![2] Very interesting. It got me thinking about how people grow and evolve.

September 11, 2001, was the day of the Democratic primary election. The favored Democratic candidate for mayor of New York was Mark Green, one of my best friends, and he was by far the favorite candidate to win in both the primary and the general election in November. The night before the election, Mark had arranged to pick me up to go campaign with him the next day. Then I got a call from him at about nine in the morning saying, "Marc, have you seen what's on television? I'm not going to be able pick you up."

The attacks confirmed my attitudes about Muslims and Islam. Rosh Hashanah fell about a week later, and it was our largest attendance ever at The Hampton Synagogue because people wanted to flee the city. And if I were to recall my sermons of the time, I probably spoke about the dangers of extremism and fundamentalism. I didn't even bother to single out Islam, because extremism meant Islam, fundamentalism meant Islam. You didn't even need to explain it. As for attacks against American Muslims, I had no empathy because I was oblivious. I wasn't even aware that there were American Muslims. And my curiosity wasn't at all piqued. My attitude was about Us versus Them.

In the years after the attack, I was still focused on black-Jewish work, and I was venturing into some work with Latino-Jewish relations. We'd done the first survey on attitudes between Jews and Hispanics. The person who helped me embark on my journey to Muslim-Jewish work was a journalist named Walter Ruby. At this time, he was involved in an interfaith organization with Boris Pincus, a Bukharian Jew, and Ghassan

---

2. The Jewish Defense League, founded in the late 1960s by Rabbi Meir Kahane, began as an armed self-defense group in New York City. During the movement to liberate Soviet Jewry, the JDL undertook vandalism and violence against Soviet institutions and representatives in the United States. After Kahane moved to Israel, the JDL transformed into the openly racist political party Kach.

Elcheikhali, the principal of the Razi School in Queens, the foremost Islamic day school in New York. They put together a Muslim-Jewish program at the school, and Walter invited me to address the students. I think he chose me because I was known as an Orthodox rabbi involved in liberal causes, and he knew of my work with the African American community.

I really didn't pay much attention to the reality of what I'd said yes to until I got out of my car in front of the Razi School. Suddenly, I thought, "I must be out of my mind. Will I be safe? Will I be compromising my security?" Then I remembered someone from the mayor's office would also be there, so I went ahead and walked inside the school. And, my God, I learned so much. There were boys and girls, teenagers, and they sat separately, like in a yeshiva. The young women were dressed modestly, like in a yeshiva. I had a respectful dialogue with them. They were obviously trying to make me feel comfortable. No questions about Israel. It was just before Hanukkah, so they asked about jelly donuts and the candles and why do some Jews wear forelocks. And what was supposed to be twenty minutes went on for two and a half hours.

And just as I'd had that experience at City Hall hearing the Boys Choir of Harlem, these Muslim children were my epiphany. I walked out and said to myself, "Why is there this conflict? We're all human. What is going on here? If I can have such a genuine, such a heartfelt, such an authentic exchange, what is the conflict?" You are reminded that no child is born a bigot. Bigotry develops from what children, and grown people, too, are exposed to.

I first met Shamsi Ali at a CBS television studio. Pope John Paul II had passed away in 2005, and CBS wanted to do a discussion on his impact on the other two Abrahamic religions. So it was Shamsi Ali and me. My initial impression was that he was a very sweet, lovely gentleman. He had a small mosque in Queens, and I had definitely brought my Upper East Side bias, my Hamptons bias. "He's relegated to Queens, too bad," I remember thinking. "What a pity he isn't in a more influential position."

But he seemed very genuine, and that piqued my interest. His words came from the heart; I could feel it. He genuinely wanted to reach out to other faith leaders, to other faith groups. I didn't question his credibility. I just questioned what kind of influence he had.

And then he became the head of probably the most prestigious, if not the largest, mosque in the United States, the Islamic Cultural Center of New York, which, among other things, is on the Upper East Side. It attracts a lot of top people—diplomats, ambassadors, Arab philanthropists. It was also very telling that the mosque is predominately funded by the Kuwaitis. The fact that they had supported Shamsi Ali, that he emerged as one of the great ecumenical leaders of New York, also reflected change or growth on their part.

The imam at the ICC-NY at the time of September 11, Muhammad Al-Gamei'a, whom I didn't know personally, came out with a statement that the Jews were responsible for the World Trade Center attack. He was removed soon after that, and his replacement was Omar Abu Namous, who did reach out to dialogue with me and took part in the Foundation for Ethnic Understanding's first summit of imams and rabbis. I was always made to feel very comfortable in his mosque. I even broke one of my cardinal rules: I'd never had a cup of coffee in my life. The only time was the first time I went to see Imam Namous. They had coffee and kosher cookies. It was heartfelt, sincere, and warm. But Imam Namous was a Palestinian refugee, and he had a certain degree of anger and bitterness. He wanted a one-state solution, which would be the end of Israel. Shamsi Ali was a breath of fresh air.

Shamsi and I did our first CNN dialogue in March 2008. A few months later, we were part of a public-service announcement with six imams and six rabbis denouncing both anti-Semitism and Islamophobia. It urged all Americans "to speak out against the hatred and to spread peace." Shamsi and I exchanged pulpits, we hosted visiting delegations, we went to the State Department. In July 2008, King Abdullah of Saudi Arabia invited me to Madrid as part of the World Conference on Dialogue Among Religions, and I was able to give the king a copy of our PSA.

That fall, the foundation did the first weekend of twinning between synagogues and mosques. The idea had first come up at a summit meeting in 2007 of six rabbis and six imams. For the concept of twinning, I borrowed a page from the National Conference of Christian and Jews—Brotherhood Week, Brotherhood Sabbath. Let's just substitute "mosques" for "churches," I thought. And it was Shamsi who made the formal motion that we do the program. The original goal was twenty-five of each.

We ended up with fifty mosques and fifty synagogues participating. That, in and of itself, was an achievement.

Two events really cemented our personal relationship, though. About four years ago, we were being interviewed together on Saudi TV. The subject of the holy temples in Jerusalem came up, and the host said, "Yes, it is true what the rabbi said, that David completed the conquest of Jerusalem, but we all know that Muhammad lived before David." By which he meant, Muslims had holy places in Jerusalem before Jews. So I'm thinking, "What am I supposed to say to that? There are thirty million Muslims watching this program." The only way to respond to that is to have a Muslim respond to that.

Shamsi told the host he was out of line and to go back to his history books and learn something about the chronology. I was so moved by him coming not really to my defense but to the defense of Judaism. And he's stood with our community so many times since then—on Holocaust denial, on terrorist attacks against Israelis. He would be the first one to sign a letter to Hamas from imams saying that it was not Islamic to keep Gilad Shalit as a hostage. I mean, what can you say?

The other binding event for us came in 2010, when Congressman Peter King announced that he was going to hold hearings on "Muslim subversion" in the United States. I started talking about this with Shamsi Ali and Feisal Rauf, the imam who'd been just savaged in the "Ground Zero mosque" controversy. I said to them, "Why don't we all get together, because something needs to get done." I went on to say, "Let's be honest. I have never seen Muslims publically demonstrate their allegiance to America. It is time for you to take to the street. We need to have a rally in Times Square. Not just a rally of Muslims demonstrating their allegiance to America, but a rally of other religious leaders demonstrating their solidarity with Muslims as well." We came up with this slogan. All the other religious leaders would stand up and say, "Today, I am a Muslim, too."

I stood on that stage in Times Square before five thousand people and denounced the demagogic Congressional hearings, and I declared, "Today, I am a Muslim, too." Many Muslims on the stage that day and quite a few in the audience came forward after I spoke to embrace me with tears in their eyes, thanking me profusely, and saying words to the effect of, "I never expected that a Jew—an Orthodox rabbi with a yarmulke on his head—would stand up before the world media and express solidarity for Muslims when they were under attack. That a prominent rabbi would put himself on the line for Muslims makes us feel less alone and vulnerable and more confident that we will find our place in America." It was a powerful demonstration. And it showed the Muslim community that I was a true champion and a genuine friend.

And now we need to come up with a similar campaign to address all the anti-Shari'a laws being passed in various states. I get push-back all the time from Jewish groups. There are people at our demonstrations who are there to protest against me. It's like a reincarnation of the JDL. I did a press conference in 2009 with Shamsi Ali and Sayyid Syeed, the national director of the Islamic Society of North America, denouncing the plot by four men, who happened to be Muslims, to plant bombs in two synagogues in the Bronx. And then you have Daniel Pipes and Steven Emerson saying that Sayyid Syeed is a rabid anti-Zionist.[3] People say that what I'm doing is a waste of time. But they said the same thing about my work with the African American community, and look at where we are now.

---

3. Pipes is a controversial historian and commentator who founded Campus Watch; Emerson is a journalist and the executive director of the Investigative Project on Terrorism.

PART TWO

What We Believe

CHAPTER SEVEN

The Chosen People

RABBI MARC SCHNEIER

The idea that the Jews are the chosen people is one of the most misunderstood concepts in history. Indeed, a lethal combination of misunderstanding and often deliberate distortion has caused immense suffering to the Jewish people at the hands of persecutors who point to the "chosen people" concept as evidence that the Jews claim to be superior to other religions and nations, and even that Jews covet world supremacy.

Actually, the concept of the chosen people was never meant to assert Jewish superiority or supremacy, and it certainly doesn't mean that today. Rather, the concept of chosenness designates the Jews' special mission to introduce the world to ethical monotheism. I believe that the emergence of Christianity and Islam as great world religions represents a fulfillment of that mission. When the Jews were first chosen for the mission to bring ethical monotheism to the world more than two thousand years ago, there were only Jews and pagans in the world. Today, the great majority of the world's population adheres to one of the three Abrahamic faiths, and we speak of a Judeo-Christian ethic or, more accurately, of a Judeo-Christian-Islamic ethic.

Still, while monotheism has become the norm, the special mission of the Jews is far from complete. There is still much work to be done to ensure that people around the world—including Jews, Muslims, and

Christians—truly live ethical lives, that focus primarily on service to their fellow human beings as opposed to the accumulation of wealth or the aggrandizement of power. As long as that work remains undone, Jews will continue to play their special role of serving as a voice of conscience on behalf of ethical monotheism.

Whatever the exact nature of the Jews' chosenness and special mission, which I will examine later in this chapter, it should be understood that being chosen has in fact proven to be more of a burden than a gift for the Jewish people. Because the Jews were chosen, they have suffered. Indeed, if Jews are "superior" to other peoples in any respect, it is in the staggering amount of persecution and bloodshed we have endured: two thousand years of subjugation, coercion, martyrdom, slaughter, Inquisition, pogroms, and Holocaust. All of this has been our destiny for the "privilege" of having been chosen.

Certainly, if the doctrine of the Jews as a chosen people has angered non-Jews throughout history, it has also deeply confounded many Jews, especially in modern times. As Jonathan Sacks, chief rabbi of the United Kingdom, has pointed out:

> It is fair to say, I think, that no idea is more deeply rooted in Jewish consciousness and that no idea has been more embarrassing to modern Jews. One can even say that much of what has happened to Jewry in the past two hundred years—the assimilation, the outmarriage—is what I call "the flight from particularity," the escape from this difficult and very opaque concept of "being chosen." We have about it a deep ambivalence.[1]

There is no question that the concept of chosenness is decidedly not politically correct in the context of early-twenty-first-century liberal secularist thinking. And it therefore makes many people uncomfortable—including some liberal and secular Jews who are deeply committed to the belief in the equality of all human beings and who find the notion of Jewish chosenness to be incompatible with that value. Indeed, some modern-day Jews, like the adherents of the small but influential Reconstructionist

---

1. From one in a series of Faith Lectures given by Chief Rabbi Jonathan Sacks, "Jewish Identity: The Concept of a Chosen People," May 8, 2001, London.

movement, have renounced chosenness as an unwarranted assertion of Jewish superiority that could lead us toward racism toward non-Jews. In a speech given in 1945, Rabbi Mordecai Kaplan, the founder of Reconstructionism, characterized the chosenness doctrine as "dogma and is meant to affirm that the Jewish people has [*sic*] been chosen to occupy forever the central place in the divine scheme of salvation." He added, "As such, it neither is nor can be any longer accepted by modern-minded Jews."

Yet the vast majority of modern-day Jews, ranging from Orthodox to Conservative and Reform and even many secular Jews, believe that the Jewish people were "chosen" by God for a particular mission—one that continues to be operative today. The most liberal wing of American Judaism, the Reform Movement, which at well over one million adherents dwarfs the Reconstructionists, is unambiguous in its belief in the doctrine of chosenness, as expressed in documents like its 1999 Statement of Principles, which reads in part:

> We affirm that the Jewish people are bound to God by an eternal covenant, as reflected in our varied understandings of Creation, Revelation and Redemption. . . . We are Israel, a people aspiring to holiness, singled out through our ancient covenant and our unique history among the nations to be witnesses to God's presence. We are linked by that covenant and that history to all Jews in every age and place.

Let us look briefly at how the concept of chosenness has evolved through the long arc of Jewish history.

The Torah contains a number of passages asserting that Israel's character as the land of the chosen people is unconditional, as in Deuteronomy 14:2: "For you are a holy people to the Lord, your God, and God has chosen you to be his treasured people from all the nations that are on the face of the earth." However, even at the beginning of Jewish history, Moses reminds the People of Israel that they were not at all superior to those of other nations. He tells them, "It is not because you are the most numerous of peoples that the Lord set His heart on you and chose you—indeed, you are the smallest of peoples" (Deuteronomy 7:6–8). Moses further upbraids his people: "It is not for any virtue of yours that the Lord your God is giving you this good land to possess, for you are a stiff-necked people" (Deuteronomy 9:6). While not suggesting any particular virtue on the part of those whom God chooses, the Torah does require that the chosen should respond by faithfully following God's commandments.

In the more than two thousand years since the destruction of the Second Temple in Jerusalem and the dispersion of the Jewish people into the Diaspora, Judaism's greatest thinkers have debated the implications of the Jews' chosenness. That ongoing, transgenerational discussion is also a dialectic about the Jews' relationship to the rest of humanity.

For example, the twelfth-century Jewish philosopher Judah Halevi upheld the biblical portrayal of the Jews as an essentially passive chosen people who simply fulfill God's commands. Yet Halevi's near contemporary, Moses Maimonides, gave brilliant articulation to a rabbinical notion of chosenness that had come to predominate in Jewish thought by that time and continues to predominate in all major streams of Judaism today—namely, that chosenness is the result of human action. Maimonides argued that Abraham was chosen because he, among all the people of his day, discovered God, whereas, he believed, the Jewish people were chosen because their acceptance of the Torah grants them a special relationship with God. Therefore, Maimonides argued, anyone "who sets oneself apart to stand before, to serve, to worship, and to know God . . . is consecrated to the Holy of Holies, and his portion and inheritance shall be in God forever" (Mishnah Torah, *Hilkhot Shemita v'Yovel* 13:13).

It is true that Halevi, in his philosophical book *Kuzari*, and some later kabbalistic and Hasidic mystics (such as Rabbi Shneur Zalman of Liadi, the founder of Chabad Hasidism and author of the *Tanya*) contended that the Jewish soul is fundamentally different in character from the non-Jewish one. Other Jewish mystics, however, rejected this idea and believed in the essential equality of all human souls. Clearly, the second position has been the dominant strain, both in Orthodox Judaism based on Halacha (Jewish law) as well as in the less traditional denominations. What is striking to me is how normative Judaism over the centuries has largely eschewed the temptation to assert the superiority of the Jewish people over the rest of humankind. One might have expected that many great rabbis and Jewish philosophers would have been inclined to move in that direction in response to the horrendous persecution and often bestial violence Jews endured from the non-Jews among whom they lived, especially in Christian Europe. Yet that sort of chauvinism rarely occurred. Over the centuries, with a few notable exceptions, the leading intellectual lights of Judaism said Jewish chosenness meant that we are a particular nation with a unique mission, but not that we are better than other nations.

In modern times, there has been a tendency among important Jewish thinkers to affirm that though the Jews were chosen by God for a unique mission on this planet, we are not the only people in the world to have been chosen for such a mission. This is the position to which I adhere— that many nations, perhaps all nations, were chosen to carry out one mission or another. For example, I think the Greeks may have been chosen to bring the world art and philosophy and the Romans to bring architecture. Many modern-day Americans believe that the United States has a unique, divinely inspired mission to spread the benefits of democracy around the world.

I also believe that all nations and faiths, including the Jewish people, should avoid labeling themselves "*the* chosen" or "*the* best." We may say we are "one of the best" or "one of the chosen," but to claim primacy in this respect is to implicitly denigrate other peoples, who also believe in their special dispensations. Ultimately, there are many paths to chosenness.

In discussing concepts like chosenness or the somewhat analogous Muslim concept of Kheir Ummah (best nation), it is critically important that we avoid extremism and absoluteness. If one believes that his or her people and only that people are *the* chosen, it follows that all other peoples are lesser beings.

Interestingly, when the Torah speaks of Jewish chosenness, it is clear that our mission is to bring the new monotheistic belief system to humanity rather than to bring Judaism itself to other nations. We Jews are decidedly not a proselytizing people, intent on converting the world to Judaism. Indeed, as is well known, it is very difficult to convert to Judaism. That is why we are a very small people.

Yet, thank God, we have been quite successful in fulfilling a goodly part of our mission. The proof of that accomplishment is that today we can speak of three monotheistic Abrahamic faiths—Judaism, Christianity, and Islam—as well as a Judeo-Christian-Islamic ethic. Paganism, which dominated the ancient world, has all but disappeared. I believe that transformation represents not only a long stride forward toward the fulfillment of the Jews' mission as the chosen people but also an important step forward for all of humankind.

Despite this commonality of ethical monotheism that we share with Islam and Christianity, the Jewish expression of that credo contains an important difference from the other two. Judaism is particularistic—not universalistic. Judaism is the faith of a particular nation, which, despite its insistence of maintaining its particularity, has managed to inspire much of humanity with its mission of ethnical monotheism.

The particularity of the Jewish mission ultimately transcends into universality. Consider, for example, how the story of the Exodus of the Jews from slavery in Egypt has been a source of inspiration and emulation for many oppressed peoples over the centuries—most famously, perhaps, for African Americans struggling to throw off the bonds of slavery in nineteenth-century America.

It is deeply troubling, however, that many anti-Semites down through the centuries have managed to venerate, and sometimes claim for themselves, the moral force of the Hebrew Bible while savagely demonizing the Jews as a people. And much of the expressed reason for that rancor, besides the false claim that the Jews killed Jesus Christ, is the charge that the doctrine of chosenness evinces an arrogant doctrine of Jewish superiority to the rest of humankind.

Ultimately, the meaning of chosenness in Judaism is by definition wrapped up in the larger question "Who is a Jew?" It is important to wrestle with this question if we are to successfully articulate an explanation of Jewish chosenness that will be credible to Jews and non-Jews alike and will help put to rest the calumny that Jews consider themselves superior to others.

Indeed, what makes a person a Jew? Is it blood lineage? Is it faith? Or is being Jewish an ethnicity or a nationality? My response is that it is all of these and more. Indeed, Jews of varying religious and political perspectives have made compelling cases that Judaism is a religion, a nation, an ethnic group, a common culture, and even a family. Some Jews and non-Jews—including our greatest persecutors, the Nazis—have also labeled Judaism a race. But I emphatically disagree with that definition. After all, there are Jews of various racial backgrounds, from European to Middle Eastern to African and even East Asian. While a white person cannot turn himself into a black person or an Asian, even if he so desires, a person of any racial background can become a Jew by converting to Judaism.

Clearly, Judaism is a faith. Like Islam, it is a venerable system of ideas about the nature of the universe, our world, and the way people should live their lives. This is the moral and spiritual system that is taught to Jewish children and youth. It varies in important ways between the various Jewish denominations—Orthodox, Conservative, Reform, and Reconstructionist. And in terms of customs and modes of prayer, there is variation between Ashkenazi (Western) and Sephardi (Middle Eastern) forms of Judaism. Yet the core of the belief system remains the same.

On the other hand, there are many people who call themselves Jews who are not religious at all and rarely if ever attend synagogue. Most such people eschew kosher food and do not observe other religious injunctions. These so-called "secular Jews" include up to half of the Jews in the United States and a majority of those in Israel. (Israeli secular Jews, though, are much better acquainted with the Torah and basic Jewish religious practices and customs than are many of their American cousins, since those elements are taught in the public schools in Israel as part of required study of Jewish history and culture.)

Many of these people would call themselves atheists or agnostics; however, they strongly identify as Jews. Just as significantly, religiously observant Jews also consider their secular cousins to be Jews, albeit Jews who should be encouraged to return to practicing their faith. There is across-the-board agreement that a person who is born a Jew will remain a Jew his or her entire life, even if he or she violates all religious strictures.

This reality clearly shows that Judaism is more than a religion. So, of course, does the creation of the State of Israel in the twentieth century, for if Judaism was solely a religion, Jews would neither need nor desire a state. As I noted earlier in this chapter, Jews are definitely not a race, but they certainly can be described as a "nation" or "culture" or "people" or "family." The Jews definitely have many attributes of a nation: a group of people with a common history, a common destiny, and a powerful sense of being connected to each other. The modern-day expression of this principle, *Kol Yisrael areivim zeh ba-zeh* ("All Jews are responsible for each other"), has its roots in the Torah and is also articulated as "We Are One," the slogan of the United Jewish Appeal-Federation, the main Jewish fund-raising body in the United States.

To be sure, the Jews are a nation unlike other nations in that they reside in countries around the world, speaking many different languages. They are also, of course, loyal to their countries of residence, both because they are genuinely patriotic and identify deeply with the language, culture, and history of their countries of origin, and because Jewish law requires that they should obey the law of the land. Finally, American Jews do not want to do or say anything that would validate the charge of "dual loyalty" that is often used against us by anti-Semites who charge that we are more loyal to Israel than to the United States. Nevertheless, there is a striking sense of connection, empathy, and mutual recognition and understanding among Jews, wherever they reside.

Many Jews believe the word "peoplehood" better expresses the sense of interconnection of Jews around the world than does "nationhood." Others, like the modern-day Torah sage Rabbi Adin Steinsaltz, make a strong case for the term "family," pointing out that within the Jewish family—as in other families—there are strong arguments and disagreements. Jews of varied theological and ideological stripes—Orthodox, Reform, secular and religious, left and right, dovish and hawkish on questions relating to Israel—will argue with each other in very strong terms and denounce each other with some harsh language, but such fights are *en famille*, and almost never come to violence. (The assassination of Israeli prime minister Yitzhak Rabin by a nationalist-religious Israeli Jew was one terrible exception to that rule.)

There is great concern for Jews living in countries of oppression, and Jews from the United States and Europe sometimes travel to those countries at a certain risk to themselves to try to help their brothers and sisters. This was the case during the Soviet Jewry movement, when the organized Jewish communities in the West mobilized their resources and political capital to help other Jews who were in danger. That concern, which also expressed itself in the rescue of the Jews of Ethiopia and the transplantation of the majority of them in Israel, flows from the modern-day slogan "Never Again," meaning that, in the wake of the Holocaust, we can never again stand by and allow Jews in lands of oppression to be bullied, victimized, and finally exterminated.

So, my short answer to the question of "Who (or what) is a Jew?" is "All of the above." Indeed, for centuries, Jews have had multiple identities, something that is becoming increasingly true in the twenty-first century of many other peoples as well. A resident of Brittany, for example, is simultaneously a Breton, a French person, and a European. A Muslim born in Pakistan and now living in New York is, variously, a Muslim, a Pakistani, and an American. In that sense, Jewish Americans and Muslim Americans have a lot in common.

So Jews come in many forms with many self-definitions and with multiple identities. Yet to return to the issue of chosenness, I believe that all Jews, no matter how they identify religiously, are "chosen" to manifest a special destiny, a Jewish identity. This mandate equally encompasses Jews who define their connection to Judaism and to the people of Israel as a nationality or a culture, as well as those who connect to Judaism as a faith.

I also believe that converts become "chosen" when they convert to Judaism, because when one converts to Judaism and is accepted into the fold, he or she voluntarily takes on the attributes and henceforth shares the fate of the Jewish people. So if, as I believe, the Jewish people were chosen to bring ethical monotheism and a corresponding moral outlook to the world, then the convert also takes on that fate and that mission. The vast majority of Jewish religious leaders in all the denominations would agree with that premise.

What are the implications of this belief in Jews as the chosen people for Muslim-Jewish relations? In my conversations with my dear friend Imam Shamsi Ali and with other Muslims as well, I have been pressed to explain whether I believe that the Jews as a people have a special dispensation—that they are *more* chosen—over other ethical monotheists such as Muslims and Christians. Certainly, Muslims as well as Jews are descendants of Abraham, so am I somehow asserting that the descendants of Isaac (Jews) are more worthy than the descendants of Ishmael (Muslims)? Am I claiming or implying that all Jews are exemplary human beings and therefore by default deserve to be "chosen" above all others?

As I have already noted, I do *not* believe that Jews are unique in being "chosen." Different nations were chosen for different missions, and I would never claim that Jews are superior to Muslims—our cousins who are descended from our common patriarch Abraham from Ishmael's line, rather than Isaac's—or, for that matter, to any other people.

As both a Jew and as an American, I believe deeply in the immortal words of our Declaration of Independence that all men (and women) are created equal and endowed by their Creator with certain unalienable rights, including life, liberty, and the pursuit of happiness. I believe those unalienable rights are for all people, not only or primarily for Jews. And no, I decidedly do not believe that every Jew is an exemplary human being. One who comes to mind as decidedly unexemplary is Bernie Madoff, who defrauded many people whom I know personally. Believe me, Madoff is hardly the only Jewish *gonif* (thief) or no-goodnik I have run across in my time. We have our share of such people, as does every other religion or ethnic group.

Giving voice to a clear disquiet with the chosenness doctrine among even Muslims who, like himself, are sympathetic to Jews and Judaism, Shamsi has asked me about what he views as the negative portrayal of Hagar and her son Ishmael in Jewish tradition. He has asked me forcefully whether it is the case that Ishmael is not accepted as a prophet by Jews because his mother was considered to be a concubine and not a "true wife" of Abraham—this despite the argument of Muslim scholars and a few Jewish ones that she likely renounced idol worship and followed Abraham's God, the God of the Jews. If that were indeed the case, Shamsi has asserted, Hagar and Ishmael should have been considered Jewish. If they were not, he asks, doesn't that strongly suggest that Jewish identity is primarily about race or nationality, as opposed to faith? If so, doesn't that prove that Judaism is suffused in racism, and that Jews must necessarily see non-Jews as inferior?

My response is that the Torah in no way denigrates either Hagar or Ishmael. Even though God commands Abraham to accede to Sarah's demand that he cast out Hagar and Ishmael soon after she gave birth to Isaac because "it is through Isaac that offspring shall be continued for you," He also reassures Abraham, "As for the son of the slave woman, I will make a nation of him too, for his is your seed" (Genesis 25:13). Once Hagar and Ishmael have been cast into the desert and cry out in agony, when they feel they are about to die of thirst, God calls to Hagar from heaven, saying, "What troubles you, Hagar? Fear not, for God has heeded the cry of the boy where he is. Come, lift up this boy and hold him by the hand, for I will make a great nation of him."

Indeed, as promised, God opens Hagar's eyes, and she suddenly sees a well she had not discerned before. That is only the beginning. God protects Ishmael all through his youth in the wilderness, where he becomes a bowman and eventually is married to an Egyptian wife his mother found for him. And so began the Arab nation, the other great Semitic people, who eventually adopted Islam.

Later in the Abrahamic narrative comes the story of God testing Abraham's faith by commanding him to sacrifice his son, which Abraham is about to do until God stays his hand. There is obviously a major doctrinal difference in the Jewish and Muslim narratives; the former asserts it was Isaac whom Abraham nearly sacrificed; the Qur'an says it was Ishmael. Despite this difference, and despite the bitter breach between the two families of Abraham, the half-brothers at the heart of the respective Torah and Qur'anic narratives concerning the sacrifice never lost touch with or renounced each other. This is made clear in Genesis 25:10, which records that after Abraham's death, "His sons Isaac and Ishmael buried him in the Cave of Machpelah." That is indeed a beautiful tableau of reconciliation through grief for the common father of Ishmael and Isaac and the common patriarch of our two peoples.

The story of Abraham, Sarah, Hagar, and their two sons is the kind of painful family situation that is instantly recognizable to all peoples throughout history. Here is a good man, Abraham, caught in an impossible position between two women, each of whom bore him a son and each of whom would have undoubtedly liked to be his primary spouse. While I do not necessarily agree with the theory that Hagar became Abraham's true wife or that she adopted Abraham's faith, the Torah clearly shows that Abraham felt compassion and love for Hagar and Ishmael and that God protected them.

In short, I would never assert that Sarah and Isaac were superior to Hagar and Ishmael; I would simply say that they had a different destiny. God chose Isaac to sire the people of Israel and Ishmael to sire the Arab people—a "great nation" that indeed came to outnumber the Jews many times over. Today there are perhaps 400 million Arabs and some 1.6 billion Muslims, compared with only about 14 million Jews.[2] In other words, the Muslims outnumber the Jews by more than 1,000 to 1.

One significant reason for this numerical imbalance is, as I noted above, that the Jews, unlike the Christians and Muslims, have never sought for our religion to become a universal faith that seeks to convert the entire world. Rather, we have remained a religion-nation-people-family, a small people with a large role to play in the world. We do not consider ourselves superior to Muslims and Christians but rather as different. The Jews have a separate and distinct destiny, but we are equal members of the human family.

I close this chapter by adding a significant point concerning the meaning of chosenness in the Jewish conception that may also give surcease to many who believe that, despite everything I have elucidated above, the term "chosenness" per se implies superiority. It may be that the entire controversy could have been ameliorated with a more careful and painstaking translation of the Hebrew term *am segulah,* which has generally been translated into the languages of the gentile world as "chosen people." Yet its literal meaning as expressed in the Torah (Exodus 19:5; Deuteronomy 7:6, 14:2, 26:18) can be more accurately rendered as "treasured nation." For example, in Exodus 19:5, God says to Moses, "Now then, if you will obey Me faithfully and keep My covenant, you shall be my treasured possession among all the peoples. Indeed all the earth is mine, but you shall be to Me a kingdom of priests and a holy nation."

So certainly the term *am segulah*—"treasured nation"—refers to the special relationship that God has with the Jewish people. It makes clear that, throughout the biblical period, He had a hands-on involvement with and affection for the Jewish people that He not only expressed but repeatedly acted on. And as I have stated, I believe God chose the Jewish people for a special mission, that of spreading ethical monotheism in the world, that is distinct from the missions for which He chose other peoples and faiths.

---

2. *The Global Religious Landscape: A Report on the Size and Distribution of the World's Major Religious Groups as of 2010,* Pew Forum on Religion and Public Life, December 18, 2012, http://www.pewforum.org/global-religious-landscape.aspx.

Yet "treasured nation" is, in my mind, subtly but profoundly different from "chosen people." The latter term certainly lends itself to the interpretation that God selected the Jews out of all the nations for better treatment or even to reign supreme, even though the punishment and martyrdom inflicted upon Jews through the millennia has led many Jews to ask ruefully why God does not choose another nation for a change. But awareness that the Hebrew term *am segulah* actually means "treasured nation," not "chosen people," also puts some distance between the Jewish people and any pretense to superiority or dominance over the nations. Yes, God saw us as his treasure, because during the biblical period we were the only nation that rejected the then-near-universal belief in idols and instead chose to accept the One God as the true one who accepted monotheism and its attendant manifold obligations to serve God. It is no wonder, then, that He would have called us his "treasured nation," assuming, of course, that we remained faithful to the laws that He laid down for us. As the Bible, the Talmud, and Jewish history all show, there were many times when we failed to do that.

Today, however, followers of major faiths, including Muslims and Christians, also are monotheistic. So while God may continue to view the Jews as his "treasured nation," I believe he also treasures other nations and faiths—including the Muslims—and has accorded them their own special missions.

Yet since Christians and Muslims also believe in and propagate monotheism, does this also make them equally chosen to perform the task assigned to the Jews, that is, to spread ethnical monotheism? No, I believe that the missions that the three faiths were chosen for were, and remain, distinct. As I said before, I believe that we Jews were chosen by God in the biblical period for a special mission: to introduce monotheism to the world. No other nation or religion was given this specific assignment. The emergence of Christianity and Islam as the two largest world religions is powerful evidence that the Jews were successful in carrying out the groundwork necessary to make most of the world understand that monotheism is a superior moral construct to polytheism. Yet because Muslims or Christians adopted monotheism does not mean they have also adopted the same mission as the Jews. So what is the special mission of the Muslims? Frankly, it would be presumptuous for me to say. That is for adherents of Islam to sort through, as they appear to have done, in a way, with the concept of Kheir Ummah.

Like Imam Shamsi Ali, I see many similarities between the concepts of *am segulah* and Kheir Ummah, though not a perfect overlap. One of the similarities these concepts share that Shamsi has pointed to is Maimonides's admonition that Jews can become "unchosen" if they do not fulfill their mission and that non-Jews may be among the chosen if they dedicate themselves to Godly service. In an exchange of e-mails on the subject, Shamsi wrote to me, "This would appear to leave open the possibility of including non-Jews in chosenness." Perhaps it does, but as I have already said, I don't take chosenness to mean the Jews enjoy a superior status. So, according to my lights, a righteous non-Jew who is fulfilling the mission of his people is every bit as "chosen" as a Jew fulfilling his mission.

Shamsi has shared with me that, in Islamic theology, adherents of Islam who fail to live up to the responsibilities of the best nation forfeit their place in it. What that tells me is that in Islam as well as Judaism, the accent is as much or more on responsibilities as it is on privileges. That sense of responsibility to all humankind, especially to the less fortunate, expressed in the concepts of *tikkun olam* and *islah*, does indeed, as my friend Shamsi has written, "represent a stunning intersection of our faiths."

However, there remain important differences between the two faiths that impact their respective outlooks on the concept of chosenness. As Shamsi has written to me:

> In our understanding of religion, the whole idea of being Muslim is about faith and commitment to a faith. While Muslims believe that no one is born into a specific tradition, our very nature is to be born faithful (*fitra*). The only idea of superiority is one that can be achieved by faith in action (*taqwa*, or righteousness).

On this point, I believe there is indeed a significant difference of emphasis in our two faith traditions. According to many of our great rabbis and philosophers throughout Jewish history, a person's behavior and mode of conduct are a more important indicator of his worth as a human being than his level of faith in God. The Talmud makes clear that both behaving in an ethical manner toward one's fellow human beings and believing deeply in God are important moral imperatives, but that the first attribute should take precedence over the second.

In Judaism, activity is primary and faith is secondary. Even if a person doesn't believe in God, he can be an exemplary Jew and human being if he serves his fellow men in an ethical manner. On Yom Kippur, God forgives us our transgressions against Him, including the inability of many Jews to connect with Him on a belief level. Yet if a Jew has transgressed against another human being, he or she cannot turn to God for forgiveness for that sin but must instead ask forgiveness from the person he or she wronged.

Where does that leave the Jewish people and the unique mission that we believe was assigned to us by God? To reiterate a point I made earlier in this chapter, we can take great pride in how far we have come with that mission, but we still have a very long way to go. Our mission is not over just because several billion people worldwide observe the three Abrahamic and monotheistic faiths. For even though adherents of the three faiths subscribe to a belief in ethical monotheism, that doesn't mean that all or even most of them are living up to what ethical monotheism is all about.

We see plenty of abuses and hypocrisy among adherents of all three religions, including among those who are purportedly the most pious. One is reminded of the terrible child-abuse scandals by Catholic priests in countries around the world and the inclination of some archbishops and cardinals to play down or even cover up the abuses in order to protect the good name of the Church rather than showing sufficient concern for the victims of the abuse. In the Islamic world, the last two decades have seen the emergence of a hateful and fanatical ideology spearheaded by Osama bin Laden and his Al Qaeda network, which, while supposedly upholding a pure version of Islam, in fact fundamentally has perverted the essence of a religion of peace by advocating acts of mass murder by suicide bombers against Muslims and non-Muslims alike.

We have many aspects of hypocritical zealotry in modern-day Judaism, as well, including within the Jewish state itself. The week that I wrote this chapter, ultra-Orthodox Jews in Israel spat upon and shouted epithets like "whore" at an eight-year-old religiously observant girl, claiming that she was not dressed modestly enough for their tastes. Other such fanatics dressed their children in concentration-camp garb in order to make the case that the Israeli authorities were behaving like Nazis by preventing them from further such excesses. What a terrible example of *sinat chinam* (baseless hatred) of Jew for Jew, of which there have been many in recent years.

Other supposedly deeply religious Jews have turned their venom against non-Jews, burning a mosque and destroying Palestinian olive groves to attach a "price tag" to Israeli government efforts to remove Jews from illegal settlement outposts. Some members of the same group actually attacked an Israeli army base, as well.

So we have a great deal of work ahead of us to ultimately ensure that all Jews and all followers of ethical monotheism uphold the ethical part as well as the monotheistic part of the equation. Ethical monotheists of all three faiths should strive to set an example in their own lives by modeling a system of values rather engaging than in the pursuit of valuables. They should concentrate on creating communities of worth, not wealth. It remains the role of the Jews to act as a voice of conscience. Our paramount mission must be to encourage all people to treat each other with respect, for we believe that manifesting kindness and compassion to one's fellow human being will lead to belief in God, and not the other way around.

While we are a long way from declaring that moral mission accomplished, we *have* succeeded in accomplishing something tremendously important: creating a widely accepted standard for ethical monotheism where none existed before. Unlike two thousand years ago, today the majority of humanity has come to believe there is one God, and that believers in God should honor their creator by improving the world and treating our fellow human beings with dignity.

So, we aren't there yet, but at least we know the direction home. And while it has hardly been a joyride for the Jews to be chosen to carry out our God-given mission of bringing ethical monotheism to the world, it has been, and remains, an uplifting assignment, one that gives many of us a reason for getting up every morning and doing what we know needs to be done.

CHAPTER EIGHT

Kheir Ummah

IMAM SHAMSI ALI

You are the best of the nations
raised up for [the benefit of] men.
—*Qur'an 3:110*[1]

The best nation is that which is the most beneficial and helpful to others,
which strives toward good, discourages vice, and believes in the oneness
and supremacy of God. This definition by its nature does not exclude non-
Muslims from forming part of the "best nation," or Kheir Ummah. Neither does it include all Muslims simply by virtue of their acknowledgment
of faith. Rather it is a motivation and encouragement to those who would
seek to belong to God's favored community in this life and the next.

The point is not simply to define the term. A correct understanding
of the Islamic concept of Kheir Ummah is also essential to appreciate the
difficulties many Muslims have with the notion of a single "chosen people," as well as to rectify the misapprehension that many non-Muslims
have about an Islamic "best nation" being a hegemonic threat to other
communities. Ideas of a global caliphate, *dhimmi* or vassal states, and
Dar-al-Salaam versus *Dar-al-Harb* are often colored by misunderstanding and apprehension, as are the concepts of the Jews as "chosen people"
who are divinely entitled to authority over followers of Islam.[2]

---

1. M. H. Shakir (1866–1939) interpretation, from QuranBrowser.com.
2. *Dar-al-Salaam* literally means "realm of peace" and is a term used to indicate
lands under Muslim dominion. *Dar-al-Harb* is a term used to indicate lands not under
Islamic rule—in effect, the "realm of war" to those Muslims who believe peace can only
be achieved when Islamic rule prevails.

MEANING AND CONTEXT

There are undeniable differences in the Abrahamic faiths regarding prophethood and Holy Scripture. While the revelations of God to Abraham and Moses are accepted by all three religions, the belief in Jesus as a prophet is core only to Christians and Muslims, while Muhammad's prophethood is embraced only by the Muslim community. The reason this matters is that while our holy book, the Qur'an, addresses the prophethood and revelations of both Jesus and Muhammad in addition to those of the Tanakh, it also stresses that divisions or disunity in belief are contrary to God's will. Although there may be differences in our scriptures, our prophet lines, and our oral traditions, our core beliefs are the same: the belief in one almighty God, the belief that He is the only one worthy of worship, and the belief that we should strive to behave in accordance with the guidance He has sent us in our scriptures. The purpose of religion is to bring people together in love and unity, as brothers and sisters. This is stated most eloquently in Qur'an 3:103:

> And hold fast, all together, by the rope which Allah (stretches out for you), and be not divided among yourselves; and remember with gratitude Allah's favour on you; for ye were enemies and He joined your hearts in love, so that by His Grace, ye became brethren; and ye were on the brink of the pit of fire, and He saved you from it. Thus doth Allah make His signs clear to you: That ye may be guided.[3]

Divisions, conflicts, and hatred are aberrations to God, and in the Islamic faith, there are many admonitions to the Muslim community on proper brotherly conduct:

> As for those who divide their religion and break up into sects, thou hast no part in them in the least: their affair is with Allah: He will in the end tell them the truth of all that they did.　　　*(6:159)*

> Turn ye back in repentance to Him, and fear Him: establish regular prayers, and be not ye among those who join gods with Allah, those

---

3. Unless otherwise noted, this and all subsequent Qur'an excerpts are from Abdullah Yusuf Ali, *The Meaning of the Holy Qur'an*, 11th ed. (Beltsville, MD: Amana Publications, 2006).

who split up their religion, and become (mere) sects, each party rejoicing in that which is with itself! *(30:31–32)*

If ye turn back (from the path), He will substitute in your stead another people; then they would not be like you! *(47:38)*

Because Muslims believe that righteousness is the key to happiness, we seek to submit to God's will in all aspects of life. This is the first level of belief, *Islam* itself, the submission of our individual wills to that of God's. This is followed by *iman*, the faith that is between one person and Allah, which is private and constant. The third level of faith is *ihsan*, a constant feeling of togetherness with Allah, in which one acts as if He is always present, not just during the time of prayer. The three levels together form *taqwa*, the confluence of being God-fearing, righteous, and pious. The belief that people who have *taqwa* are the most respected in the sight of Allah comes from a hadith attributed to Prophet Muhammad.[4] The hadith guides us to understand that even if people profess the faith (the *shahada*), if they do not live the principles, they have not had *iman* come into their hearts. And therefore, they have not become the best they can be, the Kheir Ummah.

The *Kheiriya* are the best people, and the *Ummah* is the greater community of believers. The Islamic concept of Kheir Ummah is explained by Ibn Abbas (a companion of Prophet Muhammad) as the "best man *for* man." In that phrase, the meaning of "for" is something that we *do*, not just believe; it is about selflessness, and doing good for others. Thus, this phrase refers not to any particular nation but to the group made up of individuals who are the best examples of living Godly principles.

There are three main criteria set forth regarding the Kheir Ummah: those who enjoin good and encourage virtue (*amr bil ma'ruuf*); those who forbid bad actions and discourage vice (*nahyi an-almunkar*); and those who do these things based on a strong faith in Allah (*iman*). It is about service, kindness, and being compassionate to others on the basis of faith.

---

4. *Hadith* are narrations, most often oral traditions passed down directly from Prophet Muhammad and those who were his closest companions. They are often cited as parallels to the accounts of the companions of Jesus in the New Testament and to the oral tradition, or Mishnah, of the Jewish peoples.

Just as the "chosen people" is a term associated with Jews, the Kheir Ummah is associated with Muslims. However, being a member of the Kheir Ummah is not a gift bestowed upon someone simply because he or she is Muslim or associates him- or herself with the religion; nor is it a status *guaranteed* to Muslims. Rather, it is an evident challenge for those who would carry out the righteous responsibilities put on their shoulders. It is a call to be a true servant both in vertical service to God, which is known as *hablun minallah*, and in horizontal service to our fellow human beings, known as *hablun minannas*.

From this *hablun minallah*, or theological standpoint, Judaism conforms most closely to the Muslim ideal because of the faith in the oneness of God (*Tawhid*) that our traditions share. The idea of the Kheir Ummah is as transnational as the Islamic *ummah*, and Islam encourages the ability of all peoples to be "the best" regardless of their differences, to compete in goodness.

As the Qur'an states in 5:48:

> To each among you have we prescribed a law and an open way. If Allah had so willed, He would have made you a single people, but (His plan is) to test you in what He hath given you; so strive as in a race in all virtues.

Under the *hablun minannas* or social aspect, we find that the Prophet Muhammad and his early followers emphasized positive actions in serving others as the right character for the best nation. And this remains the orthodox view, supported by many classical scholars. Though being "grounded in faith" is part of having the right character, it does not grant an individual any right to judge others with respect to their own faith traditions. Each individual's expression of his or her faith makes up the social aspect. In this sense, Mother Teresa would be an example of the Kheir Ummah because of her selflessness. The Qur'an itself delineates the positive contributions of the People of the Book—the followers of Abrahamic faiths.[5] As the first People of the Book, the Jews deserve special mention, and their position as the "chosen people" is discussed later in this chapter.

---

5. *People of the Book* is a term for Jews and Christians, and some scholars include Sabians and Zoroastrians as well as those who received divinely revealed scripture.

From a practical standpoint, there are many ways for people to rise to best nation status. If we look back to the time of the most profound Islamic influence, we see numerous examples of the preservation, pursuit, and dissemination of knowledge in the Islamic empire. The knowledge transfer of ancient Greek texts throughout centuries and into our modern civilization is a concrete contribution to all mankind that can be considered an example of the Kheir Ummah concept. For the good of all humanity, Islamic scholars made breakthroughs in mathematics, medicine, and engineering, and Islamic artists created enduring poetry and painting.

PERCEPTION

Unfortunately, the concept of the Muslim community and the Kheir Ummah is probably one of the most misunderstood of Islam. A regrettable combination of narrow-mindedness on the part of some Muslims and distorted perceptions by some non-Muslims has caused immense misunderstanding within and without the Muslim community. The most commonly voiced anxiety by non-Muslims is that there exists not just a wish to confer on all non-Muslims an abject and inferior status as second-rate citizens but also a plan to elevate the Muslim Kheir Ummah by "holy war" to its "rightful" position as overlord.

Although the word *dhimmi* comes from an Arabic word meaning "protected," the term is often invoked by non-Muslims to conjure up dangerous images and visceral fears of oppression and persecution. The term was applied by Arab-Muslim conquerors to indigenous non-Muslim populations who surrendered by treaty (*dhimma*) to Muslim authority. The consequent period under Muslim rule saw varied degrees of assimilation *and* autonomy, not least because of the amount of time it lasted. The payment of taxes (*jizya*) by non-Muslims to the Islamic government was a fact of empire, tradition, and practicality. Still, the misperception persists today that the Muslim ideal of Kheir Ummah equates to the subjugation of all other religions. While the implications and deep-rooted anxieties that a loss of peoplehood causes cannot be explored here, we can address the misunderstanding of what Kheir Ummah means with respect to this collective traumatic fear.

For many, it is difficult to decipher the difference between the widely held belief by Muslims in the concept of a global caliphate—that is, all Muslims are automatically a part of a worldwide community in which the *calipha*, or leader, leads by Islamic example, much as a community imam—and the more radical view espoused by groups such as Al-Muhajiroun that seem to be advocating a world under Muslim rule.[6] It is in this way that the concept of a caliphate has been misappropriated and misunderstood. While the issue of a caliphate is understood differently by many scholars, the majority of Muslim scholars say the caliphate is not meant as an establishment of a universal Muslim state but as the establishment of Muslim practices within the Muslim ummah, wherever Muslims are. For example, we can look to Medina in the seventh century CE as a civic state where Muslims practiced Islam and non-Muslims practiced their own laws. The great Umayyad leader Umar Bin Abdul Azziz often stated that Muslims did not have the right to impose Islamic laws onto non-Muslim people, and he made great efforts at reconciling differences between the Abrahamic groups under his dominion as well as the Zoroastrians. Those who believe they are being "truer" Muslims by following seventh-century examples of Prophet Muhammad and his companions make the error of not understanding the caliphate as an example of the nonliteral application of Islam. People like Osama bin Laden, who claim they are speaking on behalf of all Muslims in advocating "holy war" for furtherance of the expansion of Islam or for its global dominion, do not speak for the Muslims I know nor for any who have any sound religious basis. The concept of a global caliphate is closer in meaning to a guide for Muslims to act in accordance with Islamic precepts in addition to civic ones. This is part of being the best nation for a Muslim, since it encompasses rightful actions and submission to God's will. It does not mean the imposition of Shari'a on non-Muslims or the subjugation of non-Muslims to Muslim rule.

In Islam, the annual payment of alms in the amount of 2.5 percent of one's wealth is called *zakat* and is one of the Five Pillars, or basic rules, of the faith. These collected monies are used for the social welfare of the community. Food, shelter, protection, education, and other programs

---

6. Al-Muhajiroun is an internationally banned group that publicly makes a point of not renouncing violence in the push for a global caliphate. Others, such as Hizb ut-Tahrir, denounce violence but work toward political autonomy for the world's Muslims, extraneous to the civil laws of the geographic lands where they reside.

common to modern and ancient government were funded through *zakat.* For Muslims, there were many and specific rates of *zakat* exacted (e.g., on fruits, slaves, horses, and honey). Non-Muslims under Islamic government in the period of Islamic empire were not commanded to pay *zakat.* Instead, they paid a tributary tax called *jizya,* which granted them many of the same benefits and protections as the Muslims, though it is debated as to what extent. For the non-Muslims who were living in Muslim territories, *jizya* was imposed as a matter of custom, a tithe that all people paid much as we pay taxes to our government today. This tax was customary for peoples to pay to a government that would wage war on their behalf. As stated in the hadith of Imam Malik:

> Yahya related to me from Malik that he had heard that Umar ibn Abd al-Aziz wrote to his governors telling them to relieve any people who paid the *jizya* from paying the *jizya* if they became Muslims. Malik said, "The *sunna* is that there is no *jizya* due from women or children of People of the Book, and that *jizya* is only taken from men who have reached puberty. The people of *dhimma* and the Magians do not have to pay any *zakat* on their palms or their vines or their crops or their livestock. . . . As long as they are in the country they have agreed to live in, they do not have to pay anything on their property except the *jizya.* If, however, they trade in Muslim countries, coming and going in them, a tenth is taken from what they invest in such trade. This is because *jizya* is only imposed on them on conditions, which they have agreed on, namely that they will remain in their own countries, and that war will be waged for them on any enemy of theirs, and that if they then leave that land to go anywhere else to do business they will have to pay a tenth. . . . People of the Book and Magians do not have to pay any *zakat* on any of their property, livestock, produce or crops. The Sunnah still continues like that. They remain in the *deen* they were in, and they continue to do what they used to do."[7]

From this passage, we can see that non-Muslims paid *jizya* 1) as a matter of administrative Sunnah, or custom; 2) as a means of paying for protection by Muslim armies in times of war; 3) in lieu of *zakat* and other

---

7. Imam Malik, *Muwatta,* book 17, number 17.24.46.

tithes that Muslims were accountable for; and 4) as a business tax. There is no denying that non-Muslims did have a tax imposed on them in lands where they were governed by Muslim rulers, and the imposition of this tax on People of the Book is even stated in the Qur'an (9:29):

> Fight those who believe not in God nor the Last Day, nor hold that forbidden which hath been forbidden by God and His apostle, nor acknowledge the religion of truth, (even if they are) of the People of the Book, until they pay the *jizya* with willing submission, and feel themselves subdued.

The intention of this tax is a sore point for many descendants of those on whom it was imposed. The idea that the *dhimmi* nations that paid it were relegated to "second-class citizenship," and that it was meant as a form of subjugation, has support as well as refutation in scholarship. Here it is important to note the context of a minority group having tribute levied on them by a hegemonic power, and there is precedent in Jewish scripture for taxing non-Jews in their territories as well. The Jewish scholar Maimonides, for example, explains that acceptance of the Noahide laws, in addition to a tributary tax given to the Jewish kingdom, was imposed upon non-Jews as a way to avert war with the Jewish nation. We thus find in Hilchot Melachim 6:1:

> No war was declared against any people before peace had been offered to them, and this applied to both religious and other wars. If peace was accepted along with the seven commandments given to the descendants of Noah, none of these people were to be slain. They became tribute payers and slaves to Israel; if they agreed to pay tribute, or to be slaves only, that was not accepted. This servitude which was accepted, humbled the people and gave them lowly status so that they would not dominate in any way. They became subject to Israel and could not hold positions in Israel. The tribute which was levied was that they should be ready to serve the king with money and work like building walls, strengthening fortifications, building the king's palace and so on.[8]

---

8. *Kings, Their Wars, and the Messiah: From the Mishneh Torah of Maimonides,* H. M. Russell and Rabbi J. Wenberg, trans., Royal College of Physicians of Edinburgh (Edinburgh: Blackwood Pillans & Wilson, 1987), 11.

In effect, this tribute is no different from the payment of *jizya*. In both cases, these were cultural norms adapted for economic stability and governmental process, and in neither case would these historical norms be contemporary aims. We cannot unequivocally state that Islamic governments in the past were perfectly equitable and never offensive to those subjects who did not believe in Islam. We can only return to historical records in trying to paint an accurate picture and return to scriptural or hadith sources when trying to ascertain the intention of Islamic rulers and their convictions.

Let us not be naive: it is a fact that there are circumstances that test these convictions, and we are all prey to human emotions and fallibilities. But it is precisely during times of vulnerability that we must show our spiritual strength. This is a moral challenge that applies not only to Muslims, not even only to monotheists, but to all peoples who believe in an Almighty and look to face their day of judgment with a clear conscience. I have often and consistently called for the leaders of our spiritual communities to guide our people toward the greater good and toward a levelheaded response to quotidian issues. As spiritual leaders, it is our responsibility to enlighten and anticipate.

Islamophobia in the United States and abroad is fed by ill-guided people who call themselves people of faith and profess to be following the dictates of Islam. Under this banner, people such as Faisal Shazad, the Pakistani-born naturalized American citizen who attempted to detonate a car bomb in New York City's Times Square, have taken advantage of the benefits of the same country they then proposed to harm. Faisal Shazad pretended that his acts were meant to honor Islam, while acting in a way that was directly contravening Islamic precepts. There are so many verses in the Qur'an that point to the unequivocal sin of taking another's life that no one who studies the Qur'an should be confused. One of the most famous is 5:32:

> If any one slew a person . . . it would be as if he slew the whole people: and if any one saved a life, it would be as if he saved the life of the whole people. Then although there came to them Our apostles with clear signs, yet, even after that, many of them continued to commit excesses in the land.

There are also clear passages that state that if peace offerings are being made, one should never refuse them but embrace them with an open heart. Verse 4:90 says:

> Except those who join a group between whom and you there is a treaty (of peace), or those who approach you with hearts restraining them from fighting you as well as fighting their own people. If God had pleased, He could have given them power over you, and they would have fought you: Therefore if they withdraw from you but fight you not, and (instead) send you (Guarantees of) peace, then God Hath opened no way for you (to war against them).

The guidance provided by scripture points not just to offerings of peace at times of war, but consistent overtures of peace and friendship, collaboration, and helpfulness. We as Muslims are instructed to strive to be a boon to our neighbors and to improve the lives of others. As with any ambition, the goal may not always be achieved, but it can be sought.

For Muslims, preventing evil from happening where these values break down is not a civic responsibility but an Islamic duty. Islam obligates Muslims everywhere to keep *salaam*, or peace, and to actively prevent anything that undermines security. In so doing, Muslims must be very clear in their opposition to negative actions done by people purporting to profess Islam, and they must abstain from any tendency to place expiating qualifiers on these actions (such as those who would seek to justify criminality or malevolence as a valid reaction to US foreign policy).

Addressing actions that are wrong must be unambiguous; they must not hold caveats. Consistent and vocal opposition to wrongdoing, working with other faith communities, recognizing our similarities and respecting our differences, working with law enforcement officials and relevant government authorities to prevent any possible threat against our cities and our nation—all of these are Islamic duties. Every believer in the supremacy of God and our return to Him has a more expansive mission than that of merely applying belief and conviction to ourselves—it is our responsibility to guide those around us to the truth and the love that God wishes for us all. That is a way in which we can truly live up to being the Kheir Ummah.

KHEIR UMMAH AND THE CHOSEN PEOPLE

The concept of being the best or favored nation in the eyes of God was not limited to Muslims even in the time of Prophet Muhammad. In the Qur'an we see that He favored the Children of Israel and gave them special citation:

> O Children of Israel! call to mind the special favour which I bestowed upon you, and that I preferred you to all others. (*2:122*)

> O Children of Israel! call to mind The (special) favour which I bestowed upon you, and fulfill your covenants with Me as I fulfill My covenant with you, and fear none but Me. (*2:40*)

> We did aforetime grant to the Children of Israel the book, the power of command, and prophethood; we gave them, for sustenance, things good and pure; and we favoured them above the nations. (*45:16*)

And so Muslims believe that if Jews fulfill the covenant with God, they will receive His favor. This means they have the opportunity to be of the best nation, or the Kheir Ummah, as well. All Muslims place Moses within the prophethood chain, and he is considered an honor the Jews have, plainly detailed in the Qur'an and accepted by all Muslims. There is no theological basis for believing that Jews are not equal in opportunity or ability to show themselves to be true and virtuous.

We must not be disingenuous or ignorant of the Qur'an verses that critique Jews, but we must place them in context. Many of the critical verses refer to Jews who deviated from what Moses taught, whether it was breaking the Sabbath or challenging his teachings, and are found in the Tanakh as well. For example, Leviticus 26 details all that God expects from the Israelites as a mark of their special covenant—and equally details his retribution if they fail to keep to the covenant. These critiques are equally applicable to non-Jews (including Muslims), as it is the veering from scripture that is criticized. Receiving God's special favor is not the end; it is the beginning of the relationship. And being the best nation or the chosen people is not about being labeled Muslim or Jew; it is about the commitment to the teachings of the one Almighty God. The Jews have the Torah; the Christians, the New Testament; and the

Muslims, the Qur'an, so that each monotheistic tradition has a divine scripture to guide it.[9]

There seems to be currency among many Jews that the principle reason they are condemned in the Qur'an was their refusal to accept Muhammad as the one predicted in their teachings who would come to them as a Messenger of God and His final Prophet. It must be made clear that when Jews are spoken of in less-than-glowing terms in the Qur'an (or elsewhere), it is not because of their disbelief in Muhammad as a prophet per se but rather because they rejected the message he was dispensing, which was that all peoples were to uphold the very same scriptures and mandates found in the Tanakh. Qur'anic principles neither contrasted nor rejected Jewish ones but sought an adherence to and a continuation of them.

Jews whom I have spoken with explain that they were chosen by God to spread ethical monotheism to the world, that this is the root of the application of "chosenness" for the Jewish people. Since Christians and Muslims share this monotheistic belief and are continuing to disseminate the message received by Moses, the Abrahamic faiths must recognize their shared mission and responsibility for being the best nation. There are many more reasons to be united—in theology, friendship, and history—than there are reasons to find difference. For example, Muslims do not believe that Isaac was any more or less of a son to Abraham than Ishmael was, and consequently, Jews and Muslims are brothers, bonded by the father who recognized and taught worship of the one God we all pray to. The key to a person being a believer is that he or she is righteous, regardless of ancestry. Will a Jew believe that one descended from Abraham, that *Friend of God*—but from Ishmael's rather than Isaac's side—is excluded from God's grace because he is not of the line of Yaqub? Would a Muslim believe the same of one descended from Isaac? Neither argument seems valid.

---

9. Wael B. Hallaq, *A History of Islamic Legal Theories: An Introduction to Sunni Usūl Al-Fiqh* (Cambridge, UK: Cambridge University Press, 1997), 4–5. Alongside many other scholars, Hallaq clearly considers that each monotheistic tradition does well to follow its own scripture.

Furthermore, there is no commandment to believe in the Qur'an and disbelieve in the Tanakh, as evidenced by Verse 42:15:

> I believe in the book which Allah has sent down; and I am commanded to judge justly between you. Allah is our Lord and your Lord: for us (is the responsibility for) our deeds, and for you for your deeds. There is no contention between us and you. Allah will bring us together, and to Him is (our) final goal.

This sentiment is found elsewhere in the Qur'an, as in 29:46:

> And argue not with the People of the Scripture unless it be in (a way) that is better, save with such of them as do wrong; and say: We believe in that which hath been revealed unto us and revealed unto you; our God and your God is One, and unto Him we surrender.[10]

When Muslims call on worship of Allah,[11] they are saying that the righteous worship the *one* God. At the time of Islam's inception, this was the antithesis of the status quo in pagan Arabia and a concept that was searing in its urgency to the ummah of the time. When Muslims call for the worship of Allah, this is no different than the call of the other Abrahamic faiths, and the Qur'an indeed makes no differentiation of faiths in this sense. Consider the verses 3:64–67:

> Say: "O People of the Book! Come to an agreement between us and you: that we shall worship none but Allah, and that we shall ascribe no partner unto Him, and that none of us shall take others for lords beside Allah." And if they turn away, then say: "Bear witness that we are they who have surrendered (unto Him) . . . Abraham was not a Jew, nor yet a Christian; but he was an upright man who had surrendered (to Allah), and he was not of the idolaters."

---

10. *The Glorious Qur'an*, 2nd ed., Marmaduke Pickthall, trans. (Elmhurst, NY: Tahrike Tarsile Qur'an, 1999).

11. In Arabic, the language of the Holy Qur'an, the translation for the word *God* is *Allah*. Allah is not, as some have claimed, the "Arabic" or the "Islamic" God; He is simply God.

These verses seek to blur the self-identification of discrete groupings traditionally given as "Muslim," "Jew," or "Christian" and instead seek to demarcate the believers from the nonbelievers. If we look at the passages from 5:44 to 5:59, we note that the Qur'an confirms that the Torah and Injeel were sent down to the Jews and Christians previously, and that these books are the rules by which each people should be judged.[12] So between Muslims, they should be judged by the Qur'an, between Jews by the Torah, and between Christians by the Injeel. If we look at the language of 5:44, we note the confirmation of the Torah given to the Jewish people:

> It was we who revealed the law (to Moses): therein was guidance and light. By its standard have been judged the Jews, by the prophets who bowed (as in Islam) to Allah's will, by the rabbis and the doctors of law: for to them was entrusted the protection of Allah's book, and they were witnesses thereto.

This idea is reinforced by verse 5:48, noted previously, confirming that each group is to be judged by its own scriptures, and followed by reminders of the fallibility of human judgment, emphasizing that it is only God who has the right to punish wrongdoers (5:49):

> And this (He commands): Judge thou between them by what Allah hath revealed, and follow not their vain desires, but beware of them lest they beguile thee from any of that (teaching) which Allah hath sent down to thee. And if they turn away, be assured that for some of their crime it is Allah's purpose to punish them.

The same lesson is echoed throughout the Qur'an in a most consistent way—that those who follow God's commandments, in the guidelines sent to them (whether Torah, Injeel, or Qur'an) are those to be praised, and those who do not are not to be emulated or followed in any way.

> And the Jews say the Christians follow nothing (true), and the Christians say the Jews follow nothing (true); yet both are readers of the

---

12. The Injeel refers to the scriptures given to the Christians and also known as the Bible or the Gospel.

Scripture. Even thus speak those who know not. Allah will judge between them on the Day of Resurrection concerning that wherein they
differ. (*2:113*)[13]

This is no different than the admonitions found in the Bible, in which
pious Jews criticized those who went against the dictates of God, or when
God warned those who went astray of what their punishments would be
if they did not revert to the straight path.[14] The concern that is voiced in
multiple passages of the Qur'an, of the Holy laws being altered by human
interference, was not just a concern of Muslims. If we look at Jewish history, we can see that the same issues that are addressed in the Qur'an were
addressed by the Jews themselves. The breakaway sects that emerged from
around 150 BCE through Roman times were disturbed that so much of
the original message was being or had been revised.[15] Because oral interpretations were being added to the Torah of Mount Sinai, they felt the
Jewish community was drifting away from the True Message and that
priests, rabbis, "doctors of law," and the like were exerting too much influence on the word of God. Many tried to break away from the "official" Judaism of the time and form communities they saw as more correct, more
strictly adherent to the original message received through Moses. What
some of these communities objected to was not so different than what is
cited in the Qur'an! In fact, passage 2:218 seems to speak directly to the
Jewish people:

> Those who believed and those who suffered exile and fought (and
> strove and struggled) in the path of God,— they have the hope of the
> Mercy of God: And God is oft-forgiving, most merciful.

The guidance found in scripture is not meant to be taken only literally. Rather, we should extract the meanings, the universal teachings,
from the passages. The Qur'an was meant in the first place to teach les-

---

13. *The Glorious Qur'an*, Pickthall.
14. For example, Exod. 15, 16; Lev. 26; Deut. 4, 9; Isa. 1; Neh. 17.
15. Some were known as Dead Sea sects. See Hershel Shanks, *Understanding the
Dead Sea Scrolls* (New York: Random House, 1992). Also, Lawrence H. Schiffman, *Re-
claiming the Dead Sea Scrolls: Their True Meaning for Judaism and Christianity* (New
York: Doubleday, 1994), and Robert Eisenman and Michael Wise, *Dead Sea Scrolls
Uncovered* (New York: Penguin, 1992).

sons to the Muslims themselves, to provide guidance for those who believed in Prophet Muhammad's message. In the second place, references to the People of the Book, those who received divine guidance before Muhammad's time, were useful as examples of how to follow their monotheistic religion. As Islam is seen as a continuation of Moses's message and his teachings, the good things were to be taken as examples and the bad things were to be taken as lessons not to be repeated.

This is not to say the *historical* accounts mentioned in the Qur'an didn't happen literally as is written, but the Qur'an is not a history book, and historical accounting is not its main thrust. It is meant to be a book of guidance. We look at the footsteps of Banu Israel as formidable lessons, reminders of how to do right and where things could or did go wrong.[16] Our stance is that though the Qur'an is sometimes exact, to extrapolate the wisdom in its passages, we need not see the texts as simply static, literal words.

The criticisms leveled against the Jews in these instances were against the attitudes of a group that was not adhering to *Mosaic* teachings. Also, these criticisms were not extended to the entire Jewish population at large, down to the last person, but for any and all *wrongdoers*. In this sense, errant Muslims were being criticized as well. Members of Banu Israel did not follow Moses's teaching when they asked Aaron to create the Golden Calf, and this type of attitude is what is criticized. The punishment and criticism is meant for all people who behave in this way. Leviticus 26:3–43 lays out the rules of the covenant—obedience brings great gain, while disobedience brings nothing but ignominy and sorrow. But the mercy of God supports the covenant in Leviticus 26:44–45:

> And yet for all that, when they are in the land of their enemies, I will not cast them away, neither will I abhor them, to destroy them utterly, and to break My covenant with them; for I am the Lord their God. But I will for their sakes remember the covenant of their ancestors, whom I brought forth out of the land of Egypt in the sight of the heathen, that I might be their God: I am the Lord.[17]

---

16. *Banu Israel* refers to the tribe(s) of Israel.
17. King James Bible.

The idea of God accepting only those who are righteous is seen in Proverbs 15:8–9:

The sacrifice of the wicked is an abomination to the Lord; but the prayer of the upright is His delight. The way of the wicked is an abomination to the Lord; but He loveth him that followeth after righteousness.[18]

It is the same sentiment as in the Qur'an verses 5:27–28:

But recite unto them with truth the tale of the two sons of Adam, how they offered each a sacrifice, and it was accepted from the one of them and it was not accepted from the other. (The one) said: I will surely kill thee. (The other) answered: Allah accepteth only from those who ward off (evil). Even if thou stretch out thy hand against me to kill me, I shall not stretch out my hand against thee to kill thee, lo! I fear Allah, the Lord of the Worlds.[19]

The Qur'an addresses particular issues, times, and people within a particular context. On the one hand, Jews as a people are acknowledged as Children of Israel and addressed very respectfully; on the other hand, some Jews are scolded as individuals who did wrong within that larger community and who should have known better because of their special status. This is also how Muslims themselves are judged—some Muslims are good and some are not, and we must acknowledge both. A part of the community cannot be seen as the representation of the whole, not for Muslims or for Jews.

CONCLUSION

As Muslims, we strive to emulate the good deeds of the prophets chosen by God, those who have received His blessing and His revelations. As we have many hadith in our oral tradition regarding Prophet Muhammad, there is much guidance for us regarding his actions, and there has been much thought about how we can adapt these to our modern times.

---

18. The Hebrew Bible in English, according to the JPS 1917 edition, Jewish Publication Society.

19. *The Glorious Qur'an*, Pickthall.

One of the running themes in hadith narratives is the affirmation that God is most merciful, most beneficent (*Allahu al-rahman al-rahim*). As we should in all things strive to please God, if He is most merciful, so we should be merciful as well. If he forgives our mistakes and allows us freedom from judgment, then so too should we follow this example.

In any argument, we as fallible humans will only get partial information or insight given the limitations and perspectives of the people involved. Only God, who sees and knows all, can know the full story of any given event, which is why only God can judge and why we are not to assume that responsibility. Rather, we are to seek to change the things in ourselves that are unworthy of showing before God—whether greed, laziness, fear, ignorance, or jealousy. If there are aspects of ourselves we would be ashamed to put forth in front of God, then these are the aspects that we need to strive to improve until we are closer to a proper emulation of the values God wants us to embody.

There is a strong emphasis in Islam on education, on constantly educating ourselves in the Islamic characteristics of empathy, mercy, respect for others, and, most importantly, the constant remembrance of God. This ongoing striving is mandated for Muslims because striving to be closer to God is what makes a believer part of the best nation. It is not a question of being superior to any other creed, nation, ethnicity, or religion; it is a question of answering to God and being able in intention, effort, deed, and thought to stand before God on Judgment Day clearly having striven constantly for betterment in His eyes and drawing closer to His example.

The Holy Qur'an states:

> You are the best community that hath been raised up for mankind. Ye enjoin right conduct and forbid indecency; and ye believe in Allah. And if the People of the Scripture had believed it had been better for them. Some of them are believers; but most of them are evil-livers. They will not harm you save a trifling hurt, and if they fight against you they will turn and flee. And afterward they will not be helped. Ignominy shall be their portion wheresoever they are found save (where they grasp) a rope from Allah and a rope from men. They have incurred anger from their Lord, and wretchedness is laid upon them.

That is because they used to disbelieve the revelations of Allah, and slew the prophets wrongfully. That is because they were rebellious and used to transgress. They are not all alike. Of the People of the Scripture there is a staunch community who recite the revelations of Allah in the night season, falling prostrate (before Him). They believe in Allah and the Last Day, and enjoin right conduct and forbid indecency, and vie one with another in good works. These are of the righteous. (*3:110–114*)[20]

And verse 49:13 upholds this guidance:

O mankind! We created you from a single (pair) of a male and a female, and made you into nations and tribes, that ye may know each other (not that ye may despise each other). Verily the most honoured of you in the sight of God is (he who is) the most righteous of you.

Every particularistic religion to some extent claims a certain exclusivity of righteousness. We may have notions of "one of the best" or "chosen," but to claim exclusiveness in this respect is turning a blind eye to the other part of our teachings that sees the righteousness of others if they fulfill God's covenant. Many Qur'anic passages address "believers," not segregated as Jews or Christians or Muslims, but as those who believe in monotheism and the word of one God: Verse 48:29: "God has promised those among them who believe and do righteous deeds forgiveness, and a great reward." Verse 49:10: "The believers are but a single brotherhood: So make peace and reconciliation between your two (contending) brothers; and fear God, that ye may receive mercy."

Our oral history records Muhammad's last sermon as containing the following guidance:

Even as the fingers of the two hands are equal, so are human beings equal to one another. No one has any right, nor any preference to claim over another. You are brothers.

Under this rubric, Jews and Muslims should easily agree.

---

20. *The Glorious Qur'an*, Pickthall.

CHAPTER NINE

Amalek, the Dangers of Literalism, and the Role of Oral Tradition

RABBI MARC SCHNEIER

In March 2009, Imam Shamsi Ali was my guest at the New York Synagogue. It was the first time any imam had spoken to my congregation from the *bimah*.[1] The two of us held a thoughtful, heartfelt, and frequently inspiring dialogue on the striking commonalities between Islam and Judaism, and on the joint mission the two of us had undertaken to strengthen the fabric of Muslim-Jewish relations in America and around the world.

As might be expected, there were a few listeners in the audience who came to the event convinced that their rabbi was being led down the garden path by a leader of a religion intrinsically hostile to the Jewish people, and that all the sweet reasonableness Shamsi expressed at the event must be nothing more than a devious trick to lead the Jews astray. But the discomfort ran in both directions, as it turned out, and there was a moment when I wanted nothing more than to drop through the floor of my own synagogue. Most importantly, though, I was able to transform a situation of extreme embarrassment into a morally uplifting occasion and to use coincidence of acute theological tension as a teachable moment for the several hundred people present.

It happened that Shamsi's visit took place on the Shabbat Zachor (Sabbath of Remembrance) before Purim, the holiday during which we

---

1. A raised platform in a synagogue from which the Torah is read.

celebrate the triumph of Queen Esther and Mordecai over Haman, the evil vizier to the King of Persia who tried to destroy the Jews and ended up being destroyed himself. Haman is described in the Book of Esther in the Tanakh as a descendant of Amalek, a nation that hated and sought to destroy the Children of Israel in the aftermath of their Exodus from Egypt. In the Torah, God commands us to destroy the Amalekites utterly throughout history so that none of them will remain alive. In modern times, a few extremist Jews have identified Amalek variously with the Palestinians, Arabs, and/or Muslims. The mass murderer Baruch Goldstein, a radical settler influenced by the racist teachings of Meir Kahane, gunned down twenty-nine Palestinian Muslims at prayer before killing himself in the Cave of the Patriarchs (Machpelah) in Hebron on Purim 1994.

During the question-and-answer period, one man with the smug look of someone who believes he has found a foolproof argument to which no adequate response can be offered stood up. "Rabbi," he asked me, "if someone were able to prove to you that your guest, the imam, is a descendant of Amalek, would you not then agree that you would have a biblical imperative to have him killed?" In support of that notion the questioner went to cite several biblical passages, including Deuteronomy 25:17 and 1 Samuel 15:2–3. The first reads:

> Remember what Amalek did to you on your way out of Egypt; how he attacked you on the way when you were faint and weary, and cut off your tail, those who were lagging behind you, and he did not fear God. Therefore when the Lord your God has given you rest from all your enemies around you, in the land that the Lord your God is giving you for an inheritance to possess, you shall blot out the memory of Amalek from under heaven; you shall not forget.

The passage from Samuel states:

> Thus says the Lord of hosts, "I have noted what Amalek did to Israel in opposing them on the way when they came up out of Egypt. Now go and strike Amalek and devote to destruction all that they have. Do not spare them, but kill both man and woman, and infant, ox and sheep, camel and donkey."

At that moment, I felt deeply embarrassed—actually ashamed—that my dear friend Shamsi, who had just stretched out a hand of friendship to the Jews, had to sit there and listen to a presumably observant Jew argue that the God of Israel had commanded His people to conduct an endless war of extermination against another people—quite likely Shamsi's own. And instead of warmly welcoming Shamsi to my synagogue as a man of peace, I should rather be plotting (God forbid) to kill him. Fortunately, though, I had a theological response at hand that I knew would make clear to the audience how morally wrong and theologically un-Jewish the question directed at me really was.

So I raised my hand to calm the indignant hubbub in the audience, turned to my questioner, and said, "If Jewish law and Jewish morality were composed only of the Written Law, the Tanakh, and we were therefore obligated to follow all of its commandments to the letter, then you would be correct that I, like all Jews, would be obligated to fight the descendants of Amalek until the end of time. Even so, I would have a problem identifying the people with whom I am duty-bound to give battle, since most of our great rabbinical sages throughout the ages agree that the line of Amalek disappeared thousands of years ago. The Talmud, for example, contends in Berechot 28a that the destruction of the Kingdom of Israel by the Assyrians in the eighth century BCE and the subsequent exile of the Ten Lost Tribes and other non-Jewish nations in the Land of Israel "mixed up the nations." Therefore, the identity of many nations existing in and around the Land of Israel—including the Amalekites—was lost at that time. If that is the case, the commands in the Torah to exterminate Amalek and other Canaanite nations can no longer be considered binding, since it would clearly be wrong to wantonly kill anyone whom we cannot prove is a descendant of Amalek, including modern-day Arabs and Muslims."

Be that as it may, I explained to the questioner, there was another even more compelling reason why Imam Shamsi had no reason to fear for his life in my company. Specifically, in Judaism we do *not* take the Written Law in literal fashion. Rather, in the interpretation and implementation of Jewish law, the Written Law is secondary to the Oral Law, which is fleshed out in the Mishnah, Talmud, and the works of the great *rabbanim* (rabbis) and Torah sages who came later. Indeed, I emphasized, "It is an outright transgression, an actual sin, to read these sacred texts literally, without delving into the oral commentary that helps to explain and interpret them."

I then drew the attention of my questioner to Moshe Ben Maimon—most commonly known as Maimonides—the preeminent Jewish scholar and philosopher of the medieval period and one of the chief authoritative codifiers of Jewish law and ethics. On the subject of Amalek, Maimonides contended that the Jewish nation can never launch a war against any nation—including Amalek and the seven Canaanite nations that the Torah also calls on the Jews to destroy—without first offering "a call to peace." If, in response to this call to peace, the offending nations should accept the seven Noahide laws, then peace is made and, obviously, no war is required (Hilkhot Melachim 6:1).

In his *Guide for the Perplexed*, Maimonides goes even further. He argues that the command to wipe out Amalek should not be taken literally as a call to physically obliterate an enemy nation but rather as a call to remove Amalek-like behavior from the world. This command is not necessarily to be fulfilled through killing; preferably it can be fulfilled through moral influence and education.

I did not mention then, though I probably should have, that Maimonides spent his life in Muslim lands (primarily Spain, Morocco, and Egypt) and wrote *Guide to the Perplexed* in Arabic. His work, in tandem with that of contemporary Muslim philosophers like Averroes (Ibn Rushd), is often cited as the exemplar of a Golden Age of fruitful collaboration between Jews and Muslims, which greatly enriched world civilization. Both Maimonides and Ibn Rushd worked to rehabilitate Aristotle and develop a synthesis of Aristotelian philosophy with their respective faiths at a time when Christian Europe was shrouded in darkness and superstition.

Living among Muslims his entire life, Maimonides gave not the slightest hint that Arabs or Muslims should be considered descendants of Amalekites. Instead, he wrote that Islam, unlike Christianity, did not engage in idolatry in that it affirmed that its Prophet and founder Muhammad was a man and not the Son of God. Though Maimonides made clear his unhappiness with what he considered false charges that Islam had leveled at the Jews, and though he propagated some troubling writings on Jewish law that appear to assert Jewish superiority over non-Jews (see chapter 11, "Love Thy Neighbor or Love the Stranger?"), he nevertheless wrote in a letter to a disciple:

> The Ishmaelites are not at all idolaters; [idolatry] has long been severed from their mouths and hearts; and they attribute to God a proper unity, a unity concerning which there is no doubt. And because they lie about us, and falsely attribute to us the statement that God has a son, is no reason for us to lie about them and say that they are idolaters. . . . [I]dolatry has been severed from the mouths of all of them [including] women and children.

During a festive kiddush at the end of the program, many members of the audience came forward to warmly grasp Shamsi's hand and thank him for his inspiring presentation. Nevertheless, after the people had left, I apologized to my friend for the questioner's remarks. But I also noted that the questioner's abrasive words were an example of the challenge that Shamsi and I would face from extreme thinking in both communities. To my relief, Shamsi responded graciously that he had not been offended by the question but had been fascinated by my response. Until that moment, he explained, he had not understood the centrality and indispensability of the Oral Law within Judaism or its moderating impact on passages in the Torah that had seemed to him to evince an attitude of contempt for, or even hatred of, non-Jews. He pointed out that a very similar dynamic exists within Islam: the Oral Law (hadith) serves to interpret and elucidate the words of the Qur'an, something of which, I must acknowledge, I had been blissfully unaware.

As the two of us ruminated on the implications of the predominance of the Oral Law in both traditional Jewish law (Halacha) and Islamic law (Shari'a), we realized how important it is to the betterment of relations between our two faiths that Jews and Muslims come to grasp that both faiths are grounded in the oral tradition. Without such mutual understanding, we realized, attempts at dialogue would continue to founder, as they so often have, on the inclination of adherents of each side to provocatively quote "difficult texts" from Torah and Qur'an and then press the other to explain how they can possibly justify such seemingly repellent statements and commandments.

Indeed, Muslims often cite quotations from the Torah that appear to claim that the Jews are the chosen people and favored by God over all others (which, as we have seen, is a mistaken interpretation), and other verses that appear to unambiguously urge the Jews to wipe out not only the Amalekites but also seven Canaanite tribes that inhabited the Land of Israel before the Jewish return from Egypt. For their part, Jews often call upon Muslims to explain a series of Qur'anic quotations that appear to pour withering contempt on Judaism and Christianity and to assert that the Jews received richly deserved divine punishment for their disobedience to God. Yet, as the two of us affirmed to each other that day, many of these "difficult passages" have been taken in much more moderate, nonviolent, and humane directions in the oral traditions of both faiths.

To be sure, among the extremists on both sides pushing for a "War of Civilizations" between our two faiths, there are some who are aware that a moderating oral tradition exists in the other faith, yet purposefully and cynically leave out all mention of that truth while emphasizing only violent and hateful-sounding quotations from the written traditions of the Other. Most Jews and most Muslims, however, are simply unaware of the good news that the other side has an oral tradition that moderates the sometimes harsh language of the written law. The ignorance among the majority in both faiths allows the demagogic purveyors of hate to peddle their poison virtually unchallenged. So, it is past time that we get the word out, and that is a big part of the task that Imam Shamsi Ali and I have set for ourselves.

As I am obviously far more conversant with Judaism than Islam, let me use the remainder of this chapter to flesh out the primacy of the Oral Law in Judaism. As noted, many non-Jews have a false understanding of Judaism, citing certain Torah passages as "proof" that Judaism is a harsh and vengeful religion that worships a cruel and misanthropic "Old Testament" God. Many are completely unaware of the existence of the Oral Law, which balances out the Tanakh (the Torah, Nevi'im, and Ketuvim), makes it accessible, and brings it into the real world as the source of guidance to followers of traditional Judaism. Without the Oral Law, the Torah would seem austere and unapproachable, yet God created the Torah not as a glorious volume to be placed on a shelf and venerated but as a set of precepts that we would connect with on an ongoing basis in confronting and surmounting the challenges of our daily lives. The Oral Law is God's instrument to help us accomplish that.

The Written Law—*Torah sh ba'al ktav* ("Torah that is written")—is another name for the Tanakh, which, of course, includes the Torah, but I will accept the common usage and refer to the whole Hebrew Bible henceforth as Torah. The Oral Law—*Torah she be'al peh* ("Torah that is spoken")—is a massive, two-thousand-year-long running commentary on the Torah, explaining its meaning and how its commandments are to be observed. (By that, I mean both the Ten Commandments given by God to Moses atop Mount Sinai and the more comprehensive 613 mitzvoth.)

The Oral Law is a supple instrument that has been extraordinarily successful in connecting the Jewish people to the Torah down through several millennia in which the Jewish condition has been in endless flux. In short, the brilliance and user-friendly quality of the Oral Law, which serves as a kind of operating manual for the practice of Judaism, is the secret to the survival of the Jewish people, who somehow endured two thousand years of powerlessness and the hatred and violence directed against them, while many far more powerful empires and nations withered away.

This is not to in any way minimize the importance of the Torah, which, in my opinion, has been the most important and influential book in human history. Not only are the holy books of the other two great Abrahamic faiths, the New Testament and the Qur'an, direct offshoots of the Torah, but that book has also had a great impact on virtually every form of human endeavor—literature, history, philosophy, art, law, science, politics, government, and ethics. Basic building blocks of modern-day Western society, such as the idea of individual worth, the rule of law, the concept of a fair trial, and the importance of charity, all spring from the Torah. However, the Torah is not Judaism. The Torah, the story it tells, and the commandments it conveys are the essential building blocks of Judaism, but they are unable to stand on their own. For all of its magnificence, the Written Law (Tanakh) is quite inoperative without the Oral Law.

The first thing to point out is that, despite its name, the Oral Law in Judaism is today actually a written law, codified in the Mishnah, Gemara, and Talmud, and later in the writings of the great *rabbonim* (rabbis), including the *rishonim* ("first ones"), the rabbis of the Middle Ages (who include Maimonides), and the *achronim* ("last ones," the rabbis of modern times, starting with the period of the kabbalah in the sixteenth and seventeenth centuries and extending to recently deceased Torah giants such as Rav Joseph Soloveichik and Rav Moshe Feinstein).

So why, if the Oral Law is written down in these great volumes, does it continue to be called "oral"? Orthodox Jews believe that most of the oral traditions later recorded in the Mishnah and Talmud actually date back to God's revelation to Moses on Mount Sinai. We believe that when God gave Moses the Torah, He simultaneously provided Moses with the Oral Law as well, thereby giving him the essential information to make the Written Law operational for the Jewish people. Moses subsequently transmitted that Oral Law to his successor, Joshua, who transmitted it to his successor in a chain that is still being carried on today.

During the long biblical period, no one was allowed to write down the Oral Law. As long as there was a Jewish polity and religious hierarchy, built around a Temple with a functioning priesthood, the Oral Law could be successfully transmitted from generation to generation by word of mouth, as originally stipulated. But everything changed after the Romans destroyed the Second Temple in 70 CE, killing hundreds of thousands of Jews and emptying Eretz Israel of much of its Jewish population. That process was greatly accelerated in the wake of the Bar-Kochba Rebellion some sixty years later. Under the calamitous new circumstances, the rabbinical sages, the new leaders of the Jewish people after both the Jewish political leadership and Temple priesthood had been dismantled by the Romans, were rightfully concerned that the Jewish people, spread out in an ever-growing Diaspora, would forget the Oral Law unless it was rapidly written down. Guided by Rabbi Yohahan Ben-Zakkai, who had been permitted by the Romans to open an academy at Yavneh dedicated to the compilation of Jewish law, the rabbinical sages known as the *Tanaim* (which can be translated as "repeaters" or "teachers") wrote down much of the Oral Law. Their work was the main source for the Mishnah, which was begun in the first century of the Christian era and completed about two hundred years later; and later the Gemara, created to interpret the Mishnah. This led still later to the Jerusalem Talmud and Babylonian Talmud. From all of this centuries-long collective effort came the Halacha (or "The Way," from the word *holech*, which literally means "to go").

Yet if the *Tanaim* and their successors, the *Amoraim* ("Those who speak over the people"), saw as their primary role to compile and preserve the Oral Law for posterity, it is reasonable to ask why the Mishnah and Talmud are filled with arguments between the rabbis over the meaning of many passages in the Torah. Modern-day Orthodox Jews believe that these disputations took place either because many details of the Oral Law had already been forgotten by that time or because the Oral Law had always lacked specific teachings on many of the issues being discussed.

Ironically, these debates over the nature of the Oral Law, which had already begun to emerge in the sharp disagreements between the followers of the sages Hillel and Shammai, served to energize Judaism and make it an intellectually compelling faith at a time when the temporal power of the Jews as a people had seemingly all but vanished. Rather than turning into a sterile dogma overseen by a rigid and sometimes corrupt priesthood, as had transpired during the late Second Temple period, rabbinical Judaism became a forum for vibrant intellectual and spiritual discourse that drew to the rabbinate our people's best and brightest for hundreds of years. As noted, this vitality played a large role in ensuring the survival of a people who appeared doomed to extinction after the destruction of the Temple and the subsequent takeover of the Roman Empire by Christians who considered Jews to be a cursed people who had killed Jesus Christ.

It should be noted that modern-day Conservative and Reform Jews disagree with Orthodox Jews that Oral Law, as narrated in the Mishnah and largely codified in the Talmud, dates back to Moses on Mount Sinai and therefore can be considered "spoken Torah." Instead, they tend to see the Oral Law as having evolved from the debates among successive generations of rabbis as to how best to integrate the Written Law into the Judaism that evolved after the fall of the Temple. Despite this distancing of the Oral Law from the source, Conservative Jews nevertheless accept Halacha as divinely inspired and incumbent on the Jewish people to observe, although they feel more empowered than Orthodox Jews to modify aspects of the Oral Law they find inapplicable to modern times. Reform Jews, for their part, have felt free to reject Halacha outright and substitute their own ethical code, based largely on the message of the biblical prophets.

While Orthodox and Conservative Jews may disagree on the origins of the Oral Law, they can agree that it is needed for at least three reasons. First, the Torah contains many general commands as to how Jews are supposed to behave but often gives little or no elucidation as to how those commands are supposed to be carried out. Second, the Torah contains terms that are incomprehensible today, so we would be unable to understand what the authors were trying to say without the essential intervention of the generations of rabbis who pondered and wrote about the meaning of those expressions. The third reason is that many Jews of conscience over the centuries, including towering figures like Maimonides, have had deep moral reservations about observing some Torah laws literally without the softening interpretative framework of the Oral Law.

We have already discussed one example that illustrates the last point: the commandment to annihilate Amalek through the generations. Another example is the injunction of an "eye for an eye and a tooth for a tooth." This is laid out unambiguously in several Torah passages, including Leviticus 24.19:

> If anyone maims his fellow, as he has done so shall it be done to him: fracture for fracture, eye for eye, tooth for tooth. The injury he inflicted on another shall be inflicted on him.

This injunction gives the impression that Torah Judaism is an implacable and bloodthirsty religion, which demands that if one person blinds another, even if by accident, he himself should be blinded. Indeed, it is often cited by people who unfavorably compare the supposed implacability and even bloodlust of Old Testament Judaism with Jesus's millenarian injunction to his followers to "turn the other cheek" to those who did them wrong. Never mind that, once in control, the followers of Jesus treated defenseless Jews with extreme cruelty and violence for nearly two thousand years. I have also heard some Muslims wrongly accuse Jews— or, more often, Israelis—of behaving according to the ethos of "an eye for an eye," even though their own faith is falsely accused by Islamophobes of operating according to the same stricture.

Yet the Oral Law explains that the verse must be understood as requiring monetary compensation: the *value* of an eye is what must be paid. Thanks to the Oral Law, the example of an "eye for an eye" actually turns what seems to be an affirmation of revenge via exact retribution into the much more reasonable principle that in cases of wrongful injury, monetary compensation must be paid.

Let us consider several critically important commandments and decrees from God to the People of Israel, which we would not be able to understand and fully observe without the Oral Law. The Torah makes reference to God telling Moses that animals should be slaughtered "the way that I commanded to you." Yet one can search through the entire Tanakh and find no mention of how God commanded the Israelites to do that slaughtering. This is one of the clearest citations for why we believe that God gave Moses both written and oral laws at Sinai. Clearly, there had been an oral law that God dictated to Moses, and then gave him various interpretations of that text. The complex series of rules for how ritual slaughtering (*schechita*) of mammals and birds is to be done can be found at various points in the Oral Law and is codified with great specificity in the *Shulchan Aruch*, literally meaning "the arranged table," a compiled code of Jewish law. What is particularly compelling to me is that the act can be performed by a ritual slaughterer (*shochet*), a religious Jew who must be licensed, and that the rules of *shechita* necessitate that the animal must be killed with respect and compassion, with its throat cut instantly by a knife with an extremely sharp blade so as to minimize its suffering. There is an understanding that any killing, even of an animal, is an awesome responsibility that can be carried out only under strict rabbinical supervision and must be rendered as humanely as possible.

The fourth of the Ten Commandments decrees, "Remember the Sabbath day to make it holy" (Exodus 20:8). A second passage from Exodus (31:14) actually stipulates, "You shall keep the Sabbath, for it is holy to you; anyone who profanes it shall be put to death. For whoever does any work on that day shall be cut off from his people."

Thus, observing the Sabbath is clearly seen as of paramount importance in the Torah, more important than observing any of the holidays, including even the transcendent Days of Awe (*yamim nora'im*), Rosh Hashanah and Yom Kippur. But what is required to keep it properly? As noted in the Jewish Virtual Library's essay on the Oral Law:

When one looks for the specific biblical laws regulating how to observe the day, one finds only injunctions against lighting a fire, going away from one's dwelling, cutting down a tree, plowing and harvesting. Would merely refraining from these few activities fulfill the biblical command to make the Sabbath holy? Indeed, the Sabbath rituals that are most commonly associated with holiness—lighting of candles, reciting the *kiddush*, and the reading of the weekly Torah portion—are found not in the Torah, but in the Oral Law.[2]

The Kairites, a quasi-Judaic and nearly extinct sect that rigorously follows the Tanakh but rejects the Oral Law, give us a real-world example in their own fundamentalist forms of Sabbath observance of how circumscribed, how stultified Jewish civilization would have been without the Oral Law. In strict observance of the biblical injunctions concerning observance of the Sabbath, specifically the prohibition against burning fires or leaving one's dwelling during the Sabbath, the Kairites have for millennia sat in their houses during the dark hours of the Sabbath in total darkness. By contrast, Orthodox Jews also will not desecrate the Sabbath by lighting a candle or turning on an electric light during the hours of the Sabbath, but they figured out creative ways that would simultaneously allow them to observe the Sabbath and avoid sitting in total darkness, whether it was lighting a kerosene candle before the onset of the Sabbath that would burn for twenty-four hours or the more modern-day innovations like *shabbes* clocks to automatically operate lights and *shabbes* elevators that stop at every floor of a building, making it possible to travel easily even to the top of a high-rise without violating the Sabbath.

Another important subject on which the Torah has next to nothing to say is the Jewish marriage ceremony. In Genesis, God observes Adam, the first man, and decides that "it is not good for man to be alone; I will make a fitting helper for him." Having fashioned Eve from Adam's rib, he brought her to Adam, who responded memorably:

This one at last is bone of my bones and flesh of my flesh. This one shall be called Woman for from man was she taken. Hence a man

---

2. From "The Oral Law," Jewish Virtual Library. Source: Joseph Telushkin, *Jewish Literacy* (New York: William Morrow, 1991).

leaves his father and mother and clings to his wife so that they become one flesh.

Poetic and primal to be sure, but nothing that goes on to describe the solemn and joyous ceremony by which man and woman become one flesh, and nowhere in the entire Tanakh is a wedding ceremony described or discussed. Clearly, weddings were taking place according to an oral tradition, but it is not until the Talmud that we are given detailed information on how to perform the Jewish wedding as we know it today, with the signing of the *ketubah* (marriage contract), the service under the *chuppah* (a canopy held up on four poles, symbolic of the couple living together), the reciting by the bride and groom of the *Shevah Brachot* (seven blessings), and the groom shattering a glass by stepping on it with his right foot, symbolizing the destruction of the Temple, which Jews are expected to always remember, even at such a time of joy.

Among the Torah laws that would be incomprehensible without an oral tradition is the one articulated in the first paragraph of the *Shema*, the solemn prayer every Jew is enjoined to recite twice a day in which he declares his adherence to Judaism and faith in the God of the Jewish people. The text reads,

> And these words which I command you this day shall be upon your heart. And you shall teach them diligently to your children, and you shall talk of them when you sit in your house, when you walk on the road, when you lie down and when you rise up. And you shall bind them for a sign upon your hand, and they shall be for frontlets between your eyes. *(Deuteronomy 6:48)*

It is unclear from the text what "they" refers to and what the word "frontlets" means in the last sentence. The Hebrew word for frontlets, *totafot*, is mentioned in Torah only in this context of something to be placed between the eyes. It is the Oral Law which elucidates that both the straps wrapped around the forearm and hand and the small black-leather box filled with parchment strapped around the upper arm and forehead are actually tefillin (phylacteries). The Talmud and subsequent rabbinical writings provide voluminous details about the manufacture and contents of tefillin, who is obligated to wear them in prayer (men above the age of thirteen, except for mourners on the first day of their mourning period, bridegrooms, and men who are sick or in physical pain), when they should be worn (during the day but not at night and not on Shabbat or holy days), and how to put them on.

I believe that Jewish Law began 3,500 years ago at Mount Sinai and has served ever since as a continuous process of moving the Jewish people forward, making it possible for them to cope successfully with life conditions utterly different from what we confronted in the early days of our history. It is very much a work in progress but as vibrant and dynamic today as at any point in our history. During the first half of Jewish history, we were very much alone as the monotheistic faith in the world. Later, two other great monotheistic faiths, Christianity and Islam, emerged, each of them clearly offshoots of Judaism with a large debt to both the Written and Oral laws. But unlike Judaism, they became religions with great temporal power, striving to convert the entire world family to their respective belief systems. For a variety of reasons—doctrinal disputes, the imbalance of power between adherents of the two world religions, and the much smaller Jewish nation, the tendency of all three faiths to insist that they alone represented the truth—relations between Muslims, Christians, and Jews were often adversarial for much of the past 1,500 years, although Jews living in the Muslim world were far more likely to live in peace and relative security than those living in Christian lands.

Nevertheless, throughout that long period, some of the rabbinical sages, best exemplified by Maimonides but also including many other giants of Jewish thought in both the Christian and Muslim worlds, upheld the importance of interreligious dialogue. They made clear in their commentaries on issues like Amalek that Jewish law does not insist on perpetual conflict with the adherents of the other Abrahamic faiths but instead inclines toward understanding. Today, with a more equal power dynamic and less of an insistence by a growing number of leaders of all three faiths that they alone possess the truth, there are far more opportunities for creative, life-enhancing dialogue and coalition building than ever before. Muslims and Jews living side-by-side as minorities in North America, Europe, Latin America, Australia, and elsewhere have begun the process of building a world movement based on principles of communication, reconciliation, and cooperation.

There is nothing so inspiring for me, as a traditional Jew who lives his life according to the rhythms of Halacha, as seeing so many of my fellow Orthodox rabbis, most prominently in Europe, reaching out to imams and other leaders of the Muslim community and building ties of friendship and trust. Back in 2003, Rabbi Michel Serfaty, then sixty years old and a deeply devout Orthodox rabbi in the town of Ris-Orangis, a suburb of Paris with large concentrations of Muslims and Jews, was attacked on the street and roughed up by several young Muslim men, who shouted anti-Israel and anti-Semitic slogans. The attackers must have believed that attacking Rabbi Serfaty, a well-known figure who wears black rabbinical garb and has a white beard, would serve to drive the two communities ever further apart. Indeed, at that time, relations between the approximately five million Muslims and 500,000 Jews in France were sharply deteriorating, with more and more violent attacks by Muslims on Jews and with many Jews despairing of a future for Jews in France.

Yet instead of hardening his heart and crying for revenge, Rabbi Serfaty decided to devote his life's work to strengthening ties between the two communities. He correctly understood that the dearth of communication between Jews and Muslims allowed the most negative and destructive stereotypes of both communities about each other to fester and grow. Rabbi Serfaty created the Amitie Judeo-Musulmane de France (Judeo-Muslim Friendship Society of France), a small organization with little funding that initially evoked skepticism and even ridicule in both communities, to begin building a network of grassroots Muslim-Jewish ties.

Today, AJMF has chapters in scores of towns and cities across France, enjoys strong support from the main Jewish and Muslim communal organizations, and operates a bus filled with a small, passionately committed staff of young Muslim and Jewish community activists. They travel every day to converse with ordinary Jews and Muslims in schools, community centers, and even on the streets to shatter negative stereotypes and the widespread perception that members of the two communities are fated to be eternal enemies. Every year, Rabbi Serfaty, his staff, and volunteers head out on a nearly two-month-long Tour de France, during which they travel to every corner of the country, bringing Muslims and Jews together for discussions and celebrations in places where they have long lived alongside each other, but in mutual distrust and hostility.

Rabbi Serfaty's example shows that it is possible for observant Jews to bridge the divide between themselves and adherents of Islam and Christianity without compromising our strict adherence to Jewish Oral Law. It is the suppleness and versatility of that very law that makes possible the lifework of modern-day heroes like Rabbi Serfaty, Jewish leaders who are at once fully immersed in what is often called the "sea of Halacha," the resplendently deep and profoundly complex structure known as Jewish law, while simultaneously being fully involved in the larger society, including taking the lead in the lifesaving work of strengthening Muslim-Jewish relations.

It is the very vitality, moderation, and great good sense of the Oral Law, and my understanding that a similar dynamic exists within the Oral Law in Islam, that gives me faith that I can work fruitfully together with Muslim friends and allies like my dear friend Imam Shamsi Ali to build a better and happier world, one in which Muslims and Jews—and all peoples—will, in the immortal words of the Prophet Isaiah, "beat their swords into plowshares and their spears into pruning hooks. Nation will not take up sword against nation, nor will they train for war anymore."

CHAPTER TEN

War and Jihad

IMAM SHAMSI ALI

The concept is found in Judaism that "whoever destroys a soul, it is considered as if he destroyed an entire world. And whoever saves a life, it is considered as if he saved an entire world."[1] That very same ethos is echoed in Islam. As the Qur'an states,

> If any one slew a person . . . it would be as if he slew the whole people: And if any one saved a life, it would be as if he saved the life of the whole people.

Just a few lines after that passage, the Qur'an provides the meaning of *jihad*. And that location in the text makes an important point by itself. Contrary to the widespread assumption among non-Muslims, jihad is not a concept that justifies and encourages terrorism. The true meaning of jihad is inextricably bound to the Islamic vision of striving to live a moral life. Those non-Muslims who are already familiar with the interpretation of jihad as "striving" may wonder about the connection between striving and terrorism. *There is none.*

Verse 5:35 of the Qur'an states, "O ye who believe! Be mindful of your duty to Allah, and seek the way of approach unto Him, and strive in His

---

1. Jerusalem Talmud Tractate Sanhedrin 4:1 (22a), Mishnah Sanhedrin 4:5, Babylonian Talmud Tractate Sanhedrin 37a.

way in order that ye may succeed."² This one verse is the true epitome of jihad—it is about being careful of one's conduct, being aware that God sees all, seeking the way to become closer to Him, and in that seeking, striving under His guidance to become closer to being worthy of meriting success in this life and the next. This rather pacific meaning is extravagantly contrary to what most people think of when they hear the word *jihad*. The branding of Islam as a violent, suicidal, homicidal, rigid, misogynistic, primitive, and stifling religion has been accepted as commonplace, buttressed by images of bearded bombers, the World Trade Center towers crumbling, women shuffling downcast in their *chadors*, and Afghan children with acid-burned faces daring to attend schools. These visions of violence and oppression, the calls to war against the West and against "infidels" anywhere in order to further the establishment of Dar-al-Islam, are taken, tragically, as the "true" face of Islam for many in Muslim- and non-Muslim-majority countries alike. It does no one a service to pretend that these deliberate distortions of Muslim belief do not exist or to deny the presence of fundamentalists, extremists, despots, and theologically ignorant leaders who prefer control in this world to peace in the next.

But while the popular conception of jihad held by non-Muslims is that of a bloody and one-sided Holy War waged by the righteous Islamic leadership of the world against the heathen non-Muslims until they are subdued or killed in Islamic victory, the historical roots of war and jihad are not as easy to caricature. As we will see in this chapter, nothing is further from the reality of Islamic text and thought on the subjects of jihad specifically and war more generally. *Jihad* as an Islamic concept has more meaning than the term "holy war" suggests. It is more applicable to internal issues for individuals than external ones for groups. War as an Islamic concept began before Islamic expansion, as an element within the religion in its embryonic Meccan confines. It was a last recourse for Muslims, whose only power lay in advancing the shift in allegiances from tribal to ideological ones. The initial and still strongest basis for physical war is defensive, not offensive, though the purity of purpose has become muddled.

---

2. *The Glorious Qur'an*, Pickthall.

MEANING AND CONTEXT

The ideas promulgated in the Torah forbidding murder and killing were perpetuated by the prophets who came after Moses, and indeed were re-emphasized by Prophet Muhammad and in the Qur'an. Though the similarities in language and concept are not coincidental, neither should they be viewed reductively, as mere co-optation or assimilation. They are rather a continuation of the same message, a common foundation that unites the Abrahamic faith traditions.

Arabia at the time of the *Hijrah*, in 622 CE, was populated by various groups.[3] In the harsher northern territories, the Arab Bedouin peoples maintained a nomadic life, living and traveling in groups. In southern Arabia, one found settlements of great wealth where Jewish, Christian, and pagan groups coexisted. Jews and pagans were equally "Arab" culturally, engaged in the same concerns and markets of the region. In fact, the initial resistance to Muhammad came not on religious grounds but from merchants of his own tribe, who managed trade and worship routes through polytheistic regions and did not want their long-standing commercial interests threatened.

Post-*Hijrah*, we find treaties of collaboration among Muslims and other faith groups, with emphasis on the cohesiveness of the Medinese community. The treaty commonly known as the Constitution of Medina was a religious compact that morphed into a civically theocratic one. By agreeing to the constitution and thus being included in the treaty, these disparate groups were turning over their autonomy to Muhammad, not only forming one unit but also accepting him as their unequivocal leader. There were clauses calling for alliance under Muhammad as civic leader and/or nonintervention by resident tribes if war was threatened by the Meccans who persecuted him. The immensity of this change can only be understood in light of the prevailing attitudes of seventh-century CE Arabs. They were individualistic in many aspects, but in the customs of their "honor code," they all agreed.

The honor code of the Arabs held that "manliness" was proven

---

3. The migration of the Muslim community from the city of Mecca to the city of Medina, then called Yathrib. The *Hijrah* is celebrated annually by Muslims when they take hajj.

through valor in battle, vengeance, and the defending of kinsmen. Blood-wit, or blood money, was an entire economic system; there were regular annual installments, guarantors, organizations, and alliances (which were surprisingly similar to our mortgage system). The prevalence of the code meant that Muhammad had to keep in mind that "at the background of all this cooperation (between tribes) is the huge burden of blood and ransom for the tribal economy."[4] The existence of this economy did not, however, mean the end of revenge killings, as all cases were not settled by monetary compensation. Therefore the cycle of blood revenge in the name of honor continued, as did blood-wit in the name of finances.

The Qur'an, however, revealed that true brotherhood was not based on tribal or clan allegiance but on allegiance to God. It was for this reason that the essence of warfare shifted from internecine fighting to theological or ideological fighting. At a time when one's fidelity to tribe was paramount, verses 47:20–22 advocated fighting jihad even against "kith and kin."[5] The absolute nature of this for Muhammad and the nascent Muslim community is clear. In an account from Ibn Ishaq, the Prophet is speaking to the Khazraj tribe and asks to be protected by them as they would "protect their women and children." When asked by tribesmen for affirmation that he will not abandon them if they sever ties with their partners, Muhammad explains the allegiance that will be between them:

> Nay, blood is blood and blood is not to be paid for. I am of you and you are of me. I will war against them that war against you and be at peace with those at peace with you.[6]

This statement is again a strong departure from the norms at the time, as loyalty up until then had only been to "kith and kin." In no fewer than six of the clauses of the Constitution of Medina, direct or indirect mandate would force a person to choose definitive sides.

---

4. Michael Lecker, *The Constitution of Medina: Muhammad's First Legal Document* (Princeton, NJ: Darwin, 2004), 96.

5. This meaning of "jihad" references the Lesser Jihad, the one that is external, as opposed to the Greater Jihad discussed in chapter 3, the one against one's own evil impulses.

6. A. Guillaume, *The Life of Muhammad: A Translation of Ishaq's Sirat Rasul Allah* (Karachi: Oxford University Press, 1955), 203–4.

The sentiment is echoed almost precisely in clause 44: "Contracting parties are bound to help one another against attacks on Medina." Importantly, the bond that is being reinforced here is between Muhammad and his followers. The priority of kin alliance degenerated as personal accountability took root. War, in turn, increasingly became a matter of believers versus nonbelievers.

Thus, important milestones for the future of the Islamic state were launched by the rules of the constitution. In cases of blood vengeance, *diyah* (blood-money payments) was especially encouraged among the believers rather than revenge killings. As one contemporary scholar explains,

> The responsibility for vengeance lay not with brother for brother . . . but believer for the believers. In other words, the blood revenge which internally was merely restricted was abolished altogether. . . . Thus war became separated from . . . blood revenge . . . (and) assumed a military aspect.[7]

WAR

Against this stage of insecurity and constant tension, more Qur'anic revelations arrived. The suras revealed in Mecca had a more measured stance than those revealed in Medina, though they were equally strong in emphasizing that war was to be made on nonbelievers and those who sought to harm the Muslim community. Taking an anthropological approach, one sees that a sura revealed approximately three years before *Hijrah* is already using the new paradigm of the monotheistic Islamic community to inspire jihad, or striving, against nonbelievers (25:52).[8] Another sura reminds Muslims that those whom God favors will prevail in the end, in an almost gentle encouragement to stay the course.[9]

Once the migration to Medina took place—which coincided with

---

7. Arent Jan Wensinck, *Muhammad and the Jews of Medina*, Wolfgang Behn, trans. (Freiburg Im Breisgau: K. Schwarz, 1975, p. 132.
8. "Therefore listen not to the Unbelievers, but strive against them with the utmost strenuousness, with the Qur'an."
9. Qur'an 21:44: "We gave the good things of this life to these men and their fathers until the period grew long for them; See they not that We gradually reduce the land (in their control) from its outlying borders? Is it then they who will win?"

the signing of political treaties and gaining military numbers in the *Ansar*, or men of Medina who joined the Muslim polity—we see suras that are more immediate and direct regarding persecution against Muslims. For example, Qur'an 2:191–193 states,

> And slay them wherever ye find them, and drive them out of the places whence they drove you out, for persecution [of Muslims] is worse than slaughter [of nonbelievers] . . . and fight them until persecution is no more, and religion is for Allah.

There were major battles between Mecca and Medina in the first ten years after the *Hijrah*, and these also seem to find parallels in the Qur'anic revelations. Around 2–3AH,[10] concurrent with the Battle of Badr, for example, we find the following *ayats* (verses):

> So when you meet in battle those who disbelieve, then smite the necks until when you have overcome them, then make (them) prisoners.
>
> *(47:4)*

> O ye who believe! When ye meet those who disbelieve in battle, turn not your backs to them. Whoso on that day turneth his back to them, unless maneuvering for battle or intent to join a company, he truly hath incurred wrath from Allah, and his habitation will be hell, a hapless journey's end. *(8:15–16)*

> If thou comest on them in the war, deal with them so as to strike fear in those who are behind them, that haply they may remember. *(8:57)*

We can generally infer that there was much war in this period, and the fighting was between the new polity—made up of various tribes, religions, and socioeconomic groups/political alliances—against the old guard of Meccan tribes, polytheists, and wealthy businessmen who were against Muhammad's preaching of Islam. Although these verses could be seen to be very specific to this context and its concerns, three very important verses from this same period have had lasting repercussions:

---

10. The Muslim calendar begins with the *Hijrah*, and calendric dates are referred to as "BH," or Before *Hijrah*, and "AH," or After *Hijrah*, much as Christians use BC and AD.

And fight with them until there is no more persecution and religion should be only for Allah. $(8:39)$[11]

Let those fight in the way of Allah who sell the life of this world for the other. Whoso fighteth in the way of Allah, be he slain or be he victorious, on him We shall bestow a vast reward. $(4:74)$[12]

Not equal are those believers who sit (at home) and receive no hurt, and those who strive and fight in the cause of Allah with their goods and their persons. Allah hath granted a grade higher to those who strive and fight with their goods and persons than to those who sit (at home). Unto all (in faith) hath Allah promised good: But those who strive and fight hath He distinguished above those who sit (at home) by a special reward. $(4:95)$

These verses have been taken by terrorists and suicide bombers as instructions to propagate infinite war, glorifying those who undertake this war as martyrs. Literalist imams have supported these views and given blessings to suicide missions and attacks on innocent people, Muslim and non-Muslim alike. This is an interpretation that the majority of Muslims absolutely reject, for it cannot be reconciled with the peaceful aspect of Islam that Muslims believe forms its true intention. However, these verses have become some of the most dangerous in Islamic ideology.

Qur'an 5:33 was revealed around 7AH, after the Treaty of Hudaibiyyah was signed. At this time, the Meccans were a much stronger power than the nascent Muslims but were wary of the Muslims, who had been gaining in adherents and alliances. This treaty came about when Prophet Muhammad, as the leader of Medina, contracted a peace accord with Mecca and the Quraysh tribe, which oversaw all pilgrimage activity into the city.[13] The Muslims had been denied entry into Mecca to make the customary worship at the Ka'bah; to avoid further hostility, the treaty called for nonaggression from both sides and the right to worship at Mecca to be granted to Muslims the year following the treaty's accep-

---

11. M. H. Shakir (1866–1939) interpretation, from QuranBrowser.com.
12. *The Glorious Qur'an*, Pickthall, for this and the subsequent verse.
13. The Quraysh were the leaders of Meccan society and government—and Prophet Muhammad's own tribe.

tance. Ultimately, the treaty was dissolved because of Meccan aggression toward allies of the Medinese Muslims, and it was after this dissolution that Prophet Muhammad took possession of Mecca. Qur'an 5:33 states:

> The punishment of those who wage war against Allah and His messenger and strive to make mischief in the land is only this, that they should be murdered or crucified or their hands and their feet should be cut off on opposite sides or they should be imprisoned; this shall be as a disgrace for them in this world, and in the hereafter they shall have a grievous chastisement.[14]

The prescribing of force against those who feigned amity only to be discovered later as having worked against the Muslim community is seen in a slightly later sura as well, Qur'an 66:9: "O Prophet! Strive against the disbelievers and the hypocrites, and be stern with them. Hell will be their home, a hapless journey's end."[15]

There were many instances of people breaking their written promises to maintain neutrality in the case of Meccan attack on Medina and, in fact, of even cooperating with Meccan tribes in an attack on Medina. The reasons for this deceit were largely economic—the more prosperous of the tribes in Mecca were allied with the more prosperous tribes in Medina (Arabs and Jews, respectively). The Islamic idea of abandoning polytheistic worship, as well as much of the ritualistic commerce and trade that went with it, was anathema to the allied Meccan and Medinese tribes, who saw Muhammad as a troublesome gadfly. They had not expected Muhammad's movement to grow as quickly and extensively as it did; in opposing it, they simply were protecting their own interests. However, the same chapter warns Muslims that they must be just, even with those whom they hold in "malice."[16]

That there are many references in the Qur'an to war is undeniable. But although the Qur'an is the literal word of God passed down to

---

14. Shakir interpretation.

15. *The Glorious Qur'an*, Pickthall.

16. Muslims must hold on justice and fairness with people in every condition, even if they have enmity with them to any extent, the Qur'an warns in 5:8: "O you who believe, be steadfast for (obeying the commands of) Allah, (and) witnesses for justice. Malice against a people should not prompt you to avoid doing justice. Do justice. That is nearer to *taqwa* (piety)."

humanity and therefore inviolable, that does not mean it must all be taken literally, as many passages have eternal meanings that can be extracted from the literal verbiage. This is the same reasoning for all holy books and exegeses, where literal exhortations have been cynically co-opted to apply to contemporary situations. The Jewish-Muslim divide over Israel/Palestine, for example, has been retrofitted by some to be the war with Amalek, and the "holy war" aspect of Islamic jihad has been traced back to the wars between the nascent Muslims and the Quraysh tribe. There are parallels in Judaism and Islam that should be recognized in both the roots and the misapplications of these readings.

In the Mishnah Torah of Maimonides, there are twenty-three commandments. These include admonishments "to destroy the seven Canaanite nations" (6); "to blot out the seed of Amalek . . . and to never forget them" (8–10); and "not to offer peace to Ammon and Moab when besieged" (13). Maimonides also provides the reason for waging war on Amalek:

> The first war waged by a king must be for a religious cause . . . they were the wars against the seven Canaanite nations, the war against Amalek, and war in defense of Israel against enemy attack. After those, there were the optional wars, those fought against various peoples in order to extend the frontier of Israel or to increase its prestige.[17]

In the Tanakh, there are many exhortations such as these: to offensive war, defensive war, and war for expansion. These should be taken with a grain of salt, at the least with a spiritual analysis rather than a merely literal acceptance, just as the verses against the people of Amalek should be. According to a midrash, Amalek was Abraham's great-great grandson (1 Chronicles 1:34–36, Genesis 36:10–12). By that line of interpretation, the enmity between Amalekites and Jews is based on the rivalry between Jacob and Esau. But for those who see the Amalekites as representations of tribes that originated in Mecca or other "Ishmaelite" tribes, the conflict is basically good versus evil, period. God commanded the Jews to kill

---

17. *Kings, Their Wars, and the Messiah: From the Mishneh Torah of Maimonides,* H. M. Russell and Rabbi J. Wenberg, trans., Royal College of Physicians of Edinburgh (Edinburgh: Blackwood Pillans & Wilson, 1987).

all Amalekites, and if Jews have compassion and do *not* do this, it will only come back to haunt them. There is an argument that King Saul's decision not to kill King Agag caused the crisis that later was averted for the Jewish people by Esther. People who were descended from the house of Amalek (Haman, in this case) wanted to eradicate the Jews and advised the King of Persia to do so. Esther interceded, and so the Jews survived, but this was by the grace of God.

Yet there are also rabbinic analyses to the contrary: that the battle against Amalek may be viewed as a personal struggle against the evil within. In a May 2009 guest post to Beliefnet.com, Jonathan Edelstein noted, "To Rabbi Shraga Simmons, for instance, Amalek is the force of chaos and irreligion, and Jews may fight against it by embracing Torah." In the *Guide for the Perplexed*, Maimonides explains that the command to wipe out Amalek isn't based on hatred but on removing Amalek-like behavior from the world (Mishnah Torah 3:41). For Maimonides, then, the commandment is not necessarily fulfilled through killing; it can be fulfilled through moral influence and education. Those who purport to be leading offensive attacks in the name of Islam need follow Maimonides's guidance as well.

––––––––

In addition to the rational legalists, the mystical thinkers in the Jewish tradition have also provided useful reinterpretations. Professor Avi Sagi demonstrated the claim of many Hasidic sources that the battle against Amalek was only intended to be a spiritual war. In the sense that Sagi writes about the war against Amalek, every Muslim would agree: a war against a people who transgressed against God or claimed superiority over Him was a just war. This is similar to the war aspect of jihad, whether as a defensive measure against attackers or in the sense of commanding moral justice on those who believe their laws superior to God's own.[18]

The Qur'an advises believers to abide by justice: "And if you judge, judge between them with justice. Surely, Allah loves those who do justice." (5:42)[19] Justice is to be maintained even if it goes against near and

––––––––

18. Avi Sagi, "The Punishment of Amalek in Jewish Tradition: Coping with the Moral Problem," *Harvard Theological Review* 87, no. 3 (July 1994): 326ff.

19. Shakir interpretation.

dear ones: "O you who believe! Stand out firmly for justice, as witnesses to Allah, even though it be against yourselves, or your parents, or your kin." (4:135)[20] Even in warfare, inflicting injury on women, children, civilians, and those exempted from participation in military action is forbidden. Also, crops cannot be burned, means of livelihood cannot be destroyed, captives cannot be tortured, and dead bodies cannot be mutilated under any circumstances. The rights of human beings are defined by Islamic law and are protected by this law, which embraces not only Muslims but also followers of other religions who are considered "People of the Book" (*Kitab Ahl al*). Where this precept is violated in Islamic society, the failure is due not to the teachings of Islam but to the imperfections of the human recipients of the Divine Message. As Qur'an 2:190 instructs us, "Fight in the cause of God those who fight you, but do not transgress limits; for God loveth not transgressors."

I often hear complaints that Muslims tend to be very angry and violent. If, as Muslims say, Islam is a religion of peace, and if the Qur'an does not condone violence, and if the Prophet Muhammad's Sunnah is an example of friendship and patience, then why do we see the Osama bin Ladens of the world flourish?

In response, I would argue that violence and extremism are not inspired by religion per se but rather by politics, socioeconomics, and a pervasive sense of injustice. The Muslim sense of liberty is to be free from foreign oppression, which throughout modern history had meant the Western colonial powers. Many Muslims feel that the Western nations do not understand this deeply held point of view. Muslims recall that in the Islamic empire's golden age, other religious communities were allowed to flourish—most famously, perhaps, in Andalucia—and there was at least a nominal sense of peaceful cohabitation. They then see in the modern age a world where Israel took over Palestinian land, where the Balfour agreement was a colonial deception, where invasions of Iraq and Afghanistan were supported by false premises, and where hegemonic powers dictate what countries can and cannot do in their own sovereign nations.

---

20. Drs. Muhammad Taqi-ud-Din Al-Hilali and Muhammad Muhsin Khan, trans., *Interpretation of the Meanings of the Noble Qur'an in the English Language*, 15th rev. ed. (Riyadh: Darussalam, 1996).

Even for a layman, it should be easy to see why there is a sense of being wronged in the Arab Muslim world. To top this off, there are a great many disaffected youths with minds full of ideas and nowhere to put these ideas to use; and with families to support, or families to begin, with no means of gaining a paycheck in order to do so. Put these factors together and you have the soil in which the seeds of bitterness and revolt can be sown. In saying this, I do not validate suicide bombers or justify terror and violence as tools, for these things do indeed go against Islamic doctrine. But there is a context for those who are disenfranchised and choose the wrong path, and it is a context we need to understand if we are to make any inroads in addressing the issue.

I have heard some non-Muslims suggest that when Muslims are weak they do not attack, that it is only when they are strong that they do so. And, indeed, there is a reading of the Qur'an that contemplates a tiered schematic for war and jihad. In this schematic, the first stage for the nascent Muslim community was to ignore those who attacked them. This was in the Meccan period, when the powerful tribes were violently opposed to Muhammad's teachings of monotheism. This resistance was especially expressed among members of his own tribe, the Quraysh, who stood to lose income from the polytheistic trade and worship routes they controlled. The second stage was after the movement of the community to Medina, where the early Muslims began to gain strength and build alliances.[21] At this point, turning the other cheek was replaced by standing one's ground and fighting if attacked. The third stage occurred when Islam was entrenched and political alliances had been solidified. At that point in history, the Muslim community returned to Mecca and took the city. It was also then that the theological nature of war began a shift from defense to offense.

After the death of Prophet Muhammad, the caliphate of Umar undertook the major expansion of the Islamic empire. And at this stage many Qur'anic references to war began to be interpreted in an aggressive and open-ended way. It was a time of intense political and imperial upheaval and conflict, with the Persian, Byzantine, and Sassanid empires vying for power.

---

21. Qur'an 47:20.

Historical Islam had its share of war and sword, just as other empires did—but its means of conquest were no worse than those of the standards of the time, and in most cases, the ensuing Islamic rule was more lenient and tolerant than that of other empires before or after. Harmony between Muslim and non-Muslim alike is reinforced in the Qur'an itself. Our holy book propounds the precepts that "there is no compulsion in religion," that Muslims believe in the same ideals as other Abrahamic religions, and that judgment is only to be granted by God.[22] In addition, a number of hadith address the fairness with which Prophet Muhammad sought to treat non-Muslims:

> Beware! Whoever is cruel and hard on a non-Muslim minority, or curtails their rights, or burdens them with more than they can bear, or takes anything from them against their free will; I (Prophet Muhammad) will complain against the person on the Day of Judgment.
> *(Abu Dawud)*[23]

Faith is something that may grow or wane depending on one's company, and that is why many hadith give guidance on believers surrounding themselves with those who are like-minded—those who fear God—to augment the circumstances for increased faith. This has led many to mistakenly assume that Muslims are commanded not to be friends with non-Muslims. What is actually forbidden is not having non-Muslim friends but taking as protectors, guides, or teachers those people who act in ways not honouring Allah. Surah Al-Ma'idah has an often-cited *ayat* used wrongly to sow hatred of Jews and Christians. Sometimes 5:51 is translated as

> O ye who believe! Take not the Jews and the Christians for your friends and protectors: They are but friends and protectors to each other. And he amongst you that turns to them (for friendship) is of them. Verily God guideth not a people unjust.

But a better translation is this:

---

22. Qur'an 2:25, 2:62, 2:136, 3:84, and 5:69, among others.
23. The collected hadith of Abu Dawud are considered canonical for the majority of Muslims.

O you who believe! Do not take Jews and Christians as your *patrons.* [*Emphasis added.*] They are patrons of their own people. He among you who will turn to them for patronage is one of them. Verily Allah guides not a people unjust.[24]

On the one hand, surrounding oneself with righteous people, including taking them as friends, is considered part of one's own path to goodness. The Arabic word *auliya* is open to several different interpretations; in Qur'an 42:44, 45:10, and 45:19, the word is consistently translated as "protectors" rather than as "friends." Self-serving interests choose the most negative interpretation of the Other. This citation should not mean refusing non-Muslims as friends; it simply means not taking non-Muslim practices or beliefs *over* Muslim ones. This is the same spirit for all Abrahamic religions, which hold that the practices one follows are mandated by God and our allegiance is only to Him.

JIHAD

Among many concepts in Islam, one of the most misunderstood is the concept of jihad. The term *jihad* has become highly loaded and even synonymous with "armed conflict," usually of an offensive and aggressive nature. For the uninformed, the word conjures images of the suicide bomber or the terrorist network. There is the angry young man egged on and supported by a network of armed combatants, glorified in videos, and seduced by the seventy beautiful virgins awaiting him in the hereafter. But this is not what jihad meant for the Muslims who first heard of it, revealed in the Meccan time, premigration to Medina.

As I noted earlier, the word *jihad* most closely means "struggle" or "striving" in English translation, and there are different forms of jihad, the Greater Jihads and Lesser Jihads. There are also many ways that it can be used. The Noble Qur'an gives one version:

Praise be to Allah who has ordained Al-Jihad, 1. With the heart (intentions or feelings), 2. With the hand (weapons), 3. With the tongue (speeches, etc., in the cause of Allah).[25]

---

24. "E. H. Palmer, *Sacred Books of the East* (vol. 6) (1880)," Sacred-text.com, http://www.sacred-texts.com. It is annotated as Qur'an 5:56 in the Palmer interpretation.
25. Al-Hilali and Khan, trans., *Interpretation of the Meanings of the Noble Qur'an.*

That is, Greater Jihad is the war we fight with ourselves, while Lesser Jihad is the war that we fight with others. That is, the Greater Jihads are struggles that are universally common to all of us—the struggles to be honest, be faithful, not covet, give charity, refrain from vanity, and to abhor envy, lies, and pride. Greater Jihad urges us to surmount the millions of things that we as humans tend to fail at, at one time or another, in our lives. We should strive to conquer these flaws and faults in order to become better people. These are internal and spiritual struggles.

Lesser Jihad refers to any armed conflict. It is meant to be undertaken in defense only, though it has unfortunately been appropriated as a negative term by people who misunderstand it. People who have used the name of Islam while inciting murder or pain on others are performing acts contrary to what Allah wants and has mandated. How can one reconcile terrorist attacks designed to hurt innocents when there is a Qur'anic injunction not to commit such acts?

It is generally accepted by Muslim scholars and laymen that the place of war in Islam is as a defensive stance. This is why certain groups take issue with the United States and other Western powers militarily entering Muslim states or causing military action—what some call "liberation" and others call "occupation" or the overthrow of sovereign governments. The fact that Islam is not a hierarchical tradition means people must use their own faculties to reach an exegesis of the holy books, and misinterpretation of what the texts actually try to teach us becomes possible when those who have not attained the purity of the Greater Jihad run headfirst into propagating the Lesser Jihad. Unfortunately, this is what most often makes the news and what forms a backdrop for most Muslims who have limited knowledge or experience of their own tradition and themselves turn to media outlets for instruction on world affairs.

Apart from defensive actions, Islam does not allow for injury or harm to oneself or to others. Under this understanding, even an action such as smoking is *haram* because it is a path to the destruction of one of God's creations. The application of jihad in all its forms has a direct connection to the community in which it finds itself. Where there are support systems for communities (such as social welfare, education, and the like), it becomes easier for people to deal with individual jihads such as smoking or seeking forgiveness. Where these are lacking, the individual frustrations are quicker to fester and emerge in wrongful actions, without theological understanding.

Before the early Muslim community's first ten years in Medina, the following verses had been revealed (Qur'an 61:10–12):

> O ye who believe! Shall I lead you to a bargain that will save you from a grievous Penalty?— That ye believe in Allah and His Messenger, and that ye strive (your utmost) in the Cause of Allah, with your property and your persons: That will be best for you, if ye but knew! He will forgive you your sins, and admit you to Gardens beneath which Rivers flow, and to beautiful mansions in Gardens of Eternity.

That the word *jihad* (translated here as "strive") is used in this verse has been a cause for much misapplication; sura 4:95, which I referred to previously, has also become a foundational touchstone for terrorists who seek paradise in the next life regardless of the destruction they create in this one. The deliberate and misguided application of Qur'anic verses and hadith that were indicative of the contemporary concerns of seventh-century Arabian life are an insult both to Islam and to its millions of true followers. There is no way to make the false promise of murder in exchange for paradise lawful in the eyes of God or of any true Muslim, and I strongly denounce anyone who tries to. We need as much media attention on the disavowal of these practices as "Islamic" as we have currently on the false Muslims who make these claims. We need more education and other avenues for venting frustrations for those who need them.

CONCLUSION

Too much violence and atrocity have been perpetrated in the name of God and religion. It is the duty and responsibility of the faithful—those who believe and uphold a commitment to God, truth, and goodness—to rescue their ideals from abuse and misrepresentation. Islam has had its share of violence perpetrated in its name, perhaps no more and no less than other faiths. To start a dialogue from the point of finding out which religion is more prone to violence and which one is less is a non-starter. Historically and philosophically, the point is to find and create the possibility of a peaceful, meaningful, and faithful life for all humans, whatever religion they choose to profess or not to profess. There are key teachings in Islam that embody and build upon making peace and surrendering to the one and only God. This foundational principle in and of itself can be understood as a guide to eschew violence.

To read the Islamic ethos as one that glorifies worldly might and takes pride in military conquest and political expansion, commonplace as such an interpretation may have become, is not objectively accurate. Nor is such an analysis the only possible one. Its dominance in certain historical periods should be explained in light of vested interests pursued by ruling tyrants who sought to justify expansionism and conquest by claiming a religious precedent for their own acts.

Shifting the emphasis to fundamental principles and ideals of Islam opens new horizons and promises a more inclusive, compassionate interpretation of the teaching of this religion. To formulate such a reading and base it in the most authentic values of this religion is an urgent task. A key challenge is to daringly construct a new framework that seeks new possibilities beyond what has historically developed.

According to the Shari'a, Islam embraces the whole sphere of life without severing the sacred from the secular. As such, it concerns itself with force and power, and it recognizes the fact that the two categories interpenetrate. By recommending the use of force to create equilibrium and harmony, Islam puts a limit to violence and opposes any violation of the rights of both God and His creatures, as defined by the divine law. Islam condones the use of force only to undo the violations of our own nature and the chaos that reflects a state of disequilibrium. Such a use of force is not violence as usually understood. It is the exertion of human will and effort in the direction of surrendering to the will of God and in subjecting human will to divine will.

Though it is unfortunate, there is no denying that there are people who claim to be adherents of a religion but who fail to represent the very ideals of their faith. There are times in our collective histories where each of our traditions has fallen prey to this. The ancient Jews, for example, failed to retain Moses's teaching when they built a golden calf to worship, although they had been instructed not to worship any but God. Christians failed to represent Christ's teaching, as when purported "Christians" in the Nazi regime failed to "love their neighbor as themselves" when it came to our Jewish brothers. And this is the case of the Muslims as well, such as those that have called themselves "Muslim" and then proceed to cause mass bloodshed, as in the actions of September 11.

As I have demonstrated, there is extensive evidence in the Qur'an of the attitude of Islam toward violence. It is immensely frustrating to witness the distortions and misrepresentation that persist. This failure to follow the true teachings of our religions is more often than not caused by ignorance and misunderstandings of theological teachings. In our increasingly globalized world, there are many external forces exerting pressure on our communities and informing people's actions, and so, equally, our efforts to redirect religious discourse into helpful dialogues true to our faith's central values must become a shared responsibility.

As a prominent Christian scholar has put it,

> Even though people know that there are a lot of things Christians have done, they tend to talk about the teachings of Jesus as though that somehow represents Christianity, not what Christians have actually done, and then they look at Islam and don't know what the Qur'an says or what Muhammad taught through his sayings and actions, but see the behavior of extremists and think that represents Islam.[26]

This mistaken belief that Islam is inherently violent is something that all of us, Muslims and Jews alike, need to set right.

---

26. The Reverend Charles Kimball, chair, Religion Department, Wake Forest University.

CHAPTER ELEVEN

Love Thy Neighbor
or Love the Stranger?

RABBI MARC SCHNEIER

Thou shalt not avenge, nor bear any grudge
against the children of thy people,
but thou shalt love thy neighbor as thyself:
I am the Lord.
—*Leviticus 19:18*

But the stranger that dwelleth with you
shall be unto you as one born among you,
and thou shalt love him as thyself;
for ye were strangers in the land of Egypt:
I am the Lord your God.
—*Leviticus 19:34*

Not long ago, I gave a major address on Jewish-Muslim relations to a select group of opinion makers in Washington. The topic of the session was how our two faith communities—and for that matter, people of all religious backgrounds—can avoid being drawn into the dreaded "War of Civilizations" and instead build a peaceful future based on the principles of ethnical monotheism and on the premise that all of God's children deserve a place under the sun. And I contended that we are going to have to move conceptually from the teaching of "Love thy neighbor as thyself" to "Love the stranger as thyself."

The audience members responded enthusiastically to my point. Or, I should say, they responded favorably once I had explained to them the important distinction between the two commandments, which unfortunately are all too often jumbled together or confused with each other. That mistake is hardly surprising, given that these are similar-sounding commandments that God gave to Moses in the Book of Leviticus and, indeed, appear only a few paragraphs apart in the biblical text. Many people who don't pay close attention assume that the two maxims say pretty much the same thing, or that Leviticus 19:34 is essentially a restatement of Leviticus 19:18, placed in the text to drive home the point made the first time around. For reasons that I will discuss later in this chapter, Leviticus 19:18 is far better known and far more often aspired to than is Leviticus 19:34. Yet it is the latter edict that we must live up to in the coming years and decades if we are to have any hope of transforming the world for the better in the twenty-first century. And I believe that not only Jews and Muslims, but Christians, Hindus, Buddhists, and the rest of humanity, including secular humanists, need to join in this effort as well if we are to build a peaceful and productive future for our children and grandchildren, rather than one racked with terrorism and violence.

First, let me elucidate the essential difference between the two commandments, then analyze why the first edict is often emphasized over the second, and, finally, explain why it is incumbent on all people of faith—including members of my own Jewish community—to switch their emphasis from loving the neighbor to loving the stranger. Over the centuries, and especially in modern times, "Love thy neighbor" has become a kind of super-commandment, perhaps the most frequently cited of the 613 commandments that Torah-observant Jews are expected to fulfill. Unfortunately, for many Orthodox and non-Orthodox Jews, "Love the stranger" seems to have largely slipped out of sight and out of mind.

I believe we can clearly dismiss the conceit that the second edict is little more than a repetition of the first—an exclamation point, so to speak. To cite one of those clichés of recent years, "Words have meaning." If that is true today, it was surely just as true 3,500 years ago when God articulated both maxims clearly and carefully to Moses. After all, God wanted to make sure that Moses "got it," that he grasped the message he was being given and would be able to successfully articulate that message to the People of Israel, the first people to accept and adopt ethical monotheism.

In short, God surely wanted his people to love *both* the neighbor and the stranger. He understood that both forms of love would be necessary to lift first the Jews and later the other followers of ethical monotheism (Christians and Muslims) out of the morally squalid "war of all against all" that was standard operating procedure in those days. These divine instructions were essential for survival itself at a time when brother smote brother (look no further than Cain and Abel or Joseph's brothers selling him into slavery), and when extended families and tribes routinely fought against each other according to the remorseless logic of the Code of Revenge, which Muhammad would much later abolish in Arabia with the introduction of Islam.

So God knew what He was saying to Moses when He distinguished between "neighbor" and "stranger." By the first term, He clearly meant a member of one's own people, which is to say a fellow Jew. By the second term, He clearly meant someone from another tribe or people, which is to say a non-Jew. Leviticus 19:18 makes clear that "thy neighbor" is meant as part of one's own people; after all, it reads, "Thou shalt not avenge, nor bear any grudge against *the children of thy people*." (Emphasis added.) Yet Leviticus 19:34 is clearly focused on extending love outward beyond one's own people to those of other faiths and ethnicities, for in that edict God forcefully reminds the Children of Israel that only a few years earlier they themselves had been strangers in an alien land, living as a persecuted and enslaved minority in Egypt.

So, essentially, God is calling on the Hebrews—who, at that point, had managed to escape Egypt and were on their way to taking possession of their own land at God's behest—not to treat non-Jews living there in the brutal manner in which they themselves had been treated. He is asking them to remember their own history of suffering and to rise above the all-too-human inclination to fear and mistrust the Other and treat him or her as a threat. Only by building ties of communication and cooperation with the Other and eventually coming to love him or her can one break the cycle of hatred and violence that has dogged humankind throughout history. It is not enough simply to love members of one's own faith or ethnicity, though that is a critically important first step. One must come to love the Other as well.

It should be noted too that this is not the only instance in the Torah when God urges the Hebrews to be just to the stranger. Here are several others:

> You shall not wrong a stranger or oppress him.   (*Exodus 22:20*)

> There shall be one law for you and for the stranger who lives among you."   (*Exodus 12:49; Numbers 15:15*)

> Hear out your fellow man and decide justly between any man and a fellow Israelite or a stranger.   (*Deuteronomy 1:16*)

To be sure, there is an apparent, and indeed quite jarring, contradiction between these powerful calls for love, kindness, and just treatment toward the stranger and the disturbing commandments in the Torah for the Jews to exterminate the Amalekites and the seven Canaanite nations. But as Rabbi Joseph Telushkin compellingly makes the case in the second volume of his *Code of Jewish Ethics* (2009), the reason offered by the Torah for this insistence on destroying the Canaanites was not that they were in the way of the Jewish conquest of Eretz Israel or even that they worshipped idols and multiple gods but rather the immorality of practices in which they engaged, such as child sacrifice (Deuteronomy 12:31) or bestiality (Leviticus 18:23–24). Telushkin also cites Deuteronomy 20:18, which expresses the concern that if the Canaanites remain in the land, "they will lead you into doing all the abhorrent things they have done with their Gods."

Also, as I pointed out in chapter 9, these calls for eradicating the Amalekites and Canaanites were increasingly supplanted and rendered null and void by the Jewish oral tradition, including the Mishnah, Talmud, and Shulchan Aruch, and in the arguments put forth by Maimonides and other important sages of the medieval period. In their views, since the offending nations had ceased to exist by the late biblical period, the commandments to destroy them were obsolete and irrelevant, and so it was wrong to present later nations as manifestations of Amalek and its pure evil. Instead, Maimonides enjoined Jews to kill the unreasoning evil, the Amalek, within themselves.

Yet to return to the main question, given the prominence the Torah clearly accords the concept of loving the stranger, why did the "Love thy neighbor" adage ultimately gain such prominence over "Love the stranger" among Jews, Christians, and others? After all, both commandments ask people to step out of their normal comfort zones of family and friends, and embrace people they would otherwise not be inclined to connect with. Yet, a cursory understanding of human nature tells us that while loving the neighbor is admittedly a stretch for many of us, it is much easier to accomplish than loving the stranger.

The neighbor whom God asks us to love is almost certainly a fellow Jew, and the stranger a non-Jew. Both in biblical and modern times, one's neighbors—the men, women, and children in the house or apartment next door, or in the case of the Hebrews crossing the Sinai, in the tent next door—are more likely than not to be of your own faith, race, or economic status. Your neighbors' children are more likely to go to school with your children; they may well give to the same charities, belong to the same clubs, or have the same political philosophy as you do.

Of course, in a multiethnic, multiracial, and multireligious society like twenty-first-century America, it is increasingly likely that your neighbors may have important differences from you and your family that offer the possibility of a mutually enriching learning experience if you make the effort to reach out to each other. And given that you live side by side, you and your neighbors will have ample opportunity to get to know each other, explore the differences in your backgrounds, and in time to come to appreciate those differences.

That scenario is likely very different from one's encounter with a stranger, who by the very nature of the term is almost certain to be someone foreign or strange. We tell our children, "Don't talk to strangers," which, sadly, is a necessary defense mechanism in a world where there are adults capable of doing demented things to children. But to the extent that adults also follow that advice, we close ourselves off, to a greater or lesser extent, from encounters that will extend us and allow us to grow as people. In short, we need to find new opportunities to talk to strangers and hopefully to start a process that turns them into friends.

To be sure, one of the reasons that much more of the world is conscious of "Love thy neighbor" than "Love the stranger" is that most people think of the former as a Christian precept rather than a Jewish one. Indeed, that instruction is often pointed to as evidence of the loving and merciful nature of Christianity, with the figure of all-loving and all-forgiving Jesus at the center, and how it is supposedly so different from the purportedly harsh and unbending "Old Testament Judaism." Yet, as is clear in Mathew 22:36–40, Jesus cited the maxim that came to be known as the "Golden Rule" after affirming his love for the God of Israel, in an effort to demonstrate his fealty to the Law (i.e., Jewish law as laid out in Leviticus) to a skeptical lawyer connected with his Pharisee adversaries.

"Master, which is the great commandment in the law?"

Jesus said unto him, "Thou shalt love the Lord thy God with all thy heart, and with all thy soul, and with all thy mind. This is the first and great commandment. And the second is like unto it, Thou shalt love thy neighbor as thyself. On these two commandments hang all the law and the prophets."

Here, of course, is the great irony. Jesus was born and remained a Jew for his entire life and upheld the main tenets of biblical law at the heart of his teachings. And yet Christians later came to cite the Golden Rule as one of the principal maxims distinguishing Christian beliefs and behavior from that of Jews, a people whom they excoriated as evil for the better part of two millennia. Be that as it may, my larger point is that Christianity's extolling of "Love thy neighbor" ensured that dictum's supremacy over "Love the stranger" in the Western mind. It is also indisputable and very unfortunate that modern-day Christians—and modern-day Jews as well—tend to cite "Love thy neighbor" as a central component of their respective faiths, and the more powerful and more urgently needed "Love the stranger" tends to be all but forgotten in both faiths.

From the Jewish perspective, the "Love thy neighbor" formulation is often connected with the famous aphorism of the sage Hillel, a near contemporary of Jesus. When asked by a man who wished to convert to Judaism to sum up the entire Torah while standing on one foot, Hillel responded, "What is hateful to thee, do not unto thy fellow man: this is the whole Law; the rest is mere commentary. Go and learn." (Shabbat 31a)

Hillel spoke of behaving properly toward "thy fellow man," who might be either a neighbor *or* a stranger; yet his famous adage is more closely associated in the popular mind with "Love thy neighbor." It is telling that Rabbi Akiva, who lived less than a century after Hillel, identified "Love your neighbor as yourself" as "a fundamental principle of the Torah." Many of the sages who comment on Rabbi Akiva's argument explicitly identify "love thy neighbor" as meaning *ahavath Yisrael* (love of Jew by Jew), which remains the unifying principle, the ultimate glue, that held the Jewish people together through the subsequent two thousand years of far-flung Diaspora and which still holds them together today.

With Akiva, the issue at stake is clearly that Jews should stand by Jews—and no wonder! The Temple had just been destroyed and Jewish national sovereignty shattered. According to the Talmud, the reason for these tragedies was *sinat chinam*, senseless hatred between Jews. There had been myriad and extremely rancorous divisions within the Jewish camp on many issues, including relations with Rome and the wisdom of the Great Revolt, as well as doctrinal disputes between Pharisees and Saducees and other, even more heterodox sects like the Essenes and early Christians. It should not be forgotten that Rabbi Akiva endured the tragedy of the death of twenty-four thousand of his own disciples in an epidemic, which, according to subsequent sages, was caused by the failure of these students to relate to each other respectfully. However, some modern-day scholars believe that Akiva and his students were massacred en masse by the Romans for the crime of having ardently supported the Bar-Kochba Rebellion, which erupted around 130 CE, sixty years after the Great Revolt, and which ended in the complete defeat and near-annihilation of the Jewish community in Palestine.

During Talmudic times, there was a good deal of debate among sages as to whether the term *neighbor* in Leviticus referred only to Jews, to Jews and proselytes (converts), or also to non-Jews who lived among Jews. (The Samaritan community, for instance, has lived and worshipped around Mount Gerezim near Nablus for well over two thousand years, and for much of that time had a difficult relationship with the Jews. Part of what was seen as the heretical nature of Jesus's behavior was his warm embrace of the Samaritan community.) In the Bible, the word *ger* is translated as "stranger" or "sojourner." In post-biblical times, *ger* often is used to refer to proselytes, non-Jews who have accepted Judaism and live among the Jewish community. In the Talmud, *ger* is used in two senses:

ger tzedek refers to a "righteous convert," a proselyte to Judaism, and *ger toshav* to a non-Jewish inhabitant of the Land of Israel who observes the Seven Laws of Noah and has repudiated all links with idolatry.[1]

Once the vast majority of Jews had spread out throughout the Christian and Muslim worlds, leaving only a tiny remnant in the Land of Israel, the tendency to focus almost exclusively on "Love thy neighbor" in the context of *ahavath yisrael*, and to de-emphasize the idea of loving the stranger, was greatly reinforced. After all, for hundreds of years most Jews lived in ghettoes or *mellahs* in physical isolation from their non-Jewish counterparts in both the Christian and Muslim worlds. They felt belittled and demeaned by majority populations in both places, even though the level of hatred and violence against Jews was much greater in the Christian world, where Jews were officially labeled by the Vatican as "Christ-killers." The founder of Protestantism, Martin Luther, and many of his followers demonized Jews every bit as virulently.

For their part, Jewish communal leaders enforced a rigorous separation of their own population from the gentiles. There were myriad reasons for this, including the concern that the gentile authorities might otherwise be able to play some Jews off against others, thereby whipping up *sinat chinam* and demoralizing the community; and that increased contacts between the communities would cause ever-increasing intermarriage and ultimately the complete assimilation and disappearance of the Jewish communities. So the attitudes of both gentile authorities and Jewish leaders created a rigid divide between gentiles and Jews, which, for all of its negative features, served to ensure the survival of the Jews in the Diaspora for so many centuries.

The Talmud—which was largely composed in the period when the Roman Empire was still mainly pagan and when Jews still mainly lived in large numbers Eretz Israel and Babylonia—has a whole body of rulings and prohibitions that served to restrict contact between Jews and gentiles. These include a strict prohibition against intermarriage or any sexual contact with gentiles, prohibitions against eating with gentiles or partaking

---

1. According to the Jewish Virtual Library, the Seven Noahide Laws apply to non-Jews, who are expected to follow these laws presumed to date from the time of Noah; "Judaism regards any non-Jew who keeps these laws as a righteous person who is guaranteed a place in the world to come."

of any of their wine (rules obviously buttressed by Jewish dietary laws), and sharp limitations on doing business with gentiles, including lending or repaying them money or borrowing from them or being repaid by them during days preceding pagan festivals.

As Jacob Katz notes in his 1961 book *Exclusiveness and Tolerance: Studies in Jewish-Gentile Relations in Medieval and Modern Times*, the point of the Talmudic rulings governing Jewish-gentile relations was to prevent Jews from contact with idolaters and their practices. Once paganism was replaced in Europe by Christianity and the Middle East by Islam, halachists engaged in long discourse as to whether some of the prohibitions on contact with gentiles, especially in the area of business relations, had been rendered moot by the fact that the gentiles in question were no longer pagan. Another factor was that once Jews had spread out across the world, rather than being mainly collected in two compact masses in Palestine and Babylonia, it was virtually impossible for them to maintain as complete an isolation from the gentile world as they had done before. While rules forbidding social interaction with gentiles were rigorously maintained, such edicts as those forbidding the taking of interest from gentiles or of selling cattle to them were ruled inapplicable by rabbis and halachists in medieval Europe on the grounds that they should apply in cases only where practice of these laws did not entail an economic loss and were not detrimental to Jews' ability to make a living.

As is the case today, among the rabbis and sages of medieval times, there were liberals and conservatives in terms of attitudes about how much contact Jews should have with non-Jews and how they should treat them. Maimonides himself redefined Amalek not as an existing race of people but as the persistence of evil in the world and in oneself. Yet, at the same time, he also affirmed or augmented anti-gentile Talmudic language. He wrote, for example, that a Jew who kills a non-Jew is not subject to execution by Jewish law (Law of Murder 2:11), though a non-Jew who kills a Jew should be put to death. He codified a raft of clearly discriminatory rulings on how non-Jews should be treated when living under Jewish sovereignty—which was, of course, a somewhat fanciful exercise since it had been nearly one thousand years after the last period when Jews ruled any land, and would be nearly one thousand years before a Jewish state was to be reestablished. For instance, Maimonides prescribed the death penalty for non-Jews who steal even an item worth less than a prutah (penny), whereas a Jew is subject to no punishment at all for such an act. On the other hand, he ruled that a non-Jew guilty of such capital crimes as cursing God, engaging in idol worship, committing adultery, or killing another person could evade execution—and apparently any punishment at all—simply by converting to Judaism.

As Joseph Telushkin theorizes, in the harshness of these rules, Maimonides was likely responding to the traumas he had encountered in his own life. The tolerant, Muslim-ruled Córdoba of his youth was overrun by Almohide fanatics, who forced Maimonides and his family into exile, and the various Islamic laws that he encountered throughout his life prescribed much harsher punishments for crimes carried out by non-Muslims than by Muslims. Maimonides was, like all of us, a person of his times, and as a proud Jew, he felt deeply the pain of living at the sufferance of another (Muslim) religion, even though the trajectory of his own life (he became physician to the Sultan Saladin) shows how much better was the lot of Jews in the Muslim world at that time than in the Christian one. Yet in his greatest rulings, like those concerning Amalek, Maimonides set down an ethical framework that far transcended his time, a framework that in its wisdom and sublime understanding of God and man has the mark of the eternal.

Even during the long centuries when the Jews lived a precarious existence at the mercy of non-Jewish kings, barons, and sometimes mobs, many Jewish sages and rabbis enjoined their community to behave according to the precept of treating everyone—Jew and gentile alike—as they themselves would want to be treated. Telushkin reminds us that Rabbi Judah the Chasid, a fourteenth-century sage, tells the story of a Jewish man whose own children died before they themselves had children, leaving the man no descendants to whom he might leave his money. When the anguished man admits to the sage that in business dealings he had cheated a non-Jew, who later died, Rabbi Judah tells him he has been terribly punished for this sin by witnessing the death of his own children. "The Holy One, blessed be He," the rabbi explains, "takes up the cause of the oppressed whether they are Jews or non-Jews" (Safer Chasidim, paragraph 661).

Three centuries later, Rabbi Moshe Rivkis (who died in 1671), author of the Be'er HaGolah *Commentary on the Shulkhan Arukh* (the code of Jewish law), wrote, "I have seen many people become wealthy because they caused non-Jews to err in business in order to gain profit thereby. However, they did not remain successful. . . . In the end all of their wealth was lost and they had nothing for their descendants" (chapter 348).

Perhaps the most far-sighted figure in this regard was the French rabbi Menachem Meiri (1249–1310), who issued a legal ruling intended to permanently alter the status of non-Jews in Jewish law. In his work *A Treaty on Repentance*, Meiri decreed that all rulings in the Talmud intended to discriminate against non-Jews should apply only to pagans and idolaters who rejected the One God and the moral teachings of the Torah. Toward adherents of the monotheistic faiths of his own era, Meiri wrote that Jews were enjoined to behave in the same way they would act toward their fellow Jews.

It is heartening that Meiri's writings have largely carried the day in terms of modern-day Orthodox rabbinical interpretations of questions relating to Jewish-gentile relations, though extremist rabbis and scholars sometimes cite Maimonides's work on the treatment of non-Jews living under Jewish sovereignty as justifying discriminatory treatment of Arabs in the Jewish state. To be sure, some of the same people often claim that Palestinians are the modern-day version of Amalek, thereby rejecting Maimonides's important ruling on that issue. Yet extremists of all stripes are hardly known for consistency or academic rigor.

Obviously, in the centuries since the times of Meiri and Maimonides, much has transpired in the Jewish condition and in world Jewry's relations with non-Jews, for both good and ill. Emancipation of the Jews of Europe in the late eighteenth and early nineteenth centuries appeared to offer a way out of the ghetto and anti-Semitism. Tragically, however, in the late nineteenth and early twentieth centuries, as many Jews left the ghettoes and sought to find their place as contributing members of French, German, Austro-Hungarian, and Russian societies, a renewed wave of anti-Semitism erupted in all of these and other countries from large numbers of gentiles who could not abide the idea of Jews attaining full citizenship. This wave of hatred eventually culminated in the Holocaust, during which the great majority of the Jews of Europe and one out of every three Jews in the world were rounded up and murdered by the monstrous regime of Nazi Germany.

Even before the Holocaust, large numbers of European Jews had grown disillusioned with the failure of Emancipation and such mass movements as socialism and communism to end anti-Semitism and solve the Jewish question. Many of those Jews turned to a counter-movement known as Zionism, which sprang up at the end of the nineteenth century. The new movement was predicated on the belief that the only workable solution to the Jewish question lay in the recreation of a Jewish state in the Land of Israel. The success of Zionism against all odds—the birth of the State of Israel in 1948 and that state's manifest accomplishments in the sixty-three years since then—has literally revolutionized the Jewish condition, reversing two thousand years of Jewish weakness and dependency, and creating a situation of Jewish empowerment, not only in the State of Israel but in Jewish communities around the world.

There are many challenges ahead if we are to ensure a vibrant Jewish future, but it is important to acknowledge that the condition of world Jewry is enormously improved over the situation that existed one hundred years ago or even fifty years ago. Today, in the aftermath of the collapse of the Soviet bloc, there are few Jews left living in lands of active persecution (with the possible exception of Iran), though our history makes us aware that things can change dramatically for the worse at a moment's notice. Today, Jews living in the United States, Canada, and much of Europe are full and equal citizens of the countries they inhabit, something unprecedented in the history of the Diaspora.

Yes, there remain incidents of anti-Semitism in all countries, including our own; indeed, according to the Anti-Defamation League, which monitors anti-Semitism, hate crimes in the United States happen more frequently against Jews than any other religious group. Yet we Jews living in the Diaspora are in a new position today, one of considerable power and affluence. We are in a position to take a full part in American life, as well as in Jewish life; we can interact with other religious communities—Catholic, Protestant, Muslim, and others—on the basis of equality and mutual respect. And we are in a position to use our new strength to help ensure that no communities, including the American Muslim community, are unfairly stigmatized or treated as anything less than full members of the American family.

In the rest of the world, the Jewish condition, while greatly improved, still feels more perilous than it is in the United States and Canada. For good reason, Jews around the world still fear for Israel's survival, as the Jewish state remains surrounded by an Arab-Muslim world that is at best only partially reconciled to its long-term presence in the region. Ironically, at a time when the Iranian regime is poised to acquire nuclear weapons, calls for the destruction of Israel, and stocks allies like Hamas in Gaza and Hezbollah in southern Lebanon with missiles that can hit any city in Israel, it can be said that in some ways Jews in Israel are more imperiled than Jews anywhere else in the world.

The growing strength of the Muslim Brotherhood and other Islamist parties over the last year in Egypt and other countries has been deeply unsettling to Israelis and Jews everywhere. And in many European countries, Jews feel more at risk than in North America, in part because of the rapid growth of Muslim communities (which are larger than the Jewish communities in the major countries of Western Europe by factors of 5 or even 10 to 1), some of whose members have lashed out violently against Jews out of anger at the Middle East conflict.

Yet such challenging developments only sharpen the imperative for Jews to reach out to Muslims and work cooperatively to build a network of personal and organizational ties in countries around the world. At least some of the animus expressed by European Muslims against Jews stems from the mistaken belief that Jews are opposed to the mainstreaming of their community.

All of this is highly relevant to the question of whether our main priority should be to love the neighbor or love the stranger, and the Muslim stranger in particular. To be sure, we need to do both at once. The need for *ahavath Israel* is clear and compelling, both in Israel and the Diaspora. In Israel, we have seen shocking manifestations of *sinat chinam*, such as the assassination of Prime Minister Yitzhak Rabin in 1995 by a deeply devout Jew who committed the unspeakable crime of murdering the leader of the Jewish state in order to stop the peace process. This was a *hillul hashem*, a desecration of God's name, made even more horrifying because it was done in the name of Judaism.

The tendency toward extremism among some Jews continues to escalate. As I noted previously, Jews of all backgrounds were horrified by the behavior of *haredi* (ultra-Orthodox) zealots in the Israeli city of Bet Shemesh, who shouted "whore" at an eight-year-old girl from an Orthodox family because they believed that the modest dress she wore to school was not modest enough. While we have not seen anything quite that dramatic here in the United States, relations between the various streams of Judaism leave much to be desired. As in Israel, some ultra-Orthodox Jews denounce other Orthodox Jews for not being rigorous enough in their observance. Some Orthodox rabbis shun all contact with their Reform or Conservative counterparts, claiming that they are not real Jews. For their part, many liberal and secular Jews treat observant Jews as primitives to be shunned, in the process missing the opportunity to connect to and learn from the beauty and wisdom of traditional Judaism. So we as a people need to redouble our efforts if we are to begin to live up to the venerable slogan of the United Jewish Appeal, "We Are One," and at the same time, to the precept "Love thy neighbor."

Yet I believe the need is even more urgent for Jews in America and worldwide to step up in a purposeful and consistent way to make "Love the stranger" a central component of our communal agenda. It is true that over the past half century we have made some important progress in this field, especially in strengthening ties with the Christian world. This is a project that began in the early 1960s with the Second Vatican Council's adaptation of *Nostrae Etate*, a document that reversed two millennia of Catholic dogma and finally absolved the Jews of responsibility for killing Christ. Much more progress has been made since then in our relationship with both the Vatican and important Protestant denominations, and we should continue the work of strengthening the Christian-Jewish dialogue. Yet, unquestionably, today the "stranger" for both Jews and Christians in America and Europe is the Muslim, who has come to both continents in the last generation in large numbers and has yet to be fully welcomed into society in either place.

The Israeli-Palestinian conflict is the principal cause of the past hundred years of Muslim-Jewish hostility, and its resolution would go a long way to repairing it. (For a full discussion of this issue, see chapter 16, "Palestine.") Unfortunately, in the wake of the failure of the peace process of the 1990s and the renewal of violence and confrontation over the past decade, it is clear that we are still a considerable distance from resolving that conflict. However, Jews who live in close physical proximity with Muslims in countries around the world simply cannot afford the luxury of sitting back and waiting until a peace treaty is signed to do something about the perilous state of Muslim-Jewish relations in the places where they live. What moderate, far-sighted Jews around the world must do is reach out on a sustained basis to like-minded Muslims in their home countries to discover the commonalities in our two faith traditions and to begin the job of building a fabric of mutually beneficial ties.

By effectively accomplishing that ambitious assignment, we will prevent the still-unresolved Israeli-Palestinian conflict from becoming a worldwide Muslim-Jewish war. Were something like that to happen, it would imperil Jews in countries like France, Belgium, the United Kingdom, and Germany, where they are greatly outnumbered by the Muslim population. And if we are successful in building such a worldwide Muslim-Jewish movement focused on communication, reconciliation, and cooperation, that success will, in time, have an ameliorative effect on the Israeli-Palestinian conflict by reminding Jews and Muslims that we can indeed find common ground and that our two peoples—including Palestinians and Israelis—are not doomed to remain enemies for generations to come. In short, working on a sustained basis over the coming years to build ties of friendship and trust between Jews and Muslims offers hope that our children and grandchildren will live in a safer and happier world in which the Jewish people will finally be in peace. Not to make the effort almost guarantees the opposite result.

The Muslim community in my country, the United States, arrived here in large numbers much more recently than the Jewish community, with the great majority of Muslim immigrants having come in the past fifty years. As a result, the Muslim community is considerably less experienced in terms of working within the American system and considerably weaker politically than the Jewish community, although a coterie of young American-born Muslim professionals are learning the political game fast. It should also not escape our attention that there are today an estimated two million to three million Muslims in the United States. Much of this growth is first generation, and it puts their numbers closer to the more than five million American Jews than ever before.[2] The Muslim community is an eclectic one, including a mix of native-born African Americans and immigrants from South Asia, the Arab world, Africa, and elsewhere and their American-born children.

The great majority of American Muslims and most of the organizations that represent them, like the Islamic Society of North America, the Muslim Public Affairs Council, and others, strongly reject terrorism, violence, and Islamic extremism, and want only to achieve the status that once-challenged groups like American Jews and Catholics have long since attained: that of being loyal citizens who want to achieve the American Dream while simultaneously exercising their First Amendment rights to practice their faith openly and freely. In short, they want at once to be proud Americans and proud Muslims.

Unfortunately, in recent years, the American Muslim community has experienced ever-greater challenges against its very right to exist. The sense of siege that American Muslims are presently enduring began with the September 11, 2001, attacks by Osama bin Laden and his cohorts. Despite the fact that virtually all American Muslim organizations strongly denounced the murderous assault, it had the corrosive effect of casting suspicion on all American Muslims. Things have gotten much worse over the past decade, with an escalating wave of bigotry and fear-mongering directed against peaceful American Muslims. We have seen widespread opposition to the building of mosques, including the so-called Ground Zero Mosque in downtown Manhattan, and the outlawing of Islamic (Shari'a) law by a growing number of state legislatures on the bogus grounds that it somehow threatens to supplant US law. This cascade of Islamophobia has been pushed forward by prominent political figures, including some would-be and actual presidential candidates and other influential people, among them, unfortunately, several prominent Jews, all of whom are making successful careers of spreading poisonous anti-Muslim hatred in the media and on the Internet.

In rejecting the anti-Muslim hysteria of recent years, the mainstream

---

2. *The Global Religious Landscape: A Report on the Size and Distribution of the World's Major Religious Groups as of 2010*, Pew Forum on Religious and Public Life, December 18, 2012, http://www.pewforum.org/global-religious-landscape.aspx.

of American Jewry has confounded the Islamophobes who expected the Jewish community to be their allies, given that the Muslim-baiters present themselves as pro-Jewish and pro-Israel. Yes, part of the answer for that rejection lies in the lessons of recent American history, but ultimately, it goes all the way back to the source of Jewish knowledge, the Torah, back to "Love the stranger because once we were strangers in Egypt." We know in our bones what it is to be hurt, humiliated, and demonized, and we can't stand by as a people while such treatment is meted out to another people.

So we have reason for some satisfaction, but in truth we haven't yet done nearly enough to meet the challenge of the twenty-first century to "Love the stranger" and to do so by strengthening ties of communication, reconciliation, and cooperation with American Muslims. What we need to do now is get more and more Jews to become actively engaged in this effort, to convince them that doing so is both a moral imperative and a strategic necessity for our community. The reality is that millions of American Muslims are here to stay. Our choice is whether they will exist here in a fearful, angry, and alienated mood or whether, by our actions in conjunction with other Americans of conscience, they can be reassured and made to feel as much accepted and at home as all other Americans. To give young Muslims the message that their faith will never be accepted here, that they themselves will always be suspect and their chances for advancement limited by their religion or ethnicity, could push some of them toward Islamic radicalism on the despairing premise of "Well, if they hate me anyway, what do I have to lose?" It is hard to see that scenario, which, God forbid, might well lead to an upsurge of home-grown violence, as being good for the Jews.

In short, it is vitally important for ever-growing numbers of American Jews to step out of their comfort zone and reach out to the moderate majority of American Muslims. We need to let them know that we respect them and their faith and will do everything we can to help them gain full acceptance in this country. Doing that in a demonstrative way, both on the grassroots and leadership levels, helps shatter the untrue stereotype too many Muslims have that, because of the Middle East conflict, the Jews will always be their enemy and will conspire to retard their progress. When Muslims see and experience the opposite, it leads to profound changes in their thinking. I remember how many Muslims—including politically sophisticated Muslim leaders—were both amazed and deeply grateful when the Jewish mayor of New York, Michael Bloomberg, stepped forward during the Ground Zero mosque controversy and affirmed the right of Muslims, like all religious groups, to build and maintain a house of worship anywhere in the city.

I am every bit as grateful to American Muslim leaders like Imam Shamsi Ali; Congressman Keith Ellison; Dr. Sayyid Syeed, the national director of the Islamic Society of North America; Imam Feisal Rauf; and Dr. Muzammil Siddiqi, president of the Fiqh Council of America, who have spoken out on behalf of Jewish concerns. I won't forget, for example, how Dr. Syeed insistently denounced Holocaust denial by the likes of Hamas, Fatah, and Iran, and how he and Dr. Siddiqi traveled to Auschwitz to bear public witness to the horror that happened there. I won't forget Congressmen Ellison and André Carson, Dr. Syeed, and others bravely issuing a public statement calling on Hamas to release Israeli hostage Gilad Shalit several weeks before the release actually took place—in the face of considerable criticism by hard-liners in their own community.

Muslim-Jewish cooperation is very much a two-way street, and it is wonderful that leaders on both sides have stepped forward and spoken out on behalf of the "Other" when either is under attack. Thanks to the effort in which we have been engaged, Jewish leaders today speak out regularly when there are incidences of Islamophobia and Muslim leaders denounce acts of anti-Semitism.

As I think about the commandment to love the stranger, my mind races back to my first venture into Muslim-Jewish relations, which I discussed in chapter 6 of this book, when I apprehensively walked into a Muslim school in Queens in 2006 to dialogue with the students on Judaism. It was the first time I had ever visited a Muslim institution, and I was overwhelmed by the kindness and affection shown to me by the several hundred high school students gathered to greet me, including row after row of young girls in hijabs. As I spoke about practices in Orthodox Judaism, they responded that almost identical practices exist in Islam, and we experienced together a profound moment of mutual discovery and commonality that forever changed my life and led me to decide several months later, in conjunction with my close friend and collaborator Russell Simmons, to devote myself to the cause of improving Muslim-Jewish relations. That encounter in Queens was as pure an expression of "Love the stranger" as I have experienced before or since, and it illuminated for me the immense psychic rewards to those who have the courage to reach beyond their own camp and connect with the Other.

I am not naive. I know that there remain Islamist extremists around the world who are intent on committing murderous violence against America and against Jews, and who must be stopped by whatever means possible. Yet I also have come to understand over the past five years that the majority of Muslims reject that course as morally repellent and more likely to hurt Muslims than anyone else. The majority of American Muslims, who feel deeply threatened by Islamic radicalism, will respond with enthusiasm if we reach out a hand of friendship to them. So I come back to my first point: that if we are to succeed in avoiding a War of Civilizations that the extremists are seeking to ignite, Jews and Muslims of goodwill both need to step forward and say, "This time, we need to take things one step further than simply loving our neighbor. Now is the time to love the stranger. For the sake of our children and our children's children, we can do no less."

CHAPTER TWELVE

Understanding Shari'a

IMAM SHAMSI ALI

Shari'a is an Arabic word that loosely means "path," and this is how it is understood by Muslims around the world—as a path to being righteous. Interestingly, in both grammar and usage it is similar to the word for Jewish religious law, Halacha. There is no one book or set of guidelines that make up the Shari'a. Non-Muslims frequently misunderstand Shari'a to mean a legal code and expect to find definitive codes akin to what is found in law schools for educating students. While there is an aspect of legality that falls under Shari'a (the study of *fiqh*), jurisprudence is not the totality or even the dominant aspect.

Current fears of "Shari'a law" taking over or pushing out civil law in the United States and Europe display an ignorance of what Shari'a really is. The frequently called-up images of women being stoned or men being whipped are not what Shari'a means to the majority of Muslims. It is a great disservice to Islam that many in the Muslim world have defended their debauchery and self-serving purposes under the umbrella of Shari'a. We unequivocally denounce this usage. In most cases, what is falsely presented as religious law is nothing more than extremism fostered by political and economic frustrations, and devoid of theological basis.

Shari'a includes divine directives regarding every aspect of a Muslim's life and is meant to improve the harmony of individuals and communities, Muslim or not. Further, referring to Shari'a simply as "Islamic law" is incomplete—it would be as if one referred to Halacha as only what was found in the Nashim and Nezikin tractates of the Mishnah. There is a great similarity between Shari'a and Halacha in their comprehensive natures and applications. Both extend beyond societal laws and a penal system. Shari'a might be better described as an amorphous body of divine laws, rules, codes of conduct, and teachings that are intended to benefit the individual and society. There are various sources of Shari'a, which are manifest in its divine and temporal components, and it serves multiple purposes for individuals and communities through its application to daily life.

MEANING AND CONTEXT

Literally, the word *Shari'a* refers to a waterway that leads to a main water source. An analogy can be made that just as water is a necessary element of life, so is Shari'a essential to the well-being of a Muslim. We may define Shari'a as the guidance that God has provided His servants regarding belief, worship, daily affairs, manners, ethics, and all areas of life in order to organize their relationships with Him and each other, and to achieve happiness in this life and the next. Shari'a touches upon all areas of the Muslim outlook and is connected to three major areas of Islamic studies: theology, law, and ethics. This means Shari'a covers all areas of human life, either directly or indirectly, specifically or generally. The sweeping scope of Shari'a is part of what makes it ominous for non-Muslims who do not understand it—and for some who believe they understand it, as well.

The ethical guidance of the Shari'a was framed by Muslim scholars (ulama) who derived principles from the direct revelation of God to man (the Holy Qur'an). Muslims believe this divine text was revealed directly in human language to the Prophet Muhammad, and that it is exemplified in the Sunnah, or customs, that recount the Prophet's understanding of these revelations through his words and deeds. Since the *shar'* (path) to God was revealed to all the prophets of the Abrahamic succession, divine revelations given to the Jewish prophets as well as to Jesus are binding on Muslims as well, unless they are specifically abrogated in the Qur'an.

Shari'a touches on both transcendental and material experience, providing perspective and understanding for individual and community relations. The Muslim scholar Ibn al-Qayyim observed:

> Shari'a is based on wisdom and achieving people's welfare in this life and the afterlife. Shari'a is all about justice, mercy, wisdom, and good. Thus, any ruling that replaces justice with injustice, mercy with its opposite, common good with mischief, or wisdom with nonsense, is a ruling that does not belong to the Shari'a, even if it is claimed to be so according to some interpretations.[1]

Here we run into problems of interpreting the Shari'a, and this has to do with cultural versus theological norms. There are those Muslim theologians (or would-be theologians) who cite Shari'a in passing judgments, or fatwas, on contemporary issues such as foreign affairs, female autonomy, marriage, socioeconomics, and judicial considerations. The main sources of Shari'a, as I just mentioned, are the Qur'an and the Sunnah. However, Shari'a is also determined by discourse, and the Muslim polity has no "supreme head" akin to the Pope for Catholicism, nor any central corporate entity like the Vatican to propound and enforce a single, approved, and agreed-upon theological vision.

So Muslim discourse becomes highly variegated and specialized, narrowed and encompassing, with levels of validity specific to geographic regions.[2] Because of these social and historical contexts, a scholar in Indonesia may claim that it is not mandatory for a woman to veil when interpreting the Qur'anic verse usually cited as the commandment for hijab (33:59).[3] However, that same verse may be interpreted by a Wahabist

---

1. Taha Abdul Rauf Saad, ed., *I'lam Al-Muwaqi'een* (Beirut: Dar Al-Jeel, 1973).

2. According to the Pew Research Center, Sunni Islam accounts for approximately 90 percent of the world's Muslims. It has no hierarchy and no "supreme" councils, commanders, or "definitive" scholars. Shia Islam holds a more hierarchical structure, although Shia also do not all agree on one ruling per a supreme leader, as each substratum looks to its own sect leaders. It would be the equivalent of Episcopalians and Presbyterians, whose beliefs are slightly different from Catholics', though they all share the same foundation. *Muslim Americans: A National Portrait; An In-Depth Analysis of America's Most Diverse Religious Community* (Washington, DC: Gallup/CoexistFoundation, 2009).

3. "O Prophet! Tell thy wives and thy daughters and the women of the believers to draw their cloaks close round them (when they go abroad). That will be better, so that they may be recognised and not annoyed. Allah is ever Forgiving, Merciful." *The Glorious Qur'an*, Pickthall.

scholar in Saudi Arabia to mean that a woman must be completely covered except for her eyes in the belief that this is more in keeping with "modesty" in its "proper" Islamic intention. Both scholars' interpretations and fatwas are based on their contextualized discourse and cultural norms. Culture importantly informs the criteria for interpretation of the Shari'a, and it is this cultural interpretation that most often reaches the masses via media reports, and which is the cause of much misapplication of Qur'anic and Sunnic texts in the Muslim world. To better understand its reach, it is useful to understand the underpinnings of Shari'a.

The major sources of the Shari'a are the Qur'an and the Sunnah, which represent the actual speech of God and the example of how to implement it in life, as embodied by the Prophet Muhammad. Tertiary sources are *ijma, qiyas, istihan,* and *maslahah,* which are interpretive analyses of Qur'anic injunctions and normative Sunnah. If we attempt to translate this into Judaic parallels, the primary sources would be the Tanakh and Mishnah, with other Talmudic elements (such as Gemarah, Aggadic texts, Midrash, esoteric commentary) providing source material, context, elucidations, and precedent for contemporary interpretation and application.

Because Muslims hold the Holy Qur'an to be the precise words that God transmitted to the Prophet Muhammad through the angel Gabriel, it is the major source for the Shari'a. Because the Qur'an is an eternal text, it contains both literal and metaphorical aspects, and therefore it has received various interpretations in translations and exegeses. Sometimes it is direct and specific, as in the case of inheritance law and prescribed punishments, and sometimes it indicates general principles, as is the case with foundational values such as honesty, integrity, consultation, justice, and human dignity.

The second major source for understanding the Shari'a is the Sunnah of Prophet Muhammad. *Sunnah* is an Arabic word meaning "traditions," and here lie the recorded statements, actions, and silent approvals of Prophet Muhammad, which form the normative example of behavior for all Muslims. While the Prophet's example is considered to be as close to perfect as humanly possible, this does not mean that every action he took is exactly permissible or applicable today. The context in which his actions were taken must be considered.

To cite just one example, the Qur'anic allowance for up to four legal wives is much misunderstood. The basis for this specific allowance is found in Verse 4:3, which states "Marry of the women who seem good to you, two or three or four; and if ye fear that ye cannot do justice (to so many) then one (only)."[4] This statement must be understood as part of its time and place: against a backdrop of war, slavery, and nomadism, there were an abundance of orphans, widows, single mothers, and other women without means of support. In the hyperpatriarchal culture of the era and area, a lone woman could be taken as a slave or left with child after a caravan passed through, and she would have no codified legal recourse. The Qur'anic injunction was to marry women and provide the basics of food, clothing, and shelter to each wife in equal measure.[5] Lest this sound like a backdated version of Mormonism, it was actually a practice held in esteem theologically because of the precedent set by Jewish tribes, supported by the words of the Qur'an, and deemed practical for political allegiances as well as community building. This context is necessary for understanding the Sunnah in this area, though it does not necessarily translate to the modern day. Most ulama of modern times stress the part of the verse that states if a man cannot act equitably with multiple wives, that it is best to have only one, as then "it is more likely that ye will not do injustice." There are many such examples of Shari'a in practice that are corrupted by those without the correct historical and religious teaching. To this point of culture versus theology we will return.

It is important to remember that *Sunnah* is simply an Arabic indicative for "traditions." The era before Prophet Muhammad and the advent of Islam was called the *jahiliyyah*, and the normative Sunnah, or traditions, of that time were equally adhered to through ritual or cultural patterns by the peoples of each geographic region. Because Muslims believe that Prophet Muhammad and Islam did away with pagan practices and are closer to what God wishes for his followers, for Muslims the Sunnah

---

4. *The Glorious Qur'an*, Pickthall.

5. Aside from the many biblical stories of polygamy, including those of Abraham and Jacob, there are passages in the Torah believed to have been given to Moses by God Himself where the laws for keeping more than one wife were explained. For example, Exodus 21:7–10 decrees that food, clothing, and "conjugal rights" cannot be taken from one wife when a man takes another.

that is emulated is that of Prophet Muhammad (and, to a lesser extent, his Companions), rather than the pre-Islamic Sunnah, that of the *jahiliyyah* time. For this reason, it is incumbent upon Muslims to differentiate between those customs that are merely historical and/or cultural continuations, and those that come from divine guidance. Again, the important distinction is between culture and theology.

The bulk of the historical detailing of Islamic Sunnah is carried down to modern populations through hadith. Hadith are narrations of the deeds and words of Prophet Muhammad and his Companions as compiled into books called *sahih*, of which there are six canonical collections.[6]

Ijma is most commonly translated into English as "consensus." It is the verb form of the Arabic word *Ajma'a*, which has two meanings: to determine and to agree on something. Ijma is considered the third proof of Shari'a after the Qur'an and the Sunnah, and is steeped in rational analysis. When a scholarly *ijtihad* or *ta'wil* (interpretation) becomes universal, it becomes an ijma.[7] The classical definition of ijma maintains that universal consensus of the ulama is necessary for a conclusive ijma to be accepted.

However, universal ijma are indeed very few, as evidence shows that it is extremely difficult to prove ijma on issues open to ijtihad. The only form of ijma universally upheld is that of the *Sahabis* (Prophet Muhammad's Companions). Any agreement of a majority of ulama (not universal) may be taken as a proof but is not binding, and there are no valid grounds to exclude scholarly opinions from any school of Islam, as long as the school or group itself is not considered outside Islam by the Muslim majority. Ijma is therefore very inclusive and very fluid.

Qiyas literally means "measuring or ascertaining" the length, weight, or quality of something. It also means comparison, the process of establishing equality or similarity between two things. It is a rationalist doctrine whereby intellect is largely used to discover the reasoning, though personal opinion (*ra'y*) is kept subservient to divine revelation.

---

6. The sahih accepted as canonical by most Muslims are the books of Muslim, Bukhari, Dawud, Tirmidhi, Sughra, and Majah, all collected in late 9 CE/early 10 CE.

7. An *ijtihad* can best be expressed as a scholarly judgment based on analysis of various points of view. There are various types of ijtihad, which are discussed later in this chapter.

Reasoning is discovered from the texts of the Qur'an and the Sunnah, and no laws in the Qur'an or Sunnah are revised for expediency. Because qiyas is speculative and differences of opinion are accepted, laws derived through qiyas cannot carry the same authority as those of textual rulings (of the Qur'an or Sunnah). The essential requirements of qiyas are the following: the original case, that case's ruling, the cause, and the new case on which a ruling is to be given. Jurists do not consider law derived through qiyas to be "new laws." So, for example, the Muslim prohibition on narcotic drugs is a qiyas derived from analogy based on the Qur'anic prohibition on alcohol.

Istihsan literally means "to deem something preferable."[8] In its juristic sense, istihsan is a method of exercising personal opinion (*ra'y*) in order to avoid any rigidity and unfairness that might result from literal application of law. In both qiyas and istihsan, ra'y is an important component but is weighted more heavily in the case of istihsan. As a concept, it is close to "equity" in Western law and is important as a form of meeting the changing needs of society. It has been defined as a principle that authorizes departure from an established precedent in favor of a different ruling for a stronger reason.

The above considerations are all taken into account when weighing actions against the public interest (*maslahah*). On the basis of maslahah, for example, currency and prisons were established and an agricultural land tax was imposed. The actions of leaders of the Muslim community should always be in pursuit of maslahah. Authenticating and distributing copies of the definitive Qur'an to followers of Islam in order to avoid schism (as the second caliph, Usman, did) is an early example. A contemporary one may be American Muslim communities that report suspicious activity to the authorities.

LEGAL ASPECTS OF SHARI'A

Law must adapt when societies change, whether over time or by the influx of various cultures and new material conditions. As Islam spread and the borders of Muslim lands expanded, all the different civilizations, each

---

8. This branch of "law" is accepted by Sunni communities but rejected by Shia ones.

with its own culture, tradition, and codes of law, had to be incorporated into the Islamic polity. This melding process evolved into *usul al-fiqh*, or Islamic jurisprudence.

In Arabic, *fiqh* means "deep understanding" or "full comprehension." While the divine laws of Shari'a are undisputed, scholarly differences in Islamic jurisprudence do exist. There are four main Sunni schools of legal jurisprudence, called *madhabs*, all of which are considered equally orthodox. These are the Maliki, Shafi'i, Hanafi, and Hanbali legal schools. There are also three accepted madhabs in the mainstream Shia tradition, the Zaidiyya, Ja'fari, and Ismailiya. There are five main categories of acceptance in Shari'a, ranging from obligatory to prohibited, and these remain constant regardless of which school of legal analysis is followed.[9]

The madhab can, in a general way, be understood for Jews as, for example, the difference between those who follow Hillel or Shammai, with the ulama expressing a range of opinion just as the many learned rabbis do. In general, most scholars will fall under one or another of these madhab guidelines and education in interpreting fatwas. We have seen that normative bases of institutions and concepts have changed significantly over the last two centuries, and there would be no reason to believe these changes would abate.

The most integral components of Shari'a are the Five Pillars of Islam, those core beliefs universal to every Muslim, most of which are practiced on a daily basis. The application in daily life of the Five Pillars is the most important individual aspect of following Shari'a. These are

> Declaration of faith (*shahada*). This is the very first sura, or chapter, in the Holy Qur'an, *al-Fatihah*. The pronouncement and belief that there is no God but God, and that Muhammad was his messenger, is the cornerstone of faith for all Muslims.
>
> Ritual purification and prayer (*salat*). The ablutions made in preparation for prayer are called *wudu*, and they have meanings that run deeper than simple cleanliness. Washing the face indicates

---

9. The five categories are *wajib* or *fard* (obligatory, or clearly required), *mandub* (recommended, but not obligatory), *mubah* (permissible, due to lack of injunction or opinion), *makruh* (disliked and discouraged, but not prohibited), and *haram* (prohibited).

honor and dignity, respecting yourself and others. Washing the head indicates having positive thoughts and maintaining a clean mind. When one is preparing to pray, one is walking toward Allah, and the symbolic action is manifest in washing the feet before prayer.[10] There are various references to the obligatory prayers and the times in which they must be made, among them, 2:238, 11:114, and 17:78.[11] More importantly, perhaps, than the specific rituals is the discipline of praying consistently. Prayer itself is offered five times a day to remind us of and reinforce our bond with God. Prayer forces an introspection and focus throughout the day, so we can reflect on our actions and correct ourselves where we have been wrong.

Fasting (*sawm*). Fasting is undertaken not only to empathize with the poor but to encourage abstinence from all bad things, to propagate goodwill and happiness, and to better learn appreciation. The mandate is found in Qur'an 2:183–184.[12]

Charity (*zakat*). There is a formal demand of zakat for Muslims that is 2.5 percent of their annual net savings after expenses. Beyond that requirement, Muslims are expected to give many types of informal charity (*sadaka*)—a smile, a kind word,

---

10. Qur'an 5:6 explains how to perform wudu: "O ye who believe! When ye rise up for prayer, wash your faces, and your hands up to the elbows, and lightly rub your heads and (wash) your feet up to the ankles. And if ye are unclean, purify yourselves. And if ye are sick or on a journey, or one of you cometh from the closet, or ye have had contact with women, and ye find not water, then go to clean, high ground and rub your faces and your hands with some of it. Allah would not place a burden on you, but He would purify you and would perfect His grace upon you, that ye may give thanks." *The Glorious Qur'an*, Pickthall.

11. Qur'an 2:238: "Be guardians of your prayers, and of the midmost prayer, and stand up with devotion to Allah." Qur'an 11:114: "Establish worship at the two ends of the day and in some watches of the night. Lo! good deeds annul ill-deeds. This is a reminder for the mindful." Qur'an 17:78: "Establish worship at the going down of the sun until the dark of night, and (the recital of) the Qur'an at dawn. Lo! (the recital of) the Qur'an at dawn is ever witnessed." *The Glorious Qur'an*, Pickthall.

12. Qur'an 2:183–184: "O ye who believe! Fasting is prescribed for you, even as it was prescribed for those before you, that ye may ward off (evil); (Fast) a certain number of days; and (for) him who is sick among you, or on a journey, (the same) number of other days; and for those who can afford it there is a ransom: the feeding of a man in need—but whoso doeth good of his own accord, it is better for him: and that ye fast is better for you if ye did but know." *The Glorious Qur'an*, Pickthall.

assistance to friends. Anything that makes others happy is considered sadaka. These actions form part of our social responsibilities. The order to give alms and practice charity is summarized in 2:262–265:[13] A popular hadith has it that the second caliph, Umar, had insomnia caused by worry that he had not sufficiently fulfilled his social obligations to widows, orphans, the poor, and the stranger. The giving of charity in all its forms is *that* important.[14]

Pilgrimage to Mecca (hajj). The command made to visit Mecca once in one's life, whenever one is physically, emotionally, and financially able, is found in Qur'an 2:196–197.[15] The stress is on unifying the Muslim community and gathering its diversity for the purpose of worshipping God. Like the requirement of daily prayer, making the hajj is a method of disconnecting from quotidian life and reaffirming the link with one's beliefs. The hajj provides the ultimate occasion to ask forgiveness for sins, repent mistakes that were made, and seek to improve one's character.

---

13. Qur'an 2:262–265: "Those who spend their wealth for the cause of Allah and afterward make not reproach and injury to follow that which they have spent; their reward is with their Lord, and there shall no fear come upon them, neither shall they grieve. A kind word with forgiveness is better than almsgiving followed by injury.... Render not vain your almsgiving by reproach and injury, like him who spendeth his wealth only to be seen of men.... And the likeness of those who spend their wealth in search of Allah's pleasure, and for the strengthening of their souls, is as the likeness of a garden on a height.... Allah is Seer of what ye do." *The Glorious Qur'an*, Pickthall.

14. See also Qur'an 2:110, 2:254, 2:270–280, 3:92, 3:134, 9:71, 30:38, and 64:16 for references to zakat and alms-giving. Other types of charity are too numerous to detail here.

15. Qur'an 2:196–197: "Perform the pilgrimage and the visit (to Makka) for Allah. And if ye are prevented, then send such gifts as can be obtained with ease, and shave not your heads until the gifts have reached their destination. And whoever among you is sick or hath an ailment of the head must pay a ransom of fasting or almsgiving or offering. And if ye are in safety, then whosoever contenteth himself with the visit for the pilgrimage (shall give) such gifts as can be had with ease. And whosoever cannot find (such gifts), then a fast of three days while on the pilgrimage, and of seven when ye have returned; that is, ten in all. That is for him whoso folk are not present at the Inviolable Place of Worship. Observe your duty to Allah, and know that Allah is severe in punishment. The pilgrimage is (in) the well-known months, and whoever is minded to perform the pilgrimage therein (let him remember that) there is (to be) no lewdness nor abuse nor angry conversation on the pilgrimage. And whatsoever good ye do Allah knoweth it." *The Glorious Qur'an*, Pickthall.

The presence and application of Shari'a to human interaction is as limitless as human interaction itself. The general rule of thumb is that proper comportment means that we are always to behave with the knowledge that God knows all.[16] Though I cannot touch on every aspect of Shari'a here, there are areas that have consistently drawn attention, fire, condemnation, and departure from true Islamic principles. These are areas in which the intentions set down in the Qur'an have diverged and morphed into syncretized facsimiles of religion, imbued with xenophobia, ignorance, irresponsibility, and propaganda against anything or anyone not falling under the rarified and esoteric definitions of "Muslim."

To take one example, let us consider the area of family law. Sura Al-Baqarah has many chapters laying out guidance for marriage, sex, inheritance, and conduct toward orphans (Qur'an 2:220–242). Verse 228 states, "Women shall have rights similar to the rights against them (men)." We see the rights for women detailed in the Qur'an regarding *mahr*, the dowry owed to women per marriage contract (4:19); the illegality of taking back a wife's gifts upon divorce (2:229); a woman's ability to initiate divorce (*khul*); specific obligations of maintenance toward one's wife and children (2:223) and child support (2:233); monies due to a discarded bride where divorce took place before consummation (2:236–237); the obligation of men to provide inheritance and maintenance for their widows (2:240); and monetary provisions for a divorced wife similar to modern alimony (2:241). Many verses in Surah An-Nisa provide further detailed instructions with regard to marital relations, the man's obligations to support his family, and the rights of children.

Unfortunately, despite a hadith attributed to Prophet Muhammad that the mother has more right than the father to their children so long as she does not remarry, we see many instances today of women being deprived of their children upon a divorce. There are other instances of scholars upholding the principle of women being forced into marriage, divorced at will, beaten into submission, refused maintenance, and kept from education. In each of these circumstances, a combination of scripture, custom, and interpretation have been used as justification, selec-

---

16. The Hujurat chapter (Qur'an 49) goes in depth into this understanding.

tively omitting Qur'anic mandates that would negate them or hadith that would refute them.[17]

The richness of the Arabic language has been especially perversely used as justification for beating in Qur'an 4:34. That specific verse states that men are the protectors of women, and it goes on to assert that in the case of disagreements severe enough to lead to divorce, men were to first speak with their wives, then deprive them of sex. If the wife were still "disobedient," then the husband had the right of *daraba*, which can be translated as "beaten," "banished," "slapped," or "scolded."[18] Obviously, our modern world is very different from the ancient one in which men claimed supreme authority over women. Yet the acceptance of the man as the "head of the household" is a concept the remains in all patriarchal cultures; this authority is vested in Judaism, Christianity, and Islam, whether or not one agrees with it.

The issue is not one of debating the merit of such authority under religious dictate. Rather, the issue is the many men who call themselves Muslim and in their misogyny claim "beat" as the most accurate definition of *daraba*. Regardless of how many verses call for mercy, compassion, caring, and understanding of their wives (or others in their charge), the unabashed cowardice of men who claim divine right of abuse is stagger-

---

17. For example, Qur'an 58:1–4, regarding penalties on men who cast their wives aside on whim; 4:19, which treats receiving women "against their will" and has been used as analogy for forced marriage; and 16:57–58, banning female infanticide, used in analogy against female homicides outside of criminal cases. See also the hadith found in Bukhari, volume 9, book 92, number 413, "Narrated Abu Said: 'A woman came to Allah's Apostle and said, "O Allah's Apostle! Men (only) benefit by your teachings, so please devote to us from (some of) your time, a day on which we may come to you so that you may teach us of what Allah has taught you." Allah's Apostle said, "Gather on such-and-such a day at such-and-such a place." They gathered and Allah's Apostle came to them and taught them of what Allah had taught him.'" On the treatment of women, see Al-Tirmidhi: "The best of you is one who is best towards his family and I am best towards the family"; "None but a noble man treats women in an honourable manner. And none but an ignoble treats women disgracefully"; and Abu Dawud, book 11, number 2139: "Narrated Mu'awiyah al-Qushayri: 'I went to the Apostle of Allah (pbuh) and asked him: "What do you say (command) about our wives?" He replied: "Give them food what you have for yourself, and clothe them by which you clothe yourself, and do not beat them, and do not revile them."'"

18. Disobedience can mean many things, and this is an area of study in itself. While literalists maintain a woman's total agency is subservient to her husband, others disqualify as disobedience actions contrary to the husband's wishes where her emotional or physical state are in danger. Refusal to accept a second wife or to acquiesce to

ing. It is something both to be ashamed of and to be active in educating the ummah to avoid.

Even where the Qur'an is not used as justification, the Sunnah or hadith are, and to an even worse degree. Because hadith are oral transmissions passed down over centuries, their authentications are varied and do not take precedence over the Qur'an. Yet there are those Muslims who will take an unsound hadith over an interpretation of the Qur'an if it is more beneficial to them. As a spiritual leader, I would like to be very clear that there is no support in the spirit of Islam for things such as "honor killings." This is especially true in modern-day situations that are far removed from the ancient context of tribal warfare, in which custom dictated a truncated version of justice. There are, sadly, too many instances to detail here where the Qur'an has been ill-used to justify incorrect actions. These are not the actions of the righteous people, and as any faith must do, Islam must acknowledge their presence within the larger community.

Another area that catches worldwide attention is that of modesty. The incorrect application and incorrect understanding of the modesty laws— by some Muslims and non-Muslims alike—has led to the widespread, yet mistaken, perception that Islam as a religion oppresses women. In fact, in the recognition that human beings are sexual creatures at times driven by desire, guidance toward mitigating unwanted sexual arousal is provided in Qur'an 24:30–31 for *both* men and women.[19] These passages warn both male and female believers to be modest in their dress and their attitudes, although allowance is made in 24:60 for older women to be less regulated as the verse notes that a woman "past childbearing who does not expect wedlock" may discard her outer clothing.

Groups such as the Taliban, which insist that a woman's modesty is

---

unwanted sexual relations are both examples of this type of "disobedience," although there are many "softer" examples that equally are disqualified as "disobedience" against a husband.

19. Qur'an 24:30–31: "Tell the believing men to lower their gaze and be modest. That is purer for them. Lo! Allah is aware of what they do. And tell the believing women to lower their gaze and be modest, and to display of their adornment only that which is apparent, and to draw their veils over their bosoms, and not to reveal their adornment save to their own husbands or fathers or husbands' fathers, or their sons or their husbands' sons, or their brothers or their brothers' sons or sisters' sons, or their women, or their slaves, or male attendants who lack vigour, or children who know naught of women's nakedness." *The Glorious Qur'an*, Pickthall.

protected only under a burqa, are either deliberately misusing this verse as a way of proscribing women's autonomy and agency, or they are sincerely ill-educated and cannot grasp the meaning of the Arabic. As with most extremists, this misunderstanding of the actual text is both convenient and self-serving. There is no Qur'anic statement that women are not allowed out of their houses, not allowed to drive cars, or not allowed to study. Despite that, we are treated to generous retellings of exactly these circumstances for many women in Muslim-majority lands. There is no theological reason for these behaviors; they are manifestations of male insecurities supported in patriarchates and buttressed by fatwas given by men with limited knowledge who reside in the comfort zone of the status quo. If the true intention of Islam on gender relations were followed in many of these areas, not only would the GNP of those nations rise with the participation of women in the workforce but global extremism would fall, too.

Laws of inheritance are another troublesome aspect of Shari'a application. Traditional culture in place at the time of Qur'anic revelation mandated that men make full economic provision for their womenfolk. Under this understanding, women were left dependent on male agnates with no documented recourse to funds or inheritance in their own right once they were widowed or otherwise lost male protection. Codified laws of inheritance can be found in various Qur'anic suras for the most vulnerable members of the community: women and orphans. For example, verse 4:176 specifies inheritance rights of sisters to property of the deceased, while verses 89:17–20 scold those who do not encourage each other to feed the poor, who disrespect inheritance, and who over-love wealth. The themes of orphans (see 17:34), social welfare (aid to the poor), and proper inheritance distribution show up in the revelations early on. Unfortunately, in many societies today, where we see women being held to the Qur'anic inheritance of half of that of the males, we do not see the comparable commitment to abide by the Qur'anic mandates that men fully provide for their women.[20] This is an example of not only a faulty

---

20. Qur'an 4:7–12: "Unto the men (of a family) belongeth a share of that which parents and near kindred leave, and unto the women a share of that which parents and near kindred leave, whether it be little or much—a legal share.... Allah chargeth you concerning (the provision for) your children: to the male the equivalent of the portion

interpretation of scripture but the willful disregard of it. The same applies for orphans, widows, sisters, and mothers—where they are disinherited or their wealth is going to male agnates instead of to them directly, this contravenes the Qur'an. Often these deviations are due to cultural traditions that never changed and were never properly challenged.

An instance that stirred fear of Shari'a throughout the world was the 1989 fatwa against Salman Rushdie, the celebrated author. The fatwa, issued by an Iranian imam, was based on his adjudication that the author's novel *The Satanic Verses* was blasphemous and insulting to Islam. This issue of blasphemy has reemerged recently with riots by some Muslims in response both to cartoons of Prophet Muhammad in European newspapers and to the release of an amateurish American film online ridiculing him. There have even been calls for the death of apostates.

To be clear, outside of stating a belief in the monotheistic worship of Allah (God) and that Muhammad was the last prophet sent by God in a continuation from Jewish and Christian traditions, Shari'a does not impose any requirement to proselytize—or to punish those who do not choose to follow Islam.[21] Despite that fact, there have been a number of highly publicized accounts of apostates either sentenced to death or executed. The verses in the Qur'an that deal with apostasy or disbelief neither suggest nor condone execution; they state that judgment is for God alone and that those who turn to insurrection against submission to God—not specified as "Islam" and so therefore referring to those who repudiate any Abrahamic faith—are never to be forgiven in the hereafter, nor welcomed in this life.[22] A typical admonition is found in 3:84–88:

---

of two females, and if there be women more than two, then theirs is two-thirds of the inheritance . . . and if he have no son and his parents are his heirs, then to his mother appertaineth the third; and if he have brethren, then to his mother appertaineth the sixth. . . . It is an injunction from Allah. . . . And if a man or a woman have a distant heir (having left neither parent nor child), and he (or she) have a brother or a sister (only on the mother's side) then to each of them twain (the brother and the sister) the sixth, and if they be more than two, then they shall be sharers in the third." *The Glorious Qur'an*, Pickthall.

21. There is mention of discussing the religion in 22:67: "To every people have we appointed rites and ceremonies which they must follow: Let them not then dispute with thee on the matter, but do thou invite (them) to thy Lord: for thou art assuredly on the right way." But this is not a call to proselytization.

22. See verses 3:80–90, 4:137–138, 5:54, and 47:25–28.

> Say (O Muhammad): We believe in Allah and that which is revealed unto us and that which was revealed unto Abraham and Ishmael and Isaac and Jacob and the tribes, and that which was vouchsafed unto Moses and Jesus and the prophets from their Lord. We make no distinction between any of them, and unto Him we have surrendered. And whoso seeketh as religion other than the surrender (to Allah) it will not be accepted from him, and he will be a loser in the hereafter. How shall Allah guide a people who disbelieved after their belief. . . . As for such, their guerdon is that on them rests the curse of Allah and of angels and of men combined. . . . Their doom will not be lightened, neither will they be reprieved.[23]

No verse commands death for an apostate, yet many verses do warn of God's retribution. Context is again necessary, since the persecution advocated against apostates has been supported mainly by hadith, which claim that apostasy is the greatest of sins. Ironically, persecution is the key. During most of the times of the revelations cited, Muslims were fleeing persecution by members of Muhammad's own tribe, the Quraysh. Though more of the general admonishments to keep to monotheism end with descriptions of repercussions to be meted out by God in the next life, some passages directly address those who seek to corrupt the believers or raise insurrections, and even more specifically, as in 2:217, those who were persecuting the nascent Muslim community:

> They question thee (O Muhammad) with regard to warfare in the sacred month. Say: Warfare therein is a great (transgression), but to turn (men) from the way of Allah, and to disbelieve in Him and in the inviolable place of worship, and to expel His people thence, is greater with Allah; for persecution is worse than killing.

Simply put, while there are many warnings to those who would fall into polytheism, there is no Qur'anic commandment to kill those who choose a religion other than Islam.[24] There is also no call for conversions,

---

23. *The Glorious Qur'an*, Pickthall, this verse and the subsequent one.
24. Qur'an 2:256 is one of the most quoted in this respect: "There is no compulsion in religion. The right direction is henceforth distinct from error. And he who rejecteth

forced or otherwise. Although the Islamic religion spread alongside its governmental expansion, the focus of Islam was not military conquest for religious conversion. In the time of Prophet Muhammad, Islam's binding was a unified and strong polity under the greater alliance of God's leadership, rather than the norm of tribal warfare and subjugation to multiple empires. We have historical accounts of various treaties like the Constitution of Medina and the Treaty of Hudaibiyya, under which the Islamic polity entered into full relations with Christians, Jews, Zoroastrians, and even pagan groups. At times, the primary motive for conversion was not alliance with Islam but rebellion against former rulers—as when people contrasted the cruelty or injustice of the Persians, Byzantines, or Sassanids to the more tolerant rule of the invading Muslims, and converted with an eye toward greater autonomy and/or harmony. Those demagogues today who espouse the slogan of "Islam or die" are not espousing Islam but brandishing their own ambitions for power.

Considerations of power bring us to perhaps the most misunderstood and hotly debated aspect of Shari'a: war and judicial matters. Many non-Muslims believe violent aggression and terrorism are sanctioned by Shari'a and that implementation of Shari'a laws are tantamount to the dismantling of the US Constitution and US penal codes in order to make way for the Code of Hammurabi. This is not the case. There are similar guidelines in both Islamic and Judaic texts regarding witnesses, forms of evidence, and penalties. Judicial regulations found in the Tractate Makkos of the Talmud are similar to the application of Shari'a for Muslims, and both Halacha and Shari'a rest on a foundation of scripture. As supported by the Qur'an, the Sunnah, and the analytical arguments, both war and all forms of judiciary repercussion are meant 1) only for Muslim believers, 2) only in situations that are clearly demarcated and supported by theology, and 3) not to conflict with civil law.

The exact discourse between textual literality, analysis, and cultural interchange will vary for individuals based on their circumstances, yet in no case do any of the Qur'anic commandments apply to non-Muslims, nor are they expected to. A Muslim living in Indiana and therefore ex-

---

false deities and believeth in Allah hath grasped a firm handhold which will never break." *The Glorious Qur'an*, Pickthall.

pected to follow United States law is *not* supported in stoning his wife according to a literalist Qur'anic interpretation of the penalty for adultery, even if he has the Islamically required four witnesses, a videotape of the act, confessions from both parties, and fatwas from literalist imams at his disposal. In order to adhere to Shari'a, our fictional Indiana-resident Muslim would need to rely on qiyas, the previously mentioned method of applying rationalist interpretation and analogies from precedent cases onto the contemporary case being considered. In using qiyas, the laws of the land in which the believer finds him/herself are taken into consideration, and in many cases the civic law of the land supersedes any literalist interpretation of the Qur'an. It must be recognized that there are far-right members of the ulama and strict literalists who do not accept that civic law can supersede a judgment as stated in the Qur'an as a state of true Islamic living for a believer. This is the case for most extremists of any faith, and at odds with the greater Muslim community. Yet regardless of the level of literalist interpretation possible, Shari'a provides guidelines applicable only to Muslims, and these guidelines are fluid since they are also based on Muslim consensus.

CONCLUSION

Shari'a is the entire framework of moral, ethical, theological, and legal teachings of Islam. The fundamental and overriding purpose of Shari'a is to ensure individual and social welfare in this life. Classical understanding and the theological basis of the Shari'a focus on the fostering of family life, detailing obligations to support oneself and those one is responsible for, guidance for healthy eating and living, child care, and communal interaction (including judicial structures). Shari'a ranges from admonitions on wrongdoing and the prohibition of intoxicants to the encouragement of religious, ethical, moral, and intellectual knowledge.[25] Laws regulating commerce and transactions between people, in order to ensure fair dealings and economic justice, are also detailed. Proper following of the Shari'a is meant to guarantee self-determination and to prevent oppres-

---

25. A popular hadith attributable to Prophet Muhammad says, "Seek knowledge, even in China." Another hadith, quoted from Abu Bakr, says Prophet Muhammad advised the best life for one to have was that of a scholar; if not a scholar, then a student; and if not a student, then a listener.

sion, usually known as *huquuq* (rights). This refers to the responsibility of both the ruled and the rulers to establish permanent institutions designed to facilitate broad-based political participation by every member of a polity in its governance so that they can help determine both their own immediate well-being and their long-term destiny.

Respect for human dignity is at the core of all Islamic law and pertains to governmental and community applications as well as individual ones. Knowing each other in brotherhood is a contribution to communal well-being; understanding each other is the next step; and helping each other in kindness is the solidification of brotherly bonds. Qur'an 2:136–137 reinforces those bonds in the worship of the one God:

> Say ye: We believe in God, and the revelation given to us, and to Abraham, Ismail, Isaac, Jacob, and the Tribes, and that given to Moses and Jesus, and that given to (all) Prophets from their Lord: We make no difference between one and another of them and we bow to God. So if they believe as ye believe, they are indeed on the right path.

Individual dignity comes from righteous actions, and these in turn reinforce huquuq.

While the classical understanding and sources of Shari'a have been examined here, we cannot ignore the sad reality that "Shari'a" is commonly misunderstood by non-Muslims and sometimes incorrectly adapted by Muslims. The core foundation of the Shari'a, the Qur'an, does not change. The second foundation of the Shari'a, the Sunnah, has canonical and accepted traditions. The processes of qiyas and ijtihad in consideration of istihan and maslaha are fluid and based on contemporary issues. New adaptations remain beholden to the Qur'an and the Sunnah and the spirit of Islamic theology, but their specificities are malleable. The demands of some on the Far Right, that one say only the things said before, behave in accordance with the established opinions, or blindly accept the decisions of organized groups or the government of the day, seek to foreclose all possibilities of conceptual breakthroughs and enrichments of both the spiritual and temporal resources of the community.

Like Jewish and Christian canon law, Islamic law is interpreted differently due to cultural and material influences. The incorporation of Western civil law alongside traditional religious courts in many Muslim majority countries during the last two centuries has been a positive step. It has shown that Shari'a is a living thing in its legalistic guidelines and has implications beyond theology into nationalism and statehood. In the hands of moderates, religious law can be reserved and even liberal. In the hands of post-Enlightenment readers of philosophy, religious law becomes associated mainly with ritual, theology, or history and no longer regulates society or the state. There is no exclusion of the civil laws of the country a Muslim lives in simply because she or he also adheres to Shari'a. There is also no reason not to adhere to both without conflict.

Civil law and Shari'a can and should be collaborative and complementary, as both seek to support community living, peace, and stability. Shari'a is overwhelmingly concerned with *personal* religious observance such as prayer and fasting, and not with national laws. It is not static, and there is no one thing called "Shari'a"; a variety of Muslim communities exist, and each understands Shari'a in its own way. Just as in the United States, where laws vary from state to state, there is tremendous variance in the interpretation and implementation of Islamic law in Muslim societies. The Islamic ummah contains over one billion people, with interpretations by state, country, madhab, and custom. Fiqh—not just as a legal understanding but in a broader sense—is just as necessary, as is ijtihad, to grasp the most important meanings of a text.

In recent years, liberal movements within Islam have questioned the relevance and applicability of Shari'a from a variety of perspectives. Turkey has a constitution that is strongly secular, and several of the countries with the largest Muslim populations, including Indonesia, Bangladesh, and Pakistan, have largely secular constitutions and laws, with Islamic provisions mainly in family law. Many countries of the Middle East and North Africa maintain a dual system of secular courts alongside religious courts, with the religious courts primarily regulating marriage and inheritance. The culture, current circumstance, and psychology of the persons interpreting the texts all influence Shari'a, and when prevailing culture intrudes overmuch into an interpretation, the Islamic veracity tends to dissipate.[26]

---

26. The 20 CE Egyptian reformer Sayyid Qutb, for example, wrote his Qur'anic *tafsir* (exegesis) while he was in jail, and his writing has been much cited for its pronounced bent regarding waging war against oppressors.

This issue of culture versus theology is one that needs close examination and much more discussion. In many societies, cultural traditions outside of Islamic theology have taken root under the guise of religion, obfuscating correct practice. In many cases, these traditions have been detrimental to society and have reversed gains, especially for women, granted by Islam in the seventh century.[27]

Around the world, we can find numerous examples of people following so-called Islamic mandates that are, in fact, contradicting Qur'anic teachings. A lack of education and misguided fervor are to blame. Islam is meant to minimize the negative impact of cultural mores extant in any given area, and to provide for safety and kindness, comfort and self-dignity for all. It is the responsibility of spiritual leaders to correct these deviations from the correct path and the responsibility of Muslims to educate themselves on the Qur'anic guidance and intent that should inform their daily practice.

---

27. For example: "Islamic law accorded women a number of rights and privileges commensurate with the general respect for human dignity, responsibility and equality, rights and privileges which eclipsed those held by women in many (including western) pre-modern societies. The right for example of a married woman to own and inherit property in her own right, property which was not at the disposal of her husband. On the other hand, a number of debilitating social customs were able to attach themselves to Muslim values . . . either through the law itself or through popular interpretation of legal principles. So for example, while the custom of ritual excising of the external genitalia of women was never universally practiced in the Islamic world, those near eastern Muslims who did practice it were able to perpetuate and disseminate it by describing it as a means of protecting the sexual honor of Muslim women." Jonathan Berkey, *The Formation of Islam: Religion and Society in the Near East, 600–1800* (Cambridge, UK: Cambridge University Press, 2003), 122.

PART THREE

Our Shared Future

CHAPTER THIRTEEN

What Israel Means to Jews

RABBI MARC SCHNEIER

The state of Israel is not a sixty-five-year-old political aspiration of the Jewish people. It is the very core of Jewish theology. It has been our preoccupation, our magnificent obsession, over the course of three thousand years. Yet, regrettably, it is treated as if it is solely the result of some modern-day political movement. Just as Muslim clerics ask that I accept and recognize their core beliefs and conditions, they need to understand and to appreciate that the Land of Israel is at the very foundation of our religion.

That misunderstanding, even denial, of Israel's centrality to Judaism is equivalent to an attack on our other essential principles—be it belief in one god or our dietary laws. For us, the Land of Israel is a religious concept of great magnitude. It is not self-determination or nationalism in a general sense that we consider sacred; it is our ancestral land. For instance, when Theodore Herzl resurrected the Zionist movement in the late nineteenth century, it was suggested that the Jewish people settle in Uganda as a solution to the world crisis of anti-Semitism and Jewish persecution. The proposal was debated and voted on at the Zionist Congress, and it was overwhelmingly rejected. The Uganda proposal was an affront to our beliefs and our value system.

For more than two thousand years, since the exile of the Jewish people from the Holy Land, our synagogues have been physically oriented toward Jerusalem, and we have prayed three times a day for the rebuilding of Jerusalem. The groom under the wedding canopy breaks a glass to recall the shattered ruins of the Temple in Jerusalem. We conclude the Passover seder with the prayer "Next year in Jerusalem." The Land of Israel is the manifestation of our dreams.

One often hears Muslims ask, "Why are we paying the cost for the tragedy of the Holocaust?" That question can only be put forth if one believes that the Land of Israel, or the return to Israel, is a modern-day phenomenon. It's not. The question is not the cost of the Holocaust. It's the cost of more than two thousand years of persecution, of subjugation, of coercion; two-thousand years of Crusades and pogroms. We have been on a two-thousand-year quest to return to our Holy Land. Focusing on the Holocaust is to take our belief in the Land of Israel out of religious context.

Even when it is voiced by people who present themselves as sympathetic to Jews and to Israel, I question the proposition that Israel was a result of the Holocaust. I sometimes wonder how much sympathy the world actually has for the Jewish people. I cannot believe that seventy years after the Holocaust we have seen enough resurgence of anti-Semitism, especially in Europe, that a rabbi was arrested in Germany for performing a circumcision, that Jews are leaving France to escape the hatred from the Right and the Left, that the Jews in an entire city in Sweden left in fear of violence. The Holocaust was the final straw precipitating the end of a two-thousand-year campaign to return to our homeland. And even Holocaust deniers like Iran's Mahmoud Ahmadinejad are only supporting my argument. If the Holocaust never happened, then why was Israel created? Because Moses led his people out of Egypt to the Promised Land.

During the years of my interfaith work, I have had the argument about Israel on Arab television programs and at Muslim-Jewish conferences. "We're not anti-Semitic; we're anti-Zionist," they say. But if you're anti-Zionist, you *are* anti-Semitic. You cannot divorce the Jewish homeland from the Jewish people. It's like saying, "I'm not anti-Semitic; I'm just anti-kashrut, or anti-Sabbath, or anti-God." Israel is not political. It's theological. The city of Jerusalem is not political. It's theological. The topography, the geography, the city-state may be political, but the destination, the venue, the locale are theological.

I don't see the Jewish people as a nation, per se. I see Judaism as a religion, and we are the people of that religion. People who want to convert to Judaism don't need to come from Israel or move to it. But part of having this religion is having a homeland. You don't have a similar belief about land in Christianity, or even in Islam. You don't read in the Koran that Saudi Arabia or Iraq is a holy land to Muslims. You don't find in the New Testament that Rome or the Vatican is holy land to Christians. But there are seven hundred fifty references to Jerusalem in the Bible and more than two thousand references to Jerusalem in the Hebrew scriptures.

So, land has a greater hierarchy in Judaism than it does in other religions. Christianity is not about land, and Islam is not about land, but Judaism is all about holy land. We speak of a Diaspora; they do not. Christianity and Islam have capitals, but those capitals don't define the religion. Christians do make pilgrimages to Rome, and Muslims do have their hajj to Mecca and Medina, but those attachments are not to the cities but rather to specific churches and mosques and holy places.

The practical challenge for Jews today is that we do not know what the authentic definition of our land is. Drawing on our religious texts, some scholars say it extends from the Jordan River to the Mediterranean Sea, others from the Euphrates to the Mediterranean Sea. Some say it includes Jordan, Syria, Judea, and Samaria, while others say it includes just Judea and Samaria. There have been so many different formulations that there is not a single, uniformly accepted definition. At best, we have an approximation. Moreover, we have a set of geopolitical boundaries—the various borders drawn in 1948, in 1967, at the Oslo Accords.

The uncertainty of the exact extent of the Land of Israel can be an opportunity as well as a challenge, however. It can provide some of the pragmatic flexibility required in coming to a permanent resolution with the Palestinians. One of the reasons we can trade land for peace, in terms of my own belief, is that God has many names—Adonai, Elohim. And, according to the Talmud, he also has the name Shalom. Peace. He doesn't have the name Land. So peace is clearly a priority for His people. We have to arrive at a balance of land and peace. We have to achieve a fusion.

One of the dangers of lower-case orthodox fundamentalist belief in any religion is that people see things only in terms of absolutes. Those who say, "This is *my* land," those who speak in absolute terms, are expressing a terribly dangerous belief when they are referring to a small and contested area like Israel and the Palestinian territories. Jews will say, "God unequivocally promised it to us." Muslims will say, "God unequivocally promised it to us." Christians will say, "God unequivocally promised it to us." Needless to say, some of the most horrific wars in history have been fought because of such absolutism. But just as we Jews need to fight for the Other, we also need to be empathetic to the Other. We need to recognize that these other religions have claims—I'm not saying equal claims—in terms of the sanctity and the sacredness of the land to their respective beliefs.

There can be no avoiding the Israel-Palestine issue in working on Muslim-Jewish coexistence. It is critical to address the issue precisely because it is the one most likely to divide us. Once you can move past the Israel-Palestine issue, you can be more sensitive and open-minded to the claims of the other side. You can listen to what the other side is saying. You can appreciate that the other side has rights, too.

This is not a one-way street. Jews have as much to gain as do Muslims in engaging the Israel-Palestine issue, rather than avoiding it for fear of the rancor it might stir. It is critical for us as Jews to be able to tell our Muslim friends and colleagues that the Land of Israel is part of our belief. We cannot remove the Land of Israel; we cannot divorce it from our theology. Any Muslim involved in coexistence work needs to recognize that, or else the rhetoric of coexistence is, finally, empty. It would be as if I as a Jew and a rabbi were to tell a Muslim, I support you—except your muezzin call to prayer is annoying, your praying five times a day is disruptive, your halal restaurants are an eyesore.

I know that there are Muslims—as well as some Christians and even some Jews, both very secular ones on the left and anti-Zionist Orthodox on the right—who ask why Israel is so essential to Jewish life and the Judaic faith. They contend that the Jewish people have flourished in the Diaspora; they say that Jewish culture and religion as we know them today are the product of the Diaspora; or they say you cannot have Zion without the coming of the Messiah.

To all of them, I would respond: You call the Diaspora survival? Anyone who claims that the Jewish people survived for two thousand years without the Land of Israel should be ashamed of him- or herself and needs a Jewish history lesson. We became perennial scapegoats, objects of oppression. Our persecution was of a magnitude that the world has never seen. And we still suffer from that legacy, despite the creation of the State of Israel—or, as I call it, the third Jewish Commonwealth. It's only since the establishment of the State of Israel that the pride and honor and dignity and self-respect and self-esteem of the Jewish people have been restored. I cannot conceive of what it must have been like to live as a Jew before seventy years ago—not to know if you'd be living in the same town tomorrow, not to know when the next pogrom would arrive.

Then there is the argument from many Muslims that Israel and Palestine can be one unitary state. Some make that argument out of misplaced idealism, others out of a brutal desire to turn Jews back into a minority that can be subjugated. Both versions of the argument deliberately ignore some essential Jewish truths. Israel to Jews is not what Israel is to other religions. It's like my saying, "OK, why can't we have a unitary magistrate over Mecca and Medina?" That would be ridiculous. It's not Zionist propaganda to say that Jerusalem has been our holy city for thousands of years. That doesn't mean Islamic institutions in Jerusalem should not have their own autonomy, or that certain neighborhoods in East Jerusalem that are predominantly Arab and Muslim should not have their own self-determination, particularly as part of a two-state solution. But every religion has its hierarchy of holy places. And those ground rules were established thousands of years ago, not on May 14, 1948.

There is a unique role that theologians and religious leaders can play in the Israel-Palestine issue. I do not believe that they can resolve it alone, but they can complement the efforts of political leaders. The political leaders need to come up with some kind of treaty, some kind of agreement; they need to determine how to divide the land. Religious leaders, though, could serve a twofold purpose. First, any agreement can only be implemented with the force of religious leaders behind it, because I see the conflict as theological, not political. Let's say that one day we arrive at some division of Jerusalem, or Judea and Samaria, and on both sides we have fundamentalists saying, "This is against our belief; this is against our convictions." You will need religious leaders to step in and support the plan and say unequivocally, "This is consistent with our belief system, our value system." And even before that, religious leaders can lay the foundation of trust so that Muslims and Jews can understand and appreciate each other.

I have no illusions about the difficulty that Muslim and Jewish religious leaders will have in productively broaching the subject of Israel and Palestine. We have tended either to avoid it altogether or to come into immediate conflict over it. Personally, I've had some very disappointing, very discouraging episodes. I particularly recall an appearance I made on the Lebanese Broadcasting Corporation, viewed in many Arab states, for a program about the Middle East. One of the other guests was a sheik, who was speaking from Jeddah in Saudi Arabia. Our subject was Jerusalem in the Islamic, Judaic, and Christian traditions. At one point in the show, I made a reference to the Holy Temple in Jerusalem and David's conquest of the city, and the sheik said that there is no proof there was a temple.

In spite of dispiriting experiences like that one, today I am very comfortable conversing with Muslim clerics and imams. I don't agree with them on everything. But I've arrived at a place where I can agree to disagree without being disagreeable. And that is why I keep doing this work. There needs to be a natural discourse between Jews and Muslims, because we have not trusted each other.

For every two steps we move forward, even if we go one step back, we're still moving forward. I'm not saying that we are where we want to be. But if you contrast 2013 to 2003 or to 1993, it's night and day. There's been tremendous growth in Muslim-Jewish dialogue, and hopefully we'll be able at least to set a standard of what should be. People sometimes ask me, "If Martin Luther King were alive today, how would he feel about the state of black-white relations in the United States?" and I say he'd be overjoyed. In spite of some residual racism, there is mutual respect between blacks and whites. I'd like to see that between Muslims and Jews. And if we achieve that, then we're on the way to the Promised Land of Muslim-Jewish reconciliation.

CHAPTER FOURTEEN

Anti-Semitism

IMAM SHAMSI ALI

Anti-Semitism has a long and unfortunate history, with examples that are widely known as well as more subtle slights that Jews have endured from intolerant and divisive communities. I would like to clearly and strongly state that I unequivocally denounce anti-Semitism, its ideology, its misguided progress, its denigration of humanity, and its utter ignorance. In my dealing with Marc and the Jewish world, I am struck by the ferocity of rabid anti-Semites, despite the atrocities of the last hundred years. As a Muslim, I find anti-Semitism in general offensive and abhorrent; as a Muslim, I am also most frequently identified with a group of people who are not expected to feel that way. It is regrettable that to be a Muslim connotes being anti-Semitic. While I can testify myself that this is not true for the greater Islamic community, I would like to specifically address the extremists in my community who feel that anti-Semitism is justified.

The Islamic perspective on all peoples is inclusion. In the Qur'an (49:13), God says,

> O mankind! We created you from a single (pair) of a male and a female, and made you into nations and tribes, that ye may know each other (not that ye may despise [each other]). Verily the most honored of you in the sight of God is (he who is) the most righteous of you. And God has full knowledge and is well acquainted (with all things).

This inclusiveness is the foundation of human interaction—the universality of human beings, the teaching that we came from the same mother and father, that we are all brothers and sisters. Prophet Muhammad came with this message from God, and we not only believe his message was universal but that it was the same message that previous messengers had come to humanity with: the calling of all people to recognize they are of the same family, created by one God, to share this life and the hereafter, in goodness.

Based on these teachings and beliefs, I have a very strong conviction that I am obligated to reach out to my fellow human being in connection and cooperation. And to start that process, we must build understanding. In the verse I quoted above, God used the concept *taaruf*—which means knowing one another, a sense of mutuality. In order for me to be understood as a Muslim, I, as a Muslim, have to understand others.

Prophet Muhammad made many statements that affect me personally. In his last pilgrimage, he gave an extraordinary speech. It's called *Khutbatul-Wada'*—the farewell sermon. He gave it in the Uranah valley of Mount Arafat. And one of his statements, well recorded in historical Islam, is this: "Indeed your Lord is One, your Father is One, there is no superiority of an Arab or a non-Arab, except *piety, righteousness.*" (Emphasis added.) This echoes our earlier discussion of the virtues of the chosen people and the Kheir Ummah, and underlines the shared ideals of goodness expressed as fealty to our Creator.

Kindness and equanimity to each other is an idea reinforced by the Sunnah. A small but very revealing incident happened in the Prophet's lifetime. A noble Arab man had an argument with a former slave who had become a Muslim. The former slave's name was Bilal bin-Rabah, and the Arab called him "son of a black woman." In fact, Bilal's mother was from Ethiopia, but the words were intended as a racial slur. So Bilal bin-Rabah was hurt, and he reported the incident to the Prophet. And the Prophet told the noble, "You are a man who is still holding ignorance." The statement is certainly powerful. It did not matter to the Prophet that he was addressing an elite person and defending a former slave. Prophet Muhammad's teachings hold that every person is to build equal connection with others, as we are equal creations of God.

In addition, for me, there is in Islam a special community that is highly respected called Ahl al Kitab, "People of the Book." That term refers to people who follow religions that had revelations, like Judaism and Christianity, and (according to some Muslim scholars) Zoroastrianism as well. Not only does the Qur'an praise them and acknowledge their books and their prophets, but we acknowledge that their books and their prophets are part of our own faith.

So it is not solely the social interactions I've had in the United States that led me, as a human being, to build relations with Jews. It is because my faith encourages me to build this relationship with people whom I respect for their religion. Those who profess to follow Islam and can still accept anti-Semitism are not following the Qur'an, the hadith, or the Sunnah. What many use as an excuse to allow anti-Semitism, even if not to directly engage in it, is based on animosities that arose from the time of the founding of the first Muslim state, in the seventh century CE. When the Prophet migrated to Medina, there were three communities: pagan, Christian, and Jewish, each of which had been there for a very long time. After building a mosque, the second thing the Prophet did was to create a binding agreement for the people of Medina, which is known today as the Constitution of Medina, or the Medina Charter. In the process, he gathered representatives of these communities and delineated their rights and responsibilities in order to be treated equally as members of the polity of Medina. The Medina Charter specifically addresses the Jewish community of Medina several times. It recognizes that the Jews have their own religion, which does not make them separate from the unity of the state; it notes that enemies of the Jews of the pact will not be helped by any member of the unified state; and it specifies by tribe name the equality of standing they have with all other members of the contract.[1] The agreement between the communities held that everyone in Medina should unite to protect it from attack by outsiders. This was meant to unite the disparate tribes under one polity regardless of religious differences, in order to ensure security and peace.

---

1. There are various interpretations of the Medina Charter that shift the number of articles from forty-seven to sixty-three. The sixty-three outlined articles in detail can be found in Dr. Muhammad Tahir-ul-Qadri, *The Constitution of Medina: 63 Constitutional Articles* (London: Minhaj-ul-Qur'an Publications, 2012), http://www.academia .edu. See articles 20, 30–40, and 58 especially.

Later on, when there was an attack on the nascent state, some members, including some Jews, helped the groups attacking Medina, and so the Prophet, who was the governmental leader of Medina, had to administer justice. Mistrust between political factions within the coexisting polity simmered, with each group wondering if the other would one day betray them for personal gain. After Prophet Muhammad died, there was a fight in a city called Khaber, which is near Medina, and the Jews were expelled. To this day, you hear certain Muslims use the slogan "*Yaa Khaebar, Yaa Khaebar, Jaeshu Muhammadin saofa ya'uud*" ("O Khaber, O Khaber, the army of Muhammad will return")—to express their animosity and hatred toward the Jewish community.

These events have been used in subjective interpretations of history to sow further discord by Jews and Muslims alike. What the Prophet did wasn't religiously motivated, much as either side might like it to be. The Prophet was reacting to disloyalty within the Medinese community. As temporal governor, he was adjudicating against those who sought to undermine the fledgling polity—and this extended to Qurayshi tribesmen who claimed to be Muslim but worked against Medina as well. This distinction is often lost or deliberately ignored, and as a result, this dark part of history—Jews being punished, Jews being expelled, Jews leaving willingly—has exerted far too much influence on the relationship between Muslims and Jews. It has served as an excuse to believe the Other is the enemy and that such a belief is an intractable one. In most cases of tense coexistence, community anxieties flourish through fear, and the Muslim-Jewish tension from the time of Medina's founding is no different. This fear encourages negative actions, hate crimes, and ill feelings, and as much as it may seem to make anti-Semitism acceptable to an extreme Muslim group, it also serves to make Islamophobia acceptable to an extreme Jewish group. Needless to say, Marc and I are united in our rejection of either philosophy.

I have had many encounters with anti-Semitism in my community that have more to do with fear and/or mistrust than with hate, though too many scenarios seem to have Israel at their core. I still remember that when I wanted to visit Rabbi Schneier's synagogue at the first twinning, a Muslim man came to me and said, "Are you serious? You cannot trust the Jews. They will not open the door to you. They will not respect you." I asked him why, and he replied, "Look at history; they can never be trusted." I asked him to give me some examples, and the examples he chose all had to do with Israel. I pointed this out, asking, "These examples are about Israel. Tell me some examples about Jews." And he said again, "They will not respect you. They think they are chosen. People say you are selling out the Palestinian cause."

That mindset must be answered. At that time I told this man that the Qur'an talks about the children of Jacob, and that indeed *means* Jews. It praises them highly. And on the subject of being chosen, I talk about how in the Qur'an, we talk about the Kheir Ummah, the notion of Muslims as the "best nation." How do we explain that concept to people who think we are saying that Muslims must be superior to all other religions?

Many Muslims believe Jews are not genuine about building connections. "They hate you," they say; "You cannot believe it even when they are smiling." The most common problematic attitude about Jews in the Muslim community is the thinking that all Jews approve of every policy Israel has in the Middle East. This is not only very harmful; it is unrealistic. I'm sure not all Israeli policies are supported by Jews worldwide, or for that matter by all the Jews in Israel. I find I need to explain that "Jews" are not a homogenous community—not religiously and not in their political views—just as the Muslim world is not homogenous.

It is also important for Muslims to recognize that Israel's existence is not simply the result of the Holocaust. Israel is not a punishment inflicted on innocent Muslims for the crimes committed by Christians in Europe. From a religious standpoint, we know the history of the Jewish people in the Holy Land. That goes back thousands of years before the Holocaust. So when Iran's president Mahmoud Ahmadinejad, for example, connects the Holocaust and Israel, it is baseless. He wants to offer the world a viewpoint of "Why, when Europeans kill the Jews, do you take revenge against the Palestinians?" That kind of statement furthers tensions between both sides. We need to get rid of that type of rhetoric.

Muslims as individuals, especially those of us who are religious or political leaders, must take a stand against crimes based on discrimination, including anti-Semitism. When Hamas was holding the Israeli soldier Gilad Shalit captive, I signed a letter with ten other prominent Muslims—imams, professors, and the two Muslim members of the US

Congress, Keith Ellison and André Carson—to ask for his release. Why? To reiterate the first point I made in this chapter, that Islam teaches that *all* human beings are brothers and sisters. When they are in the position of being helpless, they need our help. The Prophet said, "Help your brothers, either the oppressed or the oppressors." One of his companions asked, "How should we help the oppressor?" The Prophet said, "Take his hand, so he cannot oppress." So I see this person being held, and he is helpless. For me, as the Qur'an and also the Torah tell us, killing one person is like killing all humanity. I don't see the numbers of prisoners on each side. I see all of humanity. And I hope by releasing Gilad Shalit, the people on the other side will realize their moral obligation to release their prisoners as well. I am not trading in idealistic moral arguments—we all know there are certain people who represent viable threats and who are held as prisoners in any conflict. But the idea of keeping someone imprisoned solely on the basis of his or her beliefs being different, when the underlying universal teachings are the same, is nothing but corrosive.

I felt a big effect on my soul when I went to Yad Hashem, the Holocaust memorial museum in Jerusalem. In one section, the room is darkened, and you hear the sounds of children talking, as if these are the voices of the children killed by the Nazis. I came out crying. I have five children of my own. How could people do this to helpless children? I cannot imagine how human beings can be so heartless.

Why should I cry for Jewish children? Why should I care about what anti-Semitism did to the Jews of Europe? Because I believe that the killing of Jews, especially children, is no different from the killing of any human beings, be they in Israel, Palestine, Asia, or Europe. In the simplest sense, I could also say that it is because today you may be lucky and tomorrow you may not. The Holocaust happened to the Jews yesterday, but who is to say it would not happen to Muslims tomorrow? One has only to think about Bosnia, Chechnya, or Kashmir to know that genocidal crimes of the type that arose from anti-Semitism are not restricted in scope. And why would we people of faith not band together against any form of genocide, be it in Sierra Leone or Myanmar, Rwanda or Cambodia? If at my core I feel that as human beings we must unite to protect all innocent beings, then on a spiritual level I feel even more strongly that our God commands us to help each other, to respect each other, and to help end oppression wherever it lives. As God spoke through Prophet Muhammad in the last sermon, His mercy is for all God's children.

———

Certainly, there have been challenges to advancing the work we have done between the Jewish and Muslim peoples. When I was in Jerusalem in February 2012, someone emailed me with an attachment. It was a copy of a flyer stating that I was a Jewish agent. It was being sent around New York, to mosques and other Muslim places, as a warning against me and my work. I have faced this type of attack many times, but still I trust that people know that what I am doing is for the benefit of all. When the news came out about the New York Police Department spying on Muslims, there were calls for Muslims to boycott any cooperation or involvement with the NYPD. I took another path, that of engagement. I sat down with the police commissioner and made suggestions, including, for example, intensifying the NYPD's training in Muslim culture and appointing ten Muslims to an advisory council. And the police commissioner has done those things. I see engagement as the better method; I see my way has borne fruit.

Of course, it is disturbing to be criticized by members of my own religious community. It is disheartening on spiritual and personal levels; at times it is dangerous; and on a broader level, it is frustrating, because I know that these misguided ideas serve to decelerate and obstruct work toward peace. But I am aggressive about doing good, and I will continue to do what I think is right. Sometimes when people do interfaith work, they are so careful, they worry about everything. I know the risk of working with the Jewish community because of the level of misunderstanding in both the Jewish and Muslim worlds. But as a Muslim following the guidance of God as set down in the Qur'an and following the example of Prophet Muhammad as learned from the hadith, my philosophy is to continue doing what I see as good and let God be the judge. I see no difference between anti-Semitism and Islamophobia. Each is a hurtful, denigrating, and dissociative mindset that is generated by fear, misinformation, and sadness. The desire to find justice for real or imagined wrongs and to mete out punishment for them to a generalized scapegoat group is a base one, though common to all human beings. In New York recently, a man was caught after killing three men of Middle Eastern descent, shouting anti-Semitic and anti-Muslim slogans against them. There was no personal wrong that he was trying to avenge and no good that he expected to come from his action; he was just a person filled with hate who found convenient targets in "Middle Easterners." This type of malevolence is never sated, perpetuating an infinite cycle of ignorance and anger that only feeds on itself. Hate for another is usually an easy excuse for the hater to forgive something lacking in him- or herself. The only antidote is for Jews and Muslims to unite against both anti-Semitism and Islamophobia in brotherhood and friendship, and to combat ignorance with knowledge and hate with love.

Happily, there are many examples of antidotes to hate in the contemporary world. One such example is that of Dr. Emanuel Bronner, a Jew who escaped Germany before the Nazis killed his parents. While in the United States he was committed to an insane asylum but escaped and then founded a million-dollar soap business. All his products are socially conscious, and his number-one slogan is that all the prophets (including Prophet Muhammad) bring revelation from the same God, and that we are all brothers and sisters under that God. (The soap labels declare "One for All! All for One!." His passion for this philosophy was the main reason people thought he was insane.) One of his company's projects is to import olives from a Palestinian/Israeli collaborative, which has improved the material lives of the participants and enabled them to unite over something other than conflict. Anyone who survived the Holocaust would have a reason to look for a target for their hurt and anger and loss. But Emanuel Bronner was a survivor who instead sought to make the world more peaceful and collaborative, and by peace and friendship, he succeeded. Another example is that of Hassan Askari, a young Muslim man who came to the defense of a Jewish group being attacked on the New York City subway. The reason he gave for defending the man in the group was that we are all brothers under God, and it was his Muslim duty to defend people who needed his help. I like to think that there are more people like this in the world than we realize—they just don't get as much media coverage as the negative stereotypes do.

Supporting people against the injustice done to them by those who slander their faith is a common right that deserves to be upheld by all people of faith. No true follower of God has the right to take happiness, safety, or peace, much less life, from another human being. Those who fear God believe this is strictly God's purview and that we as humans must account for ourselves and our individual actions on Judgment Day. This means that we must act to the best of our own abilities, to be good, righteous, and to live cleanly and morally. As beautifully expressed by Prophet Muhammad: People are but one body; if any part of the body is afflicted with pain, the rest of the body will feel pain as well.

As a Muslim, I experience the bitterness of Islamophobia in our society. And as I don't want this to happen to me, I also don't want it to happen to anyone else. Anti-Semitism and Islamophobia are two different names but one in their evil nature. And so it is important for both Muslim and Jewish communities to face down the evil tendencies in our midst. We all need to address the inequalities and injustices in the world, the scars that need to be healed, and the undeniable fact that we are all in this together.

CHAPTER FIFTEEN

Why Jews Should Care about Islamophobia

RABBI MARC SCHNEIER

I got involved in coexistence work for very pragmatic and very practical reasons. It became quite evident that in a world of 14 million Jews and 1.4 billion Muslims these two communities cannot remain in a state of conflict, of ever-escalating hostility. As Jews, the numbers are against us. We have to find a path to narrow the attitudinal divide that separates the two communities.

But in a deeper way, my belief in building bridges, in making alliances, goes back to Jewish responsibility and tradition. Or maybe what I mean is not Jewish responsibility but the responsibility of Jews. As I've pointed out in chapter 11, the traditional Judaic point of view is to help the stranger, indeed to love the stranger. Just to reiterate briefly, that injunction means to love the stranger who is of a different religion or sexual orientation, or who could be a different color. That is the great calling. In the Torah, we are commanded to do that thirty-six times. We are supposed to protect those who are under attack, persecuted, or misunderstood. We Jews demonstrated that commitment during the civil rights struggle of the 1950s and 1960s. And I see the modern challenge as being Muslim-Jewish reconciliation.

The Israeli-Palestinian conflict may be the elephant in the room, as I've discussed at length in chapter 13, but it is not the end to this Muslim-Jewish conflict. If Israel makes peace with the Palestinians tomorrow, you are still going to have conflict. You are still going to have the question, "Can we trust the Other?" The bottom line is that Jews and Muslims do not trust each other, not from the textual, cultural, or historical point of view. There is a lack of trust because there is a lack of knowledge. We don't know each other's our traditions, customs, and practices. That is the hard part about loving the stranger—getting to know the stranger.

In the half century since the Second Vatican Council, we have seen major progress in the relationship between world Jewry and the Roman Catholic Church, culminating in Pope John Paul II's visit to the Western Wall and Yad Vashem. The rise of so-called Christian Zionism among evangelical Christians—while not without its drawbacks in terms of their opposition to the kind of two-state solution between Israel and Palestine that I favor—has also done much to repair a historically fraught relationship between American Jews and fundamentalist, born-again Christians.

Yet there is a stronger, more specific textual basis for mutual religious respect between Jews and Muslims than between Jews and Christians. Islam is a monotheistic religion. There are no symbols or statues or icons that Jews would consider an affront. If anything, synagogues have more religious ornamentation than do mosques. The normative Judaic belief, certainly within Orthodox Jewry, is that a Jew cannot enter a church but a Jew can enter a mosque. Christianity is a form of idolatry; Islam is not. A Jew can go as far as to pray in a mosque.

Judaism is very text-oriented, as is Islam. It is clear to me that Muhammad saw Islam as the continuation of Judaism; even the dynamic of having a written law and an oral law is similar. Dietary laws, circumcision, praying five times (instead of three times) a day, the concept of one God—it's very similar to Judaism. Whenever I chant *Aleinu*, I appreciate anew that the prayer's central declaration—*bayom hahu*, God will be One and His name will be One—is the Jewish contribution to world religion. And when it comes to Islam, there is no question that Judaism is the mother religion. Christianity, in contrast, is a replacement theology, both literally and figuratively a new testament based on a new covenant. Muhammad never referred to a new testament. The Qur'an takes our forefathers and raises them up on a pedestal. Muslims trace their own lineage back through Ishmael to Isaac and to Abraham.

These are not just my own opinions or analyses. As I noted earlier in this book, no less of an authority than Maimonides, the Rambam, who lived both in Muslim Spain and in Egypt, wrote in Responsa 448, that the Ishmaelites (Muslims) "are not at all idolaters; [idolatry] has long been severed from their mouths and hearts; and they attribute to God a proper unity, a unity concerning which there is no doubt."

To cite a contemporary religious scholar, the Sephardic former chief rabbi of Israel, Ovadia Yosef, decreed, "We can see that the mosques of the Muslims are not considered houses of idolatry and one could enter there."[1] Moreover, Rav Yosef states that a Jew is "permitted to pray and learn [the Torah] there," and because Muslims worship "the One God with no blemish, there is no prohibition to pray there." The chief rabbi himself notes that he has witnessed prominent rabbis praying in the mosque at the Cave of Machpelah in Hebron, the burial site of Abraham and Sarah, Isaac and Rebecca, and Jacob and Leah.

Our religious texts, both ancient and modern, can positively affect the Jewish encounter with Muslims. I have seen this personally. At our foundation's first gathering of rabbis and imams, in November 2007 at the Islamic Center of New York, it was time for *minchah*, the afternoon worship service, and we davened in the mosque—fifteen rabbis. It felt very empowering and at the same time not familiar but familial. I felt like I was there with my extended family but expressing my own beliefs. Imams and rabbis, Muslims and Jews, we are the sons of Abraham. It's not only something you comprehend; it's also something you feel. It could be an ancestral feeling, a historical feeling, a Middle Eastern feeling. Whatever the binding force, I cannot conceive of a similar moment happening in a church. I cannot even imagine a group of rabbis chanting *Ashrei* in some basilica.

There is another basic, central tenet of Judaism that informs our approach to coexistence: the abiding concern with what we say and how we say it and of whom it is said. Of the forty-four confessions we invoke on Yom Kippur, no fewer than eleven regard sins of speech—lying, slandering, scoffing, giving evil counsel, and imputing falsely, just to cite some ex-

---

1. See "The Jewish Approach to Islam," *God's Holy Mountain*, http://www.gods holymountain.org/papers/islam.pdf.

amples. Proverbs tells us, "Life and death are in the power of the tongue." The great rabbi, the Chofetz Chaim, devoted his most important work, *Shmirat Halashon* (Guard the spoken word), to the subject of guarding against this evil. When we finish the *Amidah*, the prayer that is the oldest extant part of the Jewish liturgy, we ask God to protect us from those who speak evil and words of deceit.

So there is a clear preoccupation in Judaism with how words are to be used. And that preoccupation has been especially relevant to the discourse between American Jews and American Muslims. In the wake of September 11, I thought that it was an injustice that the entire Muslim community was being demonized. The toxic rhetoric of that time made me recall being fifteen years old at the time of the Arab oil embargo, when there were practically riots as people lined up to get gas for their cars. I still remember how Jews as an entire community were blamed for the lack of oil because of American foreign policy in the Middle East.

For me, standing with American Muslims is not just about fighting for the underdog. I'm not the type of person who just takes in the stray cat. But it is a matter of having an empathetic imagination. We have to treat injustice against Muslims as injustice against us, defamation against Muslims as defamation against us, diatribes against them as diatribes against us. Sadly, even in this modern day and age, there are backward people who find it more comfortable to hate than to love. I take my cue from Edmund Burke, the great English statesman and philosopher: *All that is necessary for evil to triumph is for good people to do nothing.*

As American Jews, and as American citizens, we have heard and seen far too many examples of Muslims portrayed as terrorists, as enemies, as subversives. There has been a broad, sweeping implication that Muslims are savages. Those stereotypes pervaded the controversy about the so-called Ground Zero mosque in New York. They pervaded the demonstrations against mosques being built in dozens of other communities. Most recently in New York, they pervaded an advertising campaign on subways and buses. Those ads used the slogans "Death to Jihad" and "Support Israel" solely in order to create unnecessary, destructive conflict and tension between Muslims and Jews.

Using language for such goals is antithetical to the teachings of Judaism. As Americans, we are grateful for the freedom of expression, the freedom of speech, but Judaism abhors following any directive to the point of extremism. We believe life is about having balance, finding a golden mean. Indeed, the Shoah taught Jews—taught the world—the lethal consequences of hateful speech. Joseph Goebbels used his powers of expression to whip the German people into the most horrific genocide in human history.

Too often, I have seen an almost willful ignorance about Muslims on the part of American Jews—and American Christians, of course, as well. Recently, Shamsi Ali and I were speaking at a program and someone in the audience asked a question about jihad. As much as the imam tried to explain to the audience the real meaning of jihad, there were people who would not hear it. To them, jihad means the apocalypse. When you deal with hate-mongers, as I have for the last several years, you see that hate takes on a life of its own. You are not dealing with the rational. You are no longer dealing with what is right and what is true. People will believe what they want to believe.

A people who fight for their own rights are only as honorable as when they fight for the rights of all people. The work that we do here is not about dialogue or exchanging pleasantries; it's about fighting for the Other. That's how I gauge if a relationship is authentic: Are you prepared to fight for me, and am I prepared to fight for you?

In the wake of the Arab Spring, at a time when the Muslim world is becoming more devout and Islamist parties are gaining strength, Jews and Muslims should be working with each other to end the cycle of mutual demonization and to allow people on both sides to appreciate that the faith of the Other has many similarities to our own. We may not agree on issues related to the Middle East conflict, but we can and must do everything possible to prevent the conflict from becoming a worldwide Jewish-Muslim one and resolve to work for peace and reconciliation between Jews and Muslims everywhere—including in the Middle East.

Fortunately, the majority of American Jews oppose raw bigotry against Muslims. I believe this is the case because we ourselves have been the victims of such attitudes and therefore have an instinctive sympathy with other groups who are unjustly maligned. Our community remembers a time not so long ago when there were unofficial quotas preventing all but a few Jews from entering many of America's top universities and from securing positions in blue-chip corporations and law firms. We remember that during the 1920s and 1930s, there were powerful figures in this country, such as Henry Ford, Father Charles Coughlin, and Gerald L. K. Smith, who used the media to preach hatred of Jews. Many American Jews risked life and limb in the 1960s to go to the South and join in the battle for civil rights for African Americans and to put an end to the national shame of segregation. A few Jews, like Andrew Goodman and Michael Schwerner, made the ultimate sacrifice in that cause.

Today, a growing number of prominent rabbis and Jewish leaders from all streams of Judaism have denounced the strident attacks on American Muslims. A coalition of Jewish groups have joined Shoulder to Shoulder, a national coalition of religious groups dedicated to fighting Islamophobia, in which I have played a leading role. And every year more synagogues and Jewish organizations, including student, women's, and youth leadership groups, have linked up with mosques and Muslim organizations in their communities to hold joint programs as part of the annual Weekend of Twinning—an event sponsored by the Foundation for Ethnic Understanding that in 2012 brought together more than two hundred fifty Jewish and Muslim communal organizations for joint programming in America and around the world. Many of the participating groups said that the anti-Muslim campaign of recent years had reinforced in them a determination to reach out to the Muslim community as a way of demonstrating their opposition to bigotry.

The stakes of this struggle became most clear to me as I looked at recent events in France, the nation with the largest Muslim and Jewish populations of any in Western Europe. France has seen a severe rise in anti-Semitic actions by Muslims. There have been appalling incidents of synagogues being defaced and cemeteries being destroyed, of Jews being beaten up in the streets. The climax of these awful events was the massacre in May 2012, when a Muslim radical shot three children and a rabbi at a Jewish school in Toulouse. In the aftermath of those murders, the pace of anti-Semitic attacks in France increased even more sharply.

Yet in that climate of hatred and fear, Rabbi Michel Serfaty of Toulouse chose not to denounce and reject French Muslims, not to use the terrorist attacks as an excuse to exacerbate tensions and drive an ever-greater wedge between peoples. Instead, he worked behind the scenes with an Islamic leader, Scheherazade Zerouala, in their French Judeo-Muslim Friendship organization to maintain dialogue and strengthen the hand of moderates. I am proud to say that my foundation, FFEU, was also deeply involved in their efforts. All this behind-the-scenes work culminated in early September 2012 with a march by seventy Jewish and Muslim faith leaders declaring zero tolerance for "hate preachers" of any religion. Imams and rabbis walked hand-in-hand, which would have been inconceivable even five years ago.

CHAPTER SIXTEEN

Palestine

IMAM SHAMSI ALI

The whole area of what is called in the Arabic language *Sham*—the Semitic area of Lebanon, Palestine, Israel, Jordan, and Syria—is considered historically important in Islam. It is mentioned repeatedly in the hadith and in the history of Islam. The first expansion of Islam took place toward that direction. The commander of the Muslim army was Khalid bin-Wihad, and the governor of Jerusalem refused to give him the key to the city, the symbol of handing over control. He said he would only give the key to the king—that is, to the caliph, Umar.[1] So Umar came all the way from Arabia to take over control from the Romans. Umar was aware of the history of Jerusalem. When he toured the holy sites and found that the places where the Jews used to worship had been turned into garbage dumps and pagan places by the Romans, he was so angry he ordered the governor to clean and restore them. Umar also gave the instruction that the Jewish community should have the right to return and settle and worship again. This is recorded in Islamic history. In my own life, I have felt encouraged to follow that great example.

Jerusalem, then, was seen as a sacred place by Umar, as well as by the Muslim people, by virtue of its importance and meaning to the previous

---

1. The caliph (or *khalifa*) is the leader of the Muslim community. This was a relevant title in the era of Islamic empire; it is used when discussing history or, if in the present, only symbolically.

People of the Book and to the prophets who came before Muhammad. But despite our respect for and deep ties to the city, Jerusalem as the capital of an independent State of Palestine has been a roadblock in various talks between Israel and Palestine. It would seem that many, including those in the Jewish community, don't understand Jerusalem's importance within the Muslim faith or its importance as a central marker of our spiritual history.

In the Holy Qur'an, Allah the Almighty says of Jerusalem (*Al-Quds*, in the Arabic language, "the holy site"), *"Baaraknaa haulahu,"* which means, "We have blessed it and its surrounding areas" (19:1). Muslims, therefore, view Jerusalem as a city blessed by the commandment of Allah. One interpretation of that blessing is the series of prophets that God has sent to that area: Abraham, Isaac, David, Solomon, and many others, including Jesus, son of Mary. We revere those prophets as our own. In fact, in some interpretations of the Qur'an, when we refer to Al-Quds, we are referring back to the time of the Canaanites. Muslim historians view the Canaanites as the Arabs who were present there before Abraham came and settled with his family in Palestine.

Another reason that Muslim scholars give for the importance of Jerusalem is directly related to an event in the life of Prophet Muhammad. When he was ascending to heaven, on the night of the journey—*Al-Isra*—he was taken from Mecca to Jerusalem.[2] And from Jerusalem, he was ascended to the heavens to receive one of the Five Pillars of Islam, the *salat*, or commandment for five daily prayers. It is said in the hadith that God enabled Prophet Muhammad to meet spiritually in heaven with the other prophets who had come before him. He met with Abraham, David, and others, and this meeting of the prophets and the instructions received from God are a foundational belief of all Muslims. Later, when the Prophet prayed five times a day, he could not face Mecca because there were so many idols surrounding the Ka'bah that it was blasphemous to pray in that direction.[3] Instead, he faced what is today known as the Al-Aqsa Mosque in al-Quds, Jerusalem.

---

2. *Al-Isra* means "night journey," in reference to the divine journey of Prophet Muhammad from Mecca in Saudi Arabia to Al-Quds (Jerusalem).

3. The Ka'bah is likely the most recognizable site in Islam for non-Muslims, as it is seen circumambulated by pilgrims around the world during the hajj, and it has rich

The Al-Aqsa mosque, which is located on Haram al-Sharif, what Muslims call the Noble Sanctuary, and what Jewish tradition calls the Temple Mount, is also mentioned in the Qur'an, in 17:1. I see this as the connection of all heavenly religions, especially the Abrahamic ones. It is also one of the strongest justifications for Al-Aqsa in Al-Quds being so important to us. It is the foundation of Muslims' psychological and faith connection to what we now call Palestine and Israel, and I hope it provides some context as to why this place is of paramount importance in our belief.

There are those who are argue that Mecca is the holiest city in Islam and thus believe that Muslims shouldn't place such importance on Jerusalem. It is true, Jerusalem is the third-holiest religious site in Islam, but we say it is the most important *historical* site in Islam, because Abraham, whom we regard as the father of the prophets, was there; because Isaac was born there; and because Jesus, who is a prophet for us as well, was there. Muhammad, Jesus, David, others—they are equal in prophethood for us. So we believe Jerusalem is the most important place *historically* in our religion. Mecca is the place of the hajj, and Medina is where we visit the grave of the last prophet, Prophet Muhammad. In all the world, there are only three mosques we are recommended to visit—the Great Mosque in Mecca, the Mosque of the Prophet in Medina, and Al-Aqsa in Jerusalem. We see all these mosques as being connected.

Jewish people—Israelis and others—talk about the fact that Israel has left the authority for Al-Aqsa in the hands of the Waqf.[4] But it is difficult for Muslims to take for granted that they will be free to worship under the control of Israel. I don't blame Israel entirely for every restriction, as I accept their concerns for security, but it is difficult for Palestinians to access the site. Even the Christians I met in Ramallah recently, during my visit to Palestine and Israel, said their most important concern was being able to visit Christian holy sites in Jerusalem and Bethlehem.

---

historical importance for Muslims. In pre-Islamic times, it was the repository of hundreds of pagan idols and a major business center catering to the pagan groups. It was the objection to this that caused the first problems for Prophet Muhammad among his own tribe, the Quraysh, since they received much material benefit from pagan business.

4. *Waqf* means a "trust" or "endowment." For Al-Aqsa, there is a special body under the Ministry of Waqf and Religious Affairs of Jordan to oversee Al-Aqsa–related issues.

While at Al-Aqsa in 2012, praying *jummah*, our midday prayer on Friday, and just after finishing the worship service, we heard shooting outside the mosque. There were Israeli soldiers all around, and we asked people what happened. They said there was a small demonstration and that the army had stormed in and shot their guns into the air to disperse the demonstrators. To feel violence surround one's place of worship to our Creator was demoralizing to me, but more saddening was the idea that for the Palestinians there, it was not in any way an unusual event; it was the norm. This is an example I have myself experienced of why Muslims believe they must have the right of access to their own holy sites in Jerusalem.

One of the other reasons Muslims care so deeply about the issue of Palestine and Israel is that the majority view the fate of Muslims in that region as an Islamic issue, based on Islamic solidarity and community—what we have referred to as our "ummah." There are some in our community who take the extreme view that this is all about religion, that the conflict is one of Muslims versus Jews. To me, that perception is damaging to the peace process, and it is erroneous. On the other side, are those who say it has nothing to do with religion at all and is just about dividing the land between Palestinians and Israelis politically and militarily. I think that view is lacking, too.

To me, the issue is about religion and land both. I can say that territorial, political issues are the ones that need to be settled by politicians. But there are other issues that are equally real and need to be addressed. I call them the "soft" issues—psychological, religious, cultural, and historical. In fact, these soft issues have already greatly influenced the peace process. Political negotiations, such as those at Camp David or Taba, have briefly allowed us to hope, only to fail en route to resolution. And one reason is that people don't give enough importance to the soft issues of the conflict. These need to be tackled very seriously. We, as Muslims, are becoming more aware that Israel is not just a political issue for Jews but also a religious issue. Even when politicians come to an agreement, if the psychological, religious, and cultural aspects of a conflict are not tackled, the result can be a fragile peace.

So interfaith engagement, interfaith dialogue, the building of trust, and the commitment of religious leaders on both sides—as well as involvement from the Christian community—are important elements of the peace process. The more we get down to the truth of individual people, the more we get to know the religious sentiments of the conflict.

The problems in the peace process are rooted in the extreme elements on both sides. On the Palestinian side, there are elements that want nothing but the destruction of Israel and who swear they will never recognize its existence. On the Israeli side, there are those who believe Palestinians are usurpers who deserve to be put in their place if allowed to stay in "Zion" at all. We have to accept the fact that Israel is a country that exists, that it is accepted by the international community, that it is in the United Nations. To say that Israel doesn't exist is unrealistic. So as a Muslim, and as a person who wants peace, I always look to the future. I envision a peace in the Middle East where Israel and Palestine exist as sovereign countries and good neighbors. Given Israeli policies that deeply hurt the Palestinians, and equally negative reactions by the Palestinians, we must take the responsibility not just to blame but also to be proactive and find solutions. We must not give up on a situation that is still bad on both sides. In fact, the difficulty of the situation has personally become a motivation for me to do more. As a Muslim, I want to see the Palestinians relieved of the burden of occupation. As a human being, I know Israel has the right to exist and to be secure.

The second problem is the inflexible and vitriolic rhetoric on both sides. It just inflames the anger and hurt already there. It is also unhelpful when each side considers itself the only victim in the conflict and uses this perceived victimhood to justify whatever it is doing, even if those actions are wrong. The best way to handle this is to raise awareness that both sides have been victimized. There are too many outsider interests, and both Palestinians and Israelis are suffering from the effects of these interests—from Iran, Syria, and the Western powers. It is important for both sides to realize independence from these outside powers. America and Europe must play a vital role in not furthering tensions by providing a neutral and just mediation for both—or by staying out of the conflict altogether. Otherwise, our hopes for democracy and friendship in the Middle East will be steered toward animosity and resentment of the United States and the rest of the Western world. Americans have strongly supported Israel and are viewed as its strongest ally in the Middle East.

But internal changes can happen quickly in the Middle East, and not always predictably. The way America handles the Palestinian-Israeli issue may endanger the future of Israel itself by giving impetus to brinksmanship that might be handled differently between Israelis and Palestinians on their own.

My own personal view, my hope and dream, is to see a two-state solution, where there is a secure Israeli state and an independent Palestinian state, side by side. That is my hope, despite the deep mistrust on both sides. This mistrust has led us to overlook and undervalue the noble parts of our shared past. When Muslims were in power in Spain, we know that many Jews managed business and trade opportunities, and held prominent positions in the government. That itself is a strong indication that instead of being suspicious of the Jewish community, we should allow trust for it to grow. And we know that when the Christians came back to power, both Muslims and Jews were executed or expelled, or forced to embrace Christianity. This history continued in Europe during the Holocaust, when Jews in Christian countries were killed, even as they were protected in Muslim ones.

Still, I have to acknowledge that the establishment of Israel has been the biggest obstacle to the process of understanding and cooperation between Muslims and Jews. In many ways, the current situation covers up or outright obliterates the peaceful cohabitations of the past, and it has been understood by Muslims as damaging Muslim-Jewish relations. And that encourages me to do something to minimize its impact, especially as we are living in a globalized world.

Just last February, I went to Israel and then to Ramallah. I met both Israelis and Palestinians—leaders and laypeople. On the Israeli side, I recall a family where the wife was Yemeni and the husband, Bulgarian. They deeply wanted to engage with Palestinians. Their children were Facebook friends with Palestinians. But they felt insecure. They were bombarded with news every day that they would be attacked, that they would be expelled from their homes if Palestinians got their independence.

When I went to Ramallah, I was introduced to a Palestinian family with seven children. I asked the kids, "What is your dream?" The daughter, who was the oldest and told me she wanted to be an engineer, said she wanted to pray at Al-Aqsa and to be friends with those who are considered enemies on the other side.

These may seem to be idealized stories, even though they are true, but my point is that the mistrust between the two communities is not going to be solved by a political solution. It can only change through religious and cultural engagement. What Marc Schneier and I are doing is tackling that aspect in particular.

In order to make the Muslim case for Palestine, it is not necessary to denigrate or deny the Jewish connection to Israel. Jews are there because of their religious and historical ties to the land. Their presence is not based simply on a desire to take over land the way a colonial or imperial power does, so calling Israel a colonizing power only makes solving the issue more difficult. Another example of the rhetoric that contributes to acrimony and tension is calling the political situation "apartheid." As we struggle to achieve peace, we need to avoid that rhetoric: comparing Israel to South Africa is not going to advance the cause of creating a Palestinian state. It will just raise more Israeli resistance and more Jewish resistance to Palestine.

On the other side, the issue of Palestine and Israel has nothing to do with how many other Muslim nations there are. Muslims believe that the Palestinian people have the right to their own sovereign state and their own freedom. And we support the Palestinian right to self-determination on that basis. We don't want to just add to the number of Muslim-majority states. It is the right of the Palestinians to have a free, sovereign Palestine. It is not fair or ethical for them to be forced to emigrate to Jordan or to Indonesia just because those countries happen to be Muslim.

Most Muslims are able to distinguish between "Israeli" and "Jewish," and they understand that not all Israeli policies are necessarily supported by all Jewish people. We understand that a Jew is not just someone who lives in Israel, that the Jewish Diaspora has great variety and is as "uniform" in its thinking as Muslim or Christian groups are. The issue most Muslims have with Jews in general and Israelis in particular is with the ethical and social justice aspect of the Palestinian issue.

We would like Israelis and Jews to acknowledge that the occupation of Palestinian land is not morally or legally acceptable. Freedom is a basic right of every human being. I have believed this all my life, since my childhood, when we studied the Indonesian constitution, which says that freedom is the right of all human beings. I therefore believe that Palestinians—besides being Muslims with whom we have solidarity—have the human right to their own state, their sovereignty. And unless Palestine has independence (a political issue), it might be difficult to see Al-Aqsa as free to access (a religious issue).

It is hard for Muslims to believe that a two-state solution is truly desired by Israel and its friends when the rights of Palestinians are routinely ignored. Even when international treaties are broken and world leaders call for the Israelis to stop building settlements on Palestinian land, the settlements continue. In a 2011 interview reported on Fox News, American presidential candidate Newt Gingrich said, "There is no such thing as a Palestinian people." This was a foolish statement, an unnecessary statement, from such a high-ranking politician, and I don't think he realized that when he says such a thing, he creates an emotional, retaliatory response among Muslims: "There is no such thing as Israel, and so why should Israel exist?" Palestinians say, "Israelis keep building houses on our land. How can we come to the table when you are violating international law?"

When Hamas, in the name of the Palestinian government, fires rockets into Israel or commits suicide killings of innocent people, I agree with the media outcry that it is condemnable. But when Benjamin Netanyahu, in the name of the Israeli government, fires rockets into Palestine or shells bombs on Gaza, killing innocent people, it seems to us that these same global media outlets justify the action as a "war against terrorism." Any loss of life, regardless of that person's faith, is absolute in its immorality.

This is why I talk about both sides feeling victimized and succumbing to victim psychology: neither side acknowledges its culpability. We need to acknowledge our shortcomings, and we must show the willingness to accept compromise, which will be painful to both sides. There are some areas of Palestinian land where Israel has no right to build, and these lands must be given back. That will be painful to the Israelis, especially the settlers. On the other hand, Palestinians must accept that they will lose some of the land they had in the past. As long as either the Palestinians or the Israelis insist on recovering every inch, the conflict cannot be settled.

There are many teachings in Islam about compromise, but to me a great example comes from Prophet Muhammad himself. In the sixth year after the migration from Mecca to Medina, God commanded Muhammad to go on the hajj, the pilgrimage to worship at the Ka'bah, which was back in Mecca. Prophet Muhammad and a small group of Muslims undertook the trip but were blocked by the Meccans. En route to Mecca they were stopped in a place known as Hudaibiyah and made to wait for Meccan leaders to arrive to negotiate passage. The new Muslims, who were with Muhammad and now settled in Medina, were very upset. Some were ready to fight—they saw no validity in pagan tribesmen blocking a commandment from God to travel and worship in His name. But Muhammad rejected that idea and sent a messenger to the Meccans to state, "We are coming to worship, not to fight." The Meccan leaders repudiated that message, as well as Muhammad's intention to worship in Mecca. So Muhammad said, "We must come to an agreement." The agreement was that the Meccans would not call him "Muhammad, the Prophet of God" but "Muhammad, son of Abdullah," and that he and his group of Muslims would not be allowed into Mecca to complete the hajj at that time but would be allowed at a future date. When these conditions were accepted, some of Muhammad's closest companions could not accept it and spoke harsh words, some still ready to fight. But Muhammad insisted on the treaty being accepted and peace being observed, and he took his group, some now doubtful of him and his veracity as a messenger of God, back to Medina to wait until relations were calmer between the groups. The pilgrimage to Mecca did, in fact, take place in the years that followed, and it was peaceful. This was one of many such agreements between Muslims and non-Muslims at the time, and I look back on this story often as an excellent example for Muslims, in particular for Palestinians and Israelis, to follow: in any conflict, peace is the best solution. In the process, there will be sacrifices required from both parties, but that is a necessary means to the end of achieving lasting peace in the Middle East.

CHAPTER SEVENTEEN

Standing Up against Holocaust Denial

RABBI MARC SCHNEIER

Several years ago, a group of Palestinian schoolchildren from Gaza came to the United States as part of a United Nations educational program. During their time here, they were brought to New York's Holocaust museum.[1] It was later discovered that representatives of both Hamas and Fatah condemned the visit of these schoolchildren, condemned the very idea of Palestinian young people being exposed to the history of the Holocaust.

That rhetorical attack did not surprise me. As we know, the Holocaust is denigrated at best and denied at worst in much of the Arab and Muslim world. At the vilest extreme, of course, is President Mahmoud Ahmadinejad of Iran, who has repeatedly cast doubt that the Holocaust occurred and convened a specious conference on that subject in Tehran. The mindset that he embodies is the same one that has made *The Protocols of the Elders of Zion* a best seller in some Arab and Muslim countries. Even putting aside Ahmadinejad and his ilk, there is a pervasive assertion among many Muslims to the effect that, "Even if we grant that the Holocaust did occur, we had nothing to do with it. It was a genocide committed by Europeans—so why should Arabs and Muslims have paid the

---

1. The official name is the Museum of Jewish Heritage—A Living Memorial to the Holocaust.

price for it in the form of Israel's creation?" And, these Muslims often contend, what the Palestinians are suffering now is a Holocaust committed *by* Jews. In other words, it is useful for such thinkers to acknowledge the factuality of the Holocaust but only to then portray today's Israelis and Jews as Nazis.

Given that context, it was sadly predictable that Palestinian leaders would object to their schoolchildren being shown an accurate historical account of the Holocaust. What was not so predictable, and what I find so promising for the future, is what happened after the Fatah and Hamas condemnations. I reached out to the general secretary of the Islamic Society of North America, Dr. Sayyid Syeed, whom I knew had a particular commitment to fighting Holocaust denial. He himself had been to Auschwitz. He wrote me a letter, which was released to the Israeli media, and in it he criticized those views and spoke of the necessity for all Arab youth to be exposed to the atrocities of the Holocaust.

From Dr. Syeed's bold and principled stance, I gained a key insight into how Muslims can and should respond to Holocaust denial. As Jews, when we are confronted with either ignorance or outright denial of the Holocaust on the part of non-Jews, we tend to advocate for more Holocaust education. I certainly do not oppose expanding the reach of Holocaust education; even within the Jewish community, such expansion is necessary, as we stand almost seventy years since the end of World War II and have a dwindling number of Holocaust survivors to give firsthand testimony. Education alone, however, does not go far enough. Sayyid Syeed was willing to speak out on the subject to his fellow Muslims on behalf of Jewish concerns and Jewish rights. Muslims learning about our tragedy simply as something to be learned is less important than their standing up for us when we've been hurt and injured.

The only effective way of combating the Ahmadinejads of the world is by challenging Muslim leaders to speak out on our behalf. It's imperative not only for Ahmadinejad and his cohorts to hear condemnation from their fellow Muslims but also for people around the world to know that Muslims do stand up to other Muslims. There is a persistent and treacherous misperception that Muslims only hear the voices of extremists. Addressing Holocaust denial is a critical step in the evolution of moderate Muslim leaders. And in order to strengthen Muslim-Jewish relations, it is imperative that the Jewish community sees the Muslim community defending Jewish concerns and Jewish issues, just as Muslims have every right to expect Jews to defend Muslims' concerns by opposing Islamophobia, for example.

I see the Holocaust at the very core of developing Muslim-Jewish relationships. You can't understand the Jew without understanding the effect of the Holocaust. It is the ghost that haunts us. To this day, we are traumatized by the extermination of six million Jews—almost 40 percent of the world population of Jews at the time. It is the basis for many decisions made by the State of Israel about the existential threats it faces.

Just as any Muslim needs to understand Israel, the Torah, and the concept of chosenness in order to understand the Jew, so one also needs to understand the role the Holocaust has played in our time: as the climax of two thousand years of Jewish persecution, coercion, and subjugation. The parallel here is that I, as a Jew, cannot understand the Muslim world without understanding the significance of the hajj, the Koran, and the atrocities Muslims suffered during the Crusades. Before you fight for the Other, you need to understand the Other.

It is historically correct for Muslims to say that the Holocaust did not take place in Arab lands. While certain Muslim leaders, like the Grand Mufti in Jerusalem, did openly support Hitler, others, like the king of Morocco, went to great lengths to protect Jews from the fascist occupation forces. But it is not morally sufficient for Muslims today to elide or diminish the importance of the Holocaust by saying simply that it happened in Europe. Because when Jews hear dismissal or denial of the Holocaust from Muslims, the reaction is, "There they go again. They hate Jews; they hate Israel; now they're leading the charge of Holocaust denial." And that is the end of meaningful interchange, much less alliance, between Muslims and Jews.

So it is incumbent on Muslim leaders to refute these charges and stand up to revisionists. Such actions will go a very long way in terms of calming Jewish fears, Jewish tensions. Muslims need to acknowledge that Jews have been hurt, have been injured by members of the Muslim community, and that those wounds have been caused by lies, by innuendo, by false rhetoric. And just as I stand up for the Muslim community when members of my community make Islamophobic comments, it's incumbent upon Muslims to do the same for my community. We must have a reciprocal relationship.

If you understand the Holocaust and know the Holocaust, then you will also know how inappropriate it is to use that terminology in the Israeli-Palestinian context. The Israelis aren't putting Palestinians into ovens and gas chambers. If, unfortunately, the Israelis have to go to war against the Palestinians, as was the case in 2009 and 2012, they send warnings, they drop leaflets from the sky. That's not exactly how the Nazis operated. So, the more you know of the Holocaust, the more you will find the correct words to describe the Israeli-Palestinian conflict. When you get to know the Other, you understand how each struggle is unique unto itself. It is fully possible for Muslims to object to Israeli policy in the Palestinian territories without making a baseless and offensive comparison of the occupation, which I personally oppose, to the Holocaust.

I see the issue of Holocaust denial within the larger context of intergroup relations. I see Jewish outrage about Holocaust denial as no different from Muslim outrage over cartoons and films designed to insult and ridicule the Prophet Muhammad and thus Islam as a religion. As a Jew, I needed to understand the pain the Muslim community felt. Only when I understand the pain can I know how to react. If someone drew a cartoon like that about Moses, I would not have the same feeling of rage and indignation, because a depiction of Moses is not blasphemous. We need to ask ourselves, "What triggered the Muslim reaction?" Instead of seeing their reaction through our eyes, we should be seeing it through their eyes. Once I was able to do so, I could understand why some Muslims reacted so strongly. That in no way gives license to violence, but at the same time, I do understand the anger.

When we brought a group of European imams and rabbis to Washington in July 2009, a highlight was the visit to the Holocaust Museum. For many of them, it was their first encounter with such a graphic display of what had happened. And when some of the rabbis spoke during a luncheon about how they survived or how their families escaped, it became something very personal and very pure. This process of exposing Muslim leaders to the reality of the Holocaust has continued; there have been visits to Auschwitz by imams and communal leaders, including Dr. Syeed.

One can ask how the Holocaust relates to Muslims. Consider my great friend and ally Shamsi Ali, who is from Indonesia. Truthfully, why should people in Indonesia have to learn about the Holocaust? It took place in a foreign land, with a foreign religion, a small religion. In a country with more than 200 million Muslims, Jews are not the primary concern.

Yet the Holocaust relates to Muslims from Indonesia—or Pakistan, or France, or South Africa, or Kansas—because it relates to their participation in working toward improving Muslim-Jewish relations. It relates to understanding the Jew, and if you understand the Jew, then you can stand up for the Jew. Holocaust denial is denial of the Jew. Holocaust denial is Judaism denial. In the field of Muslim-Jewish relations, you cannot pick and choose which issues and which historical experiences or references you're going to accept or not accept. When you say that the Holocaust never took place, that the extermination of six million Jews is a fabrication, you are denying the history of the Jewish people. It is as egregious an act as denigrating Prophet Muhammad and denying the centrality of Muhammad to the Muslim people.

CHAPTER EIGHTEEN

At Home in America

IMAM SHAMSI ALI

During the autumn of 2012, I gave a series of lectures at universities in Indonesia, Qatar, and Dubai. The question most often asked was, "How do you feel as a Muslim living in the United States?" On some occasions, there would be follow-up questions that echoed the same theme: "Do Americans accept you?" "Do Americans treat you fairly?" "Can you lead your life easily in terms of practicing your religion?" The United States, it was implied, does not give us our rights to practice Islam because this country is secular in nature, is hostile to Islam and Muslims, and is opposed to Muslims in its foreign policy.

When I responded, I hit a nerve by saying that it is not an exaggeration to say that America is more Islamic and more in line with Shari'a than many Muslim nations are. The US Constitution is actually very much in line with the principles of Islam—justice, equality, tolerance, embracing every person's rights. And even though the United States is a secular country, American people are very religious by nature. The concept of secularism in the United States is very different from the concept in many other countries, especially those in Western Europe. In the United States, secularism means the government has no right to rule over the faith of its citizens and that the country must allow all its citizens to practice their chosen faith. In certain western European nations (even previously in Turkey), secularism means that one is not allowed to show one's religious symbols in public; religion is meant to be restricted entirely to private life. Public or communal expressions of faith are seen as threatening to national cohesion. So we as Muslims feel at home in America, and we feel Islam is not a stranger in this home.

Not only is Islam in the United States not a stranger; it has been here for hundreds of years. American Islam's historical base was among African Americans. Some scholars estimate that 10 to 20 percent of the slaves brought over from Africa were Muslims. The film *Amistad* alluded to this fact, portraying Muslims aboard the slave vessel trying to perform their prayers while chained together on deck as they crossed the Atlantic. Along with those who kept or revived the Islamic heritage of West Africa, where their ancestors had come from, there was a strong draw for the marginalized pre–civil rights African American citizen. Cassius Clay became Muhammad Ali and Malcolm Little became Al-Hajj Malik Shabazz, better known as Malcolm X. Although Islam was not as well known as other religions in the United States, it was seen as a respite from troubles for the believer, just as the other Abrahamic religions were.

I am, of course, fully aware of the tensions regarding Islam in the United States since the September 11 tragedy. But as I reminded those audiences in Indonesia, Dubai, and Qatar, the September 11 tragedy may have brought us as Muslims some blessings in disguise. Though all Muslims were being blamed for the attacks, in the aftermath many Americans decided to learn more about what Islam actually is. Prior to September 11, as I say jokingly, people imagined Muslims flying to the moon on their magic prayer mats. After September 11, many Americans came to the conclusion that Islam is not the exotic, strange, and perhaps hostile thing they thought but one of the great religions of the world.

The attitude of America toward its Muslim citizens, and of its Muslim citizens toward America, has important historical precedents. I often point out the perception of more-established Americans toward Jews when they arrived here a century or more ago: the Jews were treated very badly, they were denied certain jobs and places to live, their houses of worship were seen as objectionable. Catholic immigrants, as well, particularly those who were Irish or Italian, suffered a great deal of prejudice. Strange as it may seem to us today, there was a very real and widespread belief, as recently as the 1960s, that the Pope would try to rule America if a Catholic were elected president. Perhaps American Muslims are facing similar challenges in the present. But I remain optimistic, because Jews and Catholics, groups that faced opposition in the past, have become a strong and accepted part of the mainstream.

To cite just one example, I take heart from President Obama's first inaugural address. For the first time in the history of the United States, a president said that America is the nation of Christians and Jews and Muslims and Hindus, as well as of people who do not believe in any religion. So you have the president of the United States acknowledging that the nation is more diverse than ever. Meanwhile, the Muslim community in the United States has grown not only in terms of numbers—nearly three million as of 2011—but also in terms of political involvement and sophistication.[1] We now have an impact on the political outlook of the nation. Immigrants commonly feel like guests in their adopted countries, so becoming politically involved often takes on more significance for them.

Millions of Muslims voted in the past several presidential elections. It is no secret that the first election of George W. Bush was affected by Muslim voters. Bush campaigned very diligently for the Muslim vote in 2000. He spoke to the concerns of Muslims, as well as to Christian Arab Americans, about being racially profiled. So, the very small gap between George Bush and Al Gore in that election was very much affected by Muslim voters. In the 2012 presidential race, we saw a majority of Muslims vote for Barack Obama. Certainly, their support played a major role in his reelection.[2] There were significant numbers of Muslim voters, perhaps tens of thousands, in the pivotal state of Ohio.

The participation of Muslims in the American political process is part of our belief that Muslims are here not just to take but to give back. We believe Islam is about contributing. We have two Muslim members of Congress, Keith Ellison of Minnesota and Andre Carson of Indiana. In Teaneck, New Jersey, there is a Muslim mayor, Mohammed Hameeduddin, and an Orthodox Jewish vice mayor, Adam Gussen, who have been

---

1. Figure according to "The Future of the Global Muslim Population," Pew Forum on Religion and Public Life, January 2011, http://features.pewforum.org/muslim-population-graphic/#/United%20States.

2. Marc Schneier and Shamsi Ali, "Why American Jews and Muslims Backed Obama by Huge Margins," *Washington Post*, November 9, 2012.

friends for many years. Barack Obama has appointed senior officials in his administration who happen to be Muslim, including Arif Alikhan, who served as the assistant secretary for policy development in the Department of Homeland Security; Dr. Azizah Y. al-Hibri, commissioner for the Commission on International Religious Freedom; Farah Pandith, special representative to Muslim communities at the Department of State; and Dalia Mogahed, who served on the White House Advisory Council on Faith-Based and Neighborhood Partnerships. A lot of Muslims around the world don't know that a woman who wears a scarf works with the president of the United States! Those who suffer from a fear of the unknown have equated these appointments to a "Muslim agenda." As loyal American citizens, my fellow Muslims and I proudly regard them as examples of our participation in the political process of the country we all chose to be a part of.

In New York City, my home, there has been an unfortunate pattern of surveillance of Muslim individuals and groups by the police force. Yet, despite the monitoring, Muslims are becoming more rooted in the city's political leadership and its law-enforcement corps. Two Muslims—Omar Mohammedi, a commissioner for Human Rights, and Fatima Shama, a commissioner for Immigrant Affairs—work for a Jewish mayor, Michael Bloomberg. In the New York Police Department, we have more than seven hundred Muslim officers. The police commissioner, Raymond Kelly, agreed to establish a Muslim Officers Society within the department. Muslims participate in all walks of New York public life: we have about 120,000 Muslim children in the public school system, and we assist at approximately two hundred mosques. They are educated: across the United States, 40 percent of Muslim American adults have bachelor's degrees, according to Gallup's 2009 *American Muslim Report*, which places them second in the nation to the group with the highest educational attainment—our Jewish brothers.[3] In terms of economic life, the Pew Research Center estimates that Muslims closely mirror other Americans in general terms, though it is particularly striking how similar Jews and Muslims are in the report. About one-quarter of all Muslims report

---

3. *Muslim Americans: A National Portrait; An In-Depth Analysis of America's Most Diverse Religious Community* (Washington, DC: Gallup/CoexistFoundation, 2009).

themselves as self-employed, which is higher than the US average; the second-highest number are the Jews (21 percent). More nonworking Muslims are full-time students (31 percent) than those of any other group, with, again, the second group being the Jews (14 percent). The group holding the most jobs labeled professional is the Jews at 42 percent, with the Muslims second at 30 percent.[4]

What the data shows is a group that is putting down roots. Muslims feel more and more that this country belongs to them as much as it belongs to any of its citizens, and to me, that perception is crucial. You feel differently about a country when you feel it is yours, that you are not there as a guest. The United States may not be perfect, but it is the most powerful and developed country in the world, and it is still a place one can pursue one's dreams. It gives opportunity to immigrants to better their lives and practice their religion, which will always draw the hopeful, including Muslims. The opportunities we are afforded here enable us go through some internal consultation about the causes of problems for Muslims elsewhere in the world, such as poverty and poor education. This introspection can build an enlightened community to serve as a role model for Muslims everywhere.

American Muslims are diverse, not only in terms of ethnicity and country of origin but also in their understanding of Islam. This is solid ground for Muslim Americans to represent the universal face of Islam, to adhere to the source teachings of the faith without seeing them overshadowed by local or cultural interpretation. Over time, a localized Islam will also emerge here, and it will be distinctly American.

I have learned a lot about being a better Muslim since I have been in the United States. I didn't learn about Islam as a religion from Americans, but I learned to better implement the ideals of my religion into my daily life: from cleanliness, discipline, and hard work to how to deal with my fellow human beings. In my opinion, and I've said this on several occasions, it is no exaggeration to say that the United States might be the role model for Muslims in many nations around the world. We learn a lot

---

4. Pew Research Center for the People and the Press, "Muslim Americans: No Signs of Growth in Alienation or Support for Extremism," press release, August 30, 2011, http://www.people-press.org.

from the American environment—even small things like taking the subway can teach us lessons: standing in line rather than rushing your way into a subway car, or giving your seat to an elder on the train. Rarely do we find similar practices in the Muslim-majority societies around the world, even when this is what Islam teaches (for example, to honor your elders is a part of our *khulq*, or human ethics). In this sense, I can clearly say that in America we find Islam, though there are not many Muslims, whereas in the Muslim world we find many Muslims but not very much Islam.

Since my days in the pesantren, I have learned that freedom, justice, and equality are the main foundations of both Islam and life itself. I believe Islam is about freedom; Islam without freedom is like a fish without water. It dies, slowly but surely. America has taught me what freedom, justice, and equality mean. This country makes you appreciate what it means to be free. One of the lessons I have learned from living in America is the importance of a harmonious and peaceful coexistence among citizens. My religious commitment and my obedience to my teaching do not affect or decrease my commitment to my neighbors and fellow Americans. And for me, this is another representation of my faith. The more I connect with people of diverse faiths, the more I feel growth in my own faith.

Intolerant practices may occur in any society, Muslim and non-Muslim alike. In Western countries often considered the height of freedom and tolerance, we find unfortunate attitudes afflicting all minority groups, including an acceptance of anti-Semitism and Islamophobia. Muslim countries share these prejudicial flaws. In Indonesia, for example, there are cases where churches have been destroyed by some Muslim extremists. In current-day Saudi Arabia, despite the huge number of non-Muslims allowed to stay and work in that country, it is illegal to organize any religious service other than an Islamic one. These examples do not mean that any of these nations are irredeemably or inherently "bad." In the same way, though we acknowledge the existence of some hostile behavior in the United States toward the Muslim community, we have to be careful about drawing conclusions about America as a whole. For example, Park 51, the so-called Ground Zero mosque, was not opposed until a year after it was proposed, when one of the gubernatorial candidates in New York, Rick Lazio, made it a campaign issue. The burning of a mosque in Joplin, Missouri, is an example of intolerance, but it does not reflect the real face of America. The rebuilding of the mosque was a labor aided by many non-Muslims. As a Muslim, I don't want people to say that because some persons professing to follow Islam have committed murders that all Muslims are killers. And I don't want people to say that because some Americans are bigoted, that all Americans are bigots.

In recent years, we have seen the rise of Islamophobia in the United States take many forms, including some attempts by politicians (most notably Republicans) to create legislation banning the practice of Shari'a. In my view, this is an attempt to ban Muslims from practicing their religion, since Shari'a are Islamic laws that only apply to Muslims and encompass all aspects of Islamic life. We saw Pamela Geller, a self-proclaimed enemy of Muslims, place advertisements in various New York City subway stations mocking the religion of Islam and openly advocating Islamophobic words and deeds. In the face of all this evil we are encouraged by the fact that among the first to stand up against such intolerance have been non-Muslims. My friend Rabbi Marc Schneier is a great example of this.

In my view, the media is greatly responsible for misrepresentations of Islam to America and vice versa. Therefore, it is important for both to change the way they judge one another. I take upon myself some responsibility to build that bridge, because I see this as one of the most crucial tasks in saving our shared future. Muslims must continue to become aware not only of their rights but also their responsibilities as citizens, and as I look ahead to the next ten or twenty years, my vision is for them to remain good Muslims while becoming more integrated into and deepening their participation in public life. There is no contradiction; American values and Islamic values are in line.

We want to remind our fellow Americans that our community is not "the Other" but a part of the multicultural social fabric that makes up our fifty states. We are here as a partner to you and not a threat to our own country and fellow citizens. Muslim Americans love this country and are ready to defend it from any possible threat or harm. There is no cleaving of loyalties when Muslim Americans proclaim an allegiance to the United States—loyalty to country and religion are both believed to be not only a civic duty but also a religious one. Muslim Americans represent the full diversity of the Muslim world, coming from seventy-seven countries, and can play an important role in building bridges of communication and cooperation with Muslim-majority nations.[5] This brings me to another reason why I am optimistic about Muslim Americans: the growing number of non-Muslim Americans who have turned to Islam. If before September 11, Muslims were predominantly immigrants, after the tragedy, a good number of native-born Americans accepted Islam as their new faith. For me, this phenomenon contributes positively both to the Muslim community and to America as a nation. When we are as equally accepted in mainstream US society as any other group, we are able to present our partnership in the American experiment as affirmative to the Muslim world, and America is able to reveal itself in a positive collaborative light as well.

I am the father of American Muslim children, and my hope for them is to integrate into society. We are now into the second generation. When I hear my children speaking with American accents, when I see them participating in the many aspects of American culture that do not oppose their faith, I am happy. I learn some of my English from them. They feel this is their country, this is their home, this is where they are going to live the rest of their lives. It never occurs to them that they will live anywhere else. Our kids say, "I'm here, I'm educated here, I'm going to marry here, I'm going to work here, I'm going to raise my kids here, I'm going to die here. This is my land."

---

5. Pew Research Center, "Muslim Americans."

ACKNOWLEDGMENTS

RABBI MARC SCHNEIER

My heartfelt appreciation to the following for their ongoing friendship and guidance: Russell Simmons, my partner at the Foundation for Ethnic Understanding, who on a daily basis gives of his time, energy, and resources for the advancement of our endeavors; Imam Shamsi Ali, my distinguished coauthor, friend, and fellow visionary; Danny Abraham, most generous supporter, a man of great wisdom and motivation; Ken Sunshine, cherished friend and confidant; and Walter Ruby, who was so instrumental in research and transcribing my thoughts.

As always, my beloved congregation, the Hampton Synagogue, continues to be a beacon of strength and encouragement.

IMAM SHAMSI ALI

My heartfelt appreciation goes to the following: my sister Katherine Vizcaino, without whose sincere dedication and support in writing and research this book might not have been possible; my beloved wife, Mutiah, and our children, Maryam, Utsman, Adnan, Malika, and Shakeel, for their compassionate support and understanding throughout the process; my friends Dr. Wadud Bhuyan and Akhter Hussain, for their unwavering support and valuable advice; as always, my wonderful congregations at Masjid Al-Hikmah and Jamaica Muslim Center—may they continue to be beacons of friendship and warmth; and last, but not least, my extraordinary coauthor, Rabbi Marc Schneier, a man of vision and courage whose collaboration grants us hope and optimism for a better future.

A special thank-you to the King of Morocco, His Majesty King Mohammed VI, and to Ambassador Ronald Lauder for their generosity and commitment to this project.

And to Sam Freedman, our indefatigable editor, who is a source of erudition and enlightenment; to President Bill Clinton, for elevating and ennobling this book with his foreword; and to the editorial team at Beacon Press, our gratitude for making this dream a reality.

—Rabbi Marc Schneier and Imam Shamsi Ali

Printed in the United States
By Bookmasters